Key Theories & Skills in

COUNSELLING CHILDREN & YOUNG PEOPLE

Sara Miller McCune founded SAGE Publishing in 1965 to support the dissemination of usable knowledge and educate a global community. SAGE publishes more than 1000 journals and over 800 new books each year, spanning a wide range of subject areas. Our growing selection of library products includes archives, data, case studies and video. SAGE remains majority owned by our founder and after her lifetime will become owned by a charitable trust that secures the company's continued independence.

Los Angeles | London | New Delhi | Singapore | Washington DC | Melbourne

Key Theories & Skills in

COUNSELLING CHILDREN & YOUNG PEOPLE

An Integrative Approach

REBECCA KIRKBRIDE

SAGE

Los Angeles | London | New Delhi
Singapore | Washington DC | Melbourne

SAGE

Los Angeles | London | New Delhi
Singapore | Washington DC | Melbourne

SAGE Publications Ltd
1 Oliver's Yard
55 City Road
London EC1Y 1SP

SAGE Publications Inc.
2455 Teller Road
Thousand Oaks, California 91320

SAGE Publications India Pvt Ltd
B 1/I 1 Mohan Cooperative Industrial Area
Mathura Road
New Delhi 110 044

SAGE Publications Asia-Pacific Pte Ltd
3 Church Street
#10-04 Samsung Hub
Singapore 049483

Editor: Susannah Trefgarne
Assistant editor: Ruth Lilly
Production editor: Rachel Burrows
Copyeditor: Sarah Bury
Proofreader: Bryan Campbell
Indexer: Adam Pozner
Marketing manager: Dilhara Attygalle
Cover design: Naomi Robinson
Typeset by: Knowledge Works Global Ltd.
Printed in the UK

Library of Congress Control Number: 2021932867

British Library Cataloguing in Publication data

A catalogue record for this book is available from the British Library

ISBN 978-1-5297-2966-5
ISBN 978-1-5297-2967-2 (pbk)

To Bridget
in gratitude for twenty years of unerring support
and companionship in practice

Contents

About the Author xi
Acknowledgements xiii
Introduction xv

Part I – Core Knowledge: Understanding Development from 0–18 years 1

1.1 Introduction: Development – A Dynamic Interplay Model 3
1.2 The Importance of Play 5
1.3 Theory of Mind 9
1.4 Cognitive Development 13
1.5 Attachment Theory 16
1.6 Object Relations Theory 20
1.7 Humanistic Theories of Development 25
1.8 Neurobiological Development 29
1.9 Puberty & the Adolescent Transition 32
1.10 Environmental & Systemic Factors 37
1.11 Developmental Implications for Counselling 43

Part II – Key Skills: The Therapeutic Process 47

2.1 Introduction: Core Principles of Integrative Therapy with Children, Young People & Families 49
2.2 Core Relationship Components 51
2.3 The Therapeutic Frame 58
2.4 Building Rapport 63
2.5 Contracting 68
2.6 Limit-Setting 72
2.7 Assessment & Integrative Formulation 75
2.8 Risk Assessment & Safeguarding 79

2.9 Confidentiality & Consent 84
2.10 Outcome & Process Measures 89
2.11 Cultural Competence 93
2.12 Working with Parents/Carers 97
2.13 Record-Keeping & Data Protection 101
2.14 Developing & Sustaining the Therapeutic Relationship 103
2.15 Managing Ruptures in the Therapeutic Alliance 106
2.16 Transference & Countertransference 111
2.17 Developing Advanced Empathy 114
2.18 Tracking 117
2.19 Endings 120
2.20 Ethical Issues 124
2.21 Self-Disclosure 129
2.22 Working with Other Professionals 131
2.23 Self-Care for Counsellors 134
2.24 Clinical Supervision 137

Part III – Key Skills: Interventions, Techniques & Strategies 141

3.1 Introduction: Skills & Interventions 143
3.2 Symbol & Metaphor 144
3.3 Play-Based Interventions 147
3.4 Creative-Arts Interventions 151
3.5 Therapeutic 'Chat' 154
3.6 Cognitive-Behavioural Therapy (CBT) 158
3.7 Working with Emotions 162
3.8 Mindfulness & Relaxation Techniques 168
3.9 Groups 171
3.10 Working with Risk 174
3.11 Self-Harm 179
3.12 Food & Body Issues 183
3.13 Alcohol & Substance Misuse 188
3.14 Trauma & Abuse 191
3.15 Risky Sexual Behaviour 195
3.16 Identity 199
3.17 Sexuality & Gender Identity 202
3.18 Bullying 206
3.19 Online Risk 210
3.20 Family Breakdown & Instability 214
3.21 Bereavement & Loss 218
3.22 Self-Esteem 222
3.23 Anxiety 225
3.24 Depression 229
3.25 Diagnosis, Medication & Psychiatric Presentations 233

3.26 Neurodiversity: Autistic Spectrum Disorder (ASD) & Attention-Deficit Hyperactivity Disorder (ADHD) 239
3.27 Special Educational Needs & Disabilities (SEND) 244
3.28 Visual & Hearing Impairments 247
3.29 Physical Disability 250
3.30 Chronic Illness 254
3.31 Resilience 257

Part IV – Key Considerations: Contexts & Client Groups 261

4.1 Introduction: Considerations & Contexts 263
4.2 Educational Settings 264
4.3 Private Practice 267
4.4 Child & Adolescent Mental Health Services (CAMHS) 270
4.5 Voluntary & Community Sector (VCS) Counselling Services 273
4.6 Online Counselling 276
4.7 Refugee Communities 280
4.8 Looked-After Children (LAC) 283

References 287
Index 303

About the Author

Rebecca Kirkbride is a BACP senior accredited psychotherapeutic counsellor, clinical supervisor, author and trainer. She has been practising as a therapist for 20 years and since 2018 has been convener of a new MA in Integrative Counselling and Psychotherapy for Children, Adolescents and Families at The University of Roehampton. Rebecca is author of books, chapters and articles on the subject of counselling for children and adolescents and has facilitated CPD trainings for BACP, among others.

Rebecca lives in Brighton with her family and two noisy rescue cockatiels, Stitch and Pearl.

Acknowledgements

Most of us understand there's a lot more to an apple than the twig it grows on, and books are the same. So many people have been involved in the production of this book and I'm grateful for their support and help in bringing it into being.

Thanks to SAGE for giving me another opportunity to write for them, especially Susannah Trefgarne, Ruth Lilly, Rachel Burrows and the rest of their team. Their generous support and good wishes made completing the book during the 2020 pandemic both a possibility and a pleasure.

I am grateful to colleagues and students at The University of Roehampton. This book has been written very much with these students in mind, and it's been a joy to meet those on the ICP-CAF and experience their commitment to the profession, curiosity, and bravery in embarking on this challenging path. My thanks to Roehampton colleagues including Dr Janek Dubowski, Elise Cuschieri, Dr Paula Reed, Nancy Fowler, Dr David Turgoose, Megan Stafford and Professor Mick Cooper for their support and inspiration.

My thanks to colleagues from my private practice network including my clinical supervisor, Dr Aaron Balick, Bridget Pavett, Shelley Holland and Helen Skelton. I am also indebted to my young clients, both past and present.

Lastly, thanks to my family and friends, especially my parents, Richard and Enid, my partner Richard and my daughter (and fellow Roehampton-er) Poppy. Their love, and Richard's cooking, are the roots that sustain my endeavours.

Introduction

If you have ever practised yoga, you will understand what I mean when I describe it as a 'dynamic' process. Tree pose, or 'Vrksasana', is an excellent example of this. In Vrksasana, we root through our feet into the earth, finding a firmly grounded position from which to extend upwards, arms reaching branch-like towards the sky. This pose is not static but in constant flow, the in-breath encouraging us to root down as the out-breath sends us further upwards, before flowing down again through the roots. This book is intended to encourage and facilitate a similarly dynamic relationship with the practice of integrative counselling with children and adolescents. The reader can 'ground down' into the theories and understandings which are the roots of therapeutic practice, allowing them to reach up and extend further via the skills sections, before returning once more into the roots, and so on.

The structure of this book will, I hope, reflect the dynamic nature of psychotherapeutic counselling, certainly as I have experienced it myself over two decades of practice. The book is set out in four parts, each containing entries which can be read consecutively or moved between dynamically in a way which, I imagine, will parallel many readers' experience of training in and practising therapy with children and adolescents.

My own development as a counsellor of children, adolescents and adults has been a similarly dynamic process. Having initially trained in adult psychodynamic psychotherapeutic counselling, I found myself working in Brighton & Hove as a school counsellor in the early 2000s, in response to a growing need for practitioners to enter educational settings during the 'second wave' of school counselling in the UK. This was before counsellor training provision had had a chance to catch up with the new demand for the services of those capable of responding to the emotional and psychological needs of children and young people, outside traditional therapeutic services. These services were, at the time, largely confined to the NHS or CAMHS and delivered by child psychotherapists (Kegerreis, 2006).

The task of becoming effective school counsellors required myself and colleagues to learn quickly, seeking training, reading and supervision to provide the support necessary to translate the skills and theories of adult psychotherapy, taught on our original trainings, into those required for work with children and adolescents. For myself, this meant recognising and accepting the limitations of these theories and skills if I was to work effectively with younger clients, and accepting that the therapeutic relationship needed to be built in a different way with a seven- or twelve-year-old, and that this required different skills and an alteration in the professional stance I held as a psychodynamic practitioner working with adult clients. I needed to consider new aspects of the therapeutic process; for example, the developmental stage a child had reached became significant. Was their presentation appropriate for their age, or did something seem blocked or arrested? There were new skills to be learned in creative and non-verbal interventions. I needed to understand quickly the often non-clinical context I was working in, becoming knowledgeable about schools and youth services as well as the particular cultural considerations these contexts would bring to bear on the therapeutic relationship. Training in safeguarding processes was vital in order to protect those who could not yet bear full responsibility for themselves and their safety, and I had to try to understand some of the clinical considerations experienced by young people, such as self-harm or abuse from others. I also needed to consider parents and their role in both the aetiology of the client's difficulty, but also as active and ongoing participants in their child's life and possibly their therapy, something that work with adults is generally free from. In short, there was a lot to learn in order to be able to provide effective therapeutic support for a generation of children and young people who were experiencing new challenges and pressures themselves in the form of digital technology and social media, which would have enormous implications for their individual and relational development.

Twenty years on from these developments, I am in the privileged position of providing training for a new generation of practitioners, all deeply committed to working therapeutically with the huge numbers of children and young people who benefit from therapeutic intervention today. My own experience of a continuous process of learning through training, reading and supervision, in order to reach and extend further as a practitioner, is now translated into my work as a trainer, supervisor and author. It is fed and nurtured by the learning I gain from my clients and supervisees as well as through my own continuous professional development.

As I continue working therapeutically with children and adolescents, I am ever aware of the complexities and nuances that make this a very different therapeutic endeavour from work undertaken with adults. While adult clients are often struggling with some aspect of their infantile or childhood development which prevents them from living as well as they might wish, for child and adolescent clients this development is happening 'live' and is often brought to bear directly on the therapeutic relationship and process. In my experience, the more time one spends in any field, the more the landscape expands to show just how much more there is to learn and understand. This has certainly been the case for me in my therapeutic work with all age groups and in various contexts over the years.

In this book, we engage with the process of therapy with children and adolescents in an attempt to use all that we know from theory and research as well as our understanding of development and how this can impact on the individual and the therapeutic relationship. Out of this integration of developmental understanding, theoretical approaches, research and clinical considerations emerge the skills and techniques that have been found to work most effectively in therapeutic work with children and adolescents. This is the first important place of integration in this book, but there are several more to consider within its pages.

In **Part I**, we explore human development from a range of perspectives, including humanistic, psychodynamic and attachment theory. We consider cognitive, neurological and social development, from birth through adolescence. In developmental terms this means not only looking at biological influences on growth, but also on environmental and cultural experiences of children and young people in contemporary society, approaching issues around race and oppression. This is known to be experienced not only directly by children in their everyday lives, but also indirectly through the intergenerational trauma which lies at the heart of many of our cultures and communities. Here and throughout the book, we consider the importance of understanding and engaging with this trauma if we are to provide effective interventions and culturally competent services for all who might benefit from effective therapeutic support.

Part II explores the therapeutic relationship, arguably the central component of the therapeutic process (Bordin, 1979). This provides a foundation for the reader as they gain or strengthen knowledge and skills for establishing and sustaining the therapeutic relationship. We consider the key principles of integrative practice, founded in the core relational conditions of the humanistic approach (Rogers, 1951) and informed by psychodynamic understandings of interrelational and intrapsychic dynamics. There are practical skills for contracting, limit-setting and assessment, among other important topics.

Part III continues the focus on skills development begun in Part II, growing from the secure base of the core relationship components and therapeutic alliance. This part provides examples of a variety of interventions with children and young people, including play-based work and child- or adolescent-focused cognitive-behavioural therapy. We consider the evidence-base for the clinical application of these interventions, while exploring the important integration of research and practice for the contemporary practitioner.

Part IV explores further considerations for practice with this group, looking at various contexts in which child and adolescent counselling takes place, including school, CAMHS and private practice. Here again, there are important points of integration of therapeutic practice and the particular challenges that different groups or context present. The entries in this section and the accompanying case studies are intended to support practitioners in developing the confidence to take their practice into a variety of contexts and work with groups who are in need of high-quality therapeutic support.

In recent years, there have been significant advances in the field of counselling children and young people. These have taken several forms, including the British Association for Counselling and Psychotherapy (BACP) ethical (2018) and competence frameworks (2014; 2019) for therapeutic work with children and young people aged 4–18 years, as well as the BACP training curriculum and several important research trials into the efficacy and effectiveness of child counselling and psychotherapy (Stafford et al., 2018). These represent a significant strengthening of the foundations for a contemporary approach to this field and are an integral part of my own practice and of this book.

While the book can be read straight through, the format is intended to allow the reader to move between the entries, thus strengthening the dynamic process of grounding down in knowledge and theory before extending further with skills and considerations for practice. Throughout the book, I use the terms 'counsellor', 'therapist' and 'practitioner' interchangeably to denote all those providing therapeutic interventions to children and adolescents, based on a rigorous approach and place the therapeutic alliance between client and therapist at the foundation of the therapeutic process.

Case examples are used throughout the text in various ways and are intended to bring the theory and skills 'to life'. They are all fictitious examples and any relation to real persons is purely coincidental. Each section includes signposting to other relevant entries in the book (both throughout the section and at the end) and suggested additional resources which the reader may wish to explore to further their understanding. I have included links to MindEd (www.minded.org.uk) resources in some sections. This is a comprehensive e-learning website, funded by the Department for Health and Education, which provides free continuous professional development (CPD) activities for a range of professionals working in a supportive capacity with children and adolescents.

At this time, significant shifts in personal and societal paradigms are occurring, precipitated in part by the global COVID-19 pandemic, the Black Lives Matter movement and the ongoing impact of the Climate Crisis. These shifts offer opportunities for positive change as well as provoking fears and anxiety for many. Children and adolescents growing up in these times will benefit more than ever from spaces of support and calm in which to process the developmental impact of these and other factors impacting them on their journey towards adulthood. This book is intended to support the development and practice of all those stepping forward to provide valuable service through the provision of relational counselling for children and adolescents.

Part I

Core Knowledge: Understanding Development from 0–18 years

1.1 Introduction: Development – A Dynamic Interplay Model

Therapeutic work with children and adolescents requires an awareness of the natural progression and flow of human development as well as of events which could impede this process. The first part of this book takes a dynamic approach to human development. The developmental stage a child or young person has reached, and the quality of their early relational experiences, can have a considerable bearing on the therapeutic relationship and therefore influence any approach to forming an effective working therapeutic alliance. Child psychotherapist Graham Music (2019: 10) notes:

> …many from traumatised backgrounds struggle with interpersonal attunement, reciprocity and indeed, relationships generally. They have often missed out on the building blocks of cooperation or mutual care, lacking the capacity to receive care from even benign others.

This lack of capacity to receive care is one example of a developmental factor that counsellors need to be aware of if they are to adequately support the child or young person and form the necessary bond for therapy to be effective. Part I explores several approaches to understanding human development while considering how these can be used as a foundation for effective therapeutic intervention. These approaches range from psychodynamic and humanistic theories of development and the roots of psychological disturbance, through relational and social theories such as attachment and object relations theory, while also including biological, neurobiological, cognitive and ecological-systemic approaches. The vital role of play in children's development is also considered. The task here is to immerse ourselves in the compelling world of human growth as we take an integrative approach to understanding the relationship between these approaches and how they inform our understanding of both ourselves and others as living individuals.

It is worth noting that there are significant differences the ways in which these approaches view development, as outlined here by Bateman and Holmes (1995: 28):

> Underlying different theories are different fundamental assumptions about the world: how much experience is determined by the environment, and how much it is innate; whether a basically optimistic or pessimistic viewpoint is

adopted; whether a mechanistic or humanistic view of the mind is taken; on the balance between determinism and freedom; on the emphasis on mental forces as opposed to meanings and language; whether a position of mentalism or realism is taken.

These differences of understanding can be seen throughout the entirety of human history, whether the subject is philosophy, science, religion, politics or any areas which provoke a variety of viewpoints and positions. Psychology and psychotherapy are not immune to this form of conflict, and the potential for taking a dogmatic position is considerable. In the following entries, however, theories and ideas are considered as potential aids to understanding the individual child, young person or family as best we can in order to work with them in a manner which is going to be of the most help to them in their difficulty. They can be held lightly as hypotheses which we are prepared to adapt and adjust in the face of the individual we meet in the room.

Development: A Dynamic Interplay

Our exploration of development begins with infancy and childhood, before shifting into a consideration of the impact of puberty and adolescence on the individual. We consider family systems and the significant impact they have on children and adolescents, along with cultural background and community. We consider the dynamic interplay between these intrapsychic, interpersonal, hereditary and environmental factors, which interact as the infant grows into a child, then an adolescent and, ultimately, a fully-grown adult human being.

Implications for the therapeutic process

By considering this complex range of factors, all potentially influencing the development and growth of an individual, we begin to create a picture of the complexity of the client. Early clinicians working with children and adolescents, such as Anna Freud (1946), understood the importance of viewing the child-client as a developing human. They saw therapy as vital to help promote or return the child to a healthy developmental trajectory. In the final entry in this part (see entry 1.11, p. 43), we will look closely at the implications of development for the therapeutic process, considering attachment, cognitive development and the adolescent phase, among other developmental factors.

1.2 The Importance of Play

> 'Work?' he said to me once, astonished, when I referred to our classroom activities as such. 'Do you really think that what we do is work?'
> 'What else should I call it?'
> '*I* should call it the most glorious kind of *play*.'
> (*The Secret History*, Donna Tartt, 1992)

Key Understandings

Play has long been understood to be the instinctive way through which children encounter the world and come to understand themselves, others, and their environment. Children's play changes and develops as rapidly as they do. For a baby who has recently developed the ability to 'play' with their own toes, this provides hours of amusement and occupation. For an older baby, more sophisticated material for play is required and 'toys' (objects for play) become more complex, fulfilling their growing hunger for learning and development. As children get older and their lives and relationships with others become increasingly complex, so correspondingly does their play. When children are anxious or traumatised or experiencing developmental delays, this is often expressed through their play, or indeed their lack of a capacity for play and playfulness.

What is Play?

The opening quote from Donna Tartt's 1992 novel, *The Secret History*, questions the validity of the distinction between 'play' and 'work'. Is what the characters do in their Ancient Greek class 'work'? Or could this be understood in a different way: that is, as, a form of 'glorious play'? And what is the difference anyway?

Child psychotherapist Biddy Youell (2008: 122) discusses this distinction, defining playfulness as 'a state of mind in which an individual can think flexibly, take risks with ideas (or interactions), and allow creative thoughts to emerge'. Winnicott (1971: 41) was fascinated by play and its vital role in the development of the self and the maintenance of health:

> In other words, *it is play that is the universal*, and that belongs to health: playing facilitates growth and therefore health; playing leads into group

> relationships; playing can be a form of communication in psychotherapy; and, lastly, psychoanalysis has been developed as a highly specialized form of playing in the service of communication with oneself and others. ... It must be of value to the analyst to be constantly reminded not only of what is owed to Freud but also of what we owe to the natural and universal thing called playing.

Winnicott (1971) sees the role of therapy as facilitating playfulness in the individual in order that they might live creatively and, therefore, spontaneously. Winnicott positions play as a 'transitional space', bringing the child's intrapsychic inner world into a 'safe' space between them and the external or 'real' world:

> Into this play area the child gathers objects or phenomena from external reality and uses these in the service of some sample derived from inner or personal reality. ... There is a direct development from transitional phenomena to playing, and from playing to shared playing, and from this to cultural experiences. (1971: 51)

This suggests that the capacity to play develops through relationship. Therefore, it follows that the capacity to play alone, and accordingly for separation and individuation, only develops through the experience of playing with another (Winnicott, 1990; Youell, 2008). This is an important understanding when we come to consider those children whose capacity for play and for appropriate development is impeded or limited in some way, often due to the quality of their early relational experiences.

The developmental stages of play, as well as its various forms and functions, have been conceptualised by early-years theorists over many decades (Wood & Attfield, 2005). Jennings (1993: 20) suggests the human infant is born with a capacity to symbolise and for imagination:

> ...indeed, it is the very capacity of human beings to pretend or make-believe which enables them to survive. We cannot envisage a life within which we could not imagine how things are – how they were, or how they might be.

This places emphasis on the fundamental and foundational role of imagination and play in human existence and survival. It is this capacity and drive to symbolise experience through play which has been utilised by child therapists from the early theories of Melanie Klein (1926/1975), who saw the child's play as synonymous with free association in adult psychotherapy, up to the present day and contemporary child-centred practice (Landreth et al., 2005).

Swiss psychologist, Jean Piaget (1962), defined three categories and stages of play:

Practice play – sensory motor and exploratory play based on physical activities (6 months–2 years).

Symbolic play – pretend, fantasy and socio-dramatic play, involving the use of mental representations. When play becomes representational, it is regarded as an intellectual activity (2–6 years).

Games with rules – from 6 or 7 years upwards (cited in Wood & Attfield, 2005: 39).

The Piagetian view is that play is primarily used by children as they develop the cognitive capacity to understand themselves and the world around them. Play allows them to develop the structures required to understand their world and make sense of their experiences within it. While the Piagetian stages indicate a linear developmental progression, similar to his stages of cognitive development (Piaget, 1964) (see entry 1.4, p. 13), progress between stages is dynamic, involving regression as well as progression.

Jennings (1993) developed a 'developmental paradigm' of play, which forms the basis for her 'Playtherapy' model and is widely used by contemporary play therapists and those using play-based interventions with children and young people (see Table 1.1).

Table 1.1 Jennings (1993) developmental paradigm: Embodiment-Projection-Role (EPR)

Embodiment: Most prominent during the first year of life. Sensory experience, holding, whole body and parts.

Projection: Experiences are projected out onto various toys and media. Media (e.g. sand and water) also heighten the sensory experience. Toys take on roles and relationships and child controls outcome.

Role: Child takes on the role or the character and moves into different roles; integrates activity with role and creates the story or directs the drama.

(Jennings, 1993: 22)

Jennings (1993) theorises that when the child has not had the primary experience of navigating these stages through play, they will need to be assisted with this via play therapy. As Winnicott (1971: 54) suggests: 'It is in playing and only in playing that the individual child or adult is able to be creative and use the whole personality, and it is only in being creative that the individual discovers the self.'

Play is naturally associated with childhood, so it may be difficult to imagine children who can't play or whose play is minimal, cautious and rigid, or chaotic, lacking boundaries and unsafe. As stated earlier, play is a natural part of human development and something strongly and positively associated with childhood across cultures. However, when we consider Winnicott's (1971) theories regarding play and the capacity to enter a transitional 'me-and-not-me' space of primitive separation, it makes sense that for some children, possibly because of previous experiences of trauma or abuse, entering such a space could be experienced as a threat that might profoundly hamper development. To play is to be spontaneous and take risks in entering the unknown. For many, this is what makes play exciting as well as such a rich and pleasurable experience. However, as Blake (2008: 237) notes, 'If this early anxiety about being separate is too overwhelming, then the development of real play is under threat'. Blake goes on to suggest that this threat can be particularly pronounced in severe autism, where 'the development of the self is extremely fragile, and separateness is massively denied. There are no personal pronouns. There is no transition from infantile omnipotence to external reality. There is no real play' (Blake, 2008: 237).

Summary

- Play is the natural way for infants and children to develop a sense of self and of their relationship with others.
- The capacity to play alone can only develop from the experience of playing with another.
- The capacity for play in children who have had difficult early relational experiences, suffered trauma or abuse, can be impeded or negatively affected, leading to issues more generally in their sense of self and in their ability to form necessary relationships as they get older.

Additional Resources

- Blake, P. (2008) *Child and Adolescent Psychotherapy.* London: Routledge.
- Jennings, S. (1993) *Playtherapy with Children: A Practitioner's Guide.* Oxford: Blackwell Scientific.
- Music, G. (2019) *Nurturing Children: From Trauma to Growth Using Attachment Theory, Psychoanalysis and Neurobiology.* London: Routledge.

Associated Entries

3.2 Symbol & Metaphor
3.3 Play-Based Interventions
3.4 Creative-Arts Interventions
3.5 Therapeutic 'Chat'
3.26 Neurodiversity: Autism Spectrum Disorder (ASD) & Attention-Deficit Hyperactivity Disorder (ADHD)

1.3 Theory of Mind

Theory of mind (ToM) is a concept derived from developmental psychology which helps us to understand not only the child's capacity to develop a sense of their own mind, but also of the mind of another. This leads to:

> the developmental acquisition that permits children to respond not only to another person's behavior, but to the children's *conception* of others' beliefs, feelings, attitudes, desires, hopes, knowledge, imagination, pretense, deceit, intentions, plans and so on. Reflective function, or mentalization, enables children to 'read' other people's minds. (Meins et al., 2003: 24)

In this entry we consider the development of ToM and its relevance for the therapeutic process.

Key Understandings

We have already considered how infants encounter and begin to understand themselves and others through play and the capacity to symbolise (see entry 1.2, p. 5), but as Youell (2008) indicated, this is a process which is also dependent on the quality of the relationship between the child's mind and the minds of those with whom they are in close early contact. In recent years, clinicians such as Peter Fonagy (Fonagy et al., 2004) have begun to consider how early relational experiences can impact on the development of ToM and what the repercussions of this could be for the therapeutic relationship.

Interest and research into understanding an infant's capacity to understand others' minds and feeling states began in the late 1980s to early 1990s (Dunn et al., 1991). The concept of ToM developed from this research and has since been tested and developed to offer greater understanding in this area.

Test to Establish Theory of Mind

A test used to establish whether a child has developed ToM is the 'Sally–Anne' test. This involves three stages:

1. Child is told that Sally puts a marble in a basket and then goes out to play.
2. Child is told that while Sally is playing, Anne takes the marble and puts it in a box.
3. The child is asked, 'When Sally comes back, where will she look for the marble?'

Children under the age of four tend not to get the answer right (Astington & Gopnik, 1991), answering that Sally will look in the box. As the child knows where the marble is, they assume Sally will as well. They have not yet understood that Sally's mind is not the same as theirs. They are still in the stage Piaget (1964) described as 'ego-centredness' (see entry 1.4, p. 13).

Research suggests the child's capacity in this respect is greatly influenced by their caregivers' responses to them, rather than being an aspect of development which simply 'appears' at a certain age. Meins et al. (2003) developed the concept of 'mind-mindedness' (MM), which is defined as 'the proclivity to treat one's infant as an individual with a mind, rather than merely an entity with needs that must be satisfied' (Meins et al., 2003: 1194). In other words, if the carer is able to use their own mind to imagine that their infant also has a mind and to respond accordingly, this increases the child's own capacity for mind-mindedness. Repeated studies (Meins et al., 2003, 2013) have found that parents' demonstration of MM in response to their infant's mental states, for example by using appropriate 'mental state language' to accurately reflect their infant's current state of mind, predicts later security of attachment.

There are many complex processes at work here, all within what we might consider to be the most 'ordinary' of human interactions – that of a parent connecting with their baby's experience and offering an explanation and/or emotional response accordingly. For example, an infant hears a visitor's dog barking outside. The noise is unfamiliar and the baby starts to cry, communicating confusion and distress. Dad picks up baby and soothes him, saying 'don't worry baby, it's only the dog downstairs. He won't hurt you.' In this interaction, not only is baby soothed and his affect validated as a reasonable response, but he also has the beginning of a mental framework for the sound of a dog bark, language to describe what this is along with a sense of how this should be responded to. Had dad simply soothed him without either connecting empathically with the fear response, or by giving an explanation which draws on his own mind and capacity to mentalise, then the baby would perhaps be calmer, but still lacking a mental picture of what had just happened.

This is closely linked to Fonagy et al.'s (2004) concept of mentalisation and the need for development to be supported by connection with a parent who themselves has developed the capacity to mentalise or to be 'mind-minded'. These ideas are closely linked to those of Winnicott (1960), who suggested that 'there is no such thing as an infant', highlighting the impossibility of seeing an individual without also seeing the profound influences of the parents on the developing psyche, and those of Bion (1962) and his theories of 'maternal reverie' and the 'containment' of projected material (see entry 1.6, p. 20). Further research into attachment, mentalisation and ToM (Fonagy et al., 2004; Bateman & Fonagy, 2013) suggests that deficits in the capacity to mentalise are at the root of a range of mental health issues experienced by children and young people, including personality disorders, peer relationships, self-esteem and conduct issues, among others. Music (2017: 54) writes that 'being able to reflect on mental states is a crucial capacity, the lack of which links with poor psychological health'. Children and adolescents presenting for therapy may be seeking a relational experience which can assist them in developing a sense of their own mind as well as the separate mind of another.

Given what we have outlined so far in terms of the relational component of developing ToM, it follows that those who experience neglect, trauma and abuse may experience difficulty developing this capacity, causing later relational difficulties. We will consider the impact of such difficulties in Part III.

Summary

- Theory of mind (ToM) is a concept from developmental psychology describing the capacity to understand one's own mind and its separate nature from the mind of another.
- ToM is thought to be fully developed around the age of 4–5 years, but there are indications of developing ToM as early as infancy.
- The development of ToM and its particular quality in an individual is now understood to be dependent partly on the early relational experiences of the infant, including whether the parent is capable of 'mind-mindedness'.
- These experiences lead to the development of the capacity to 'mentalise', which is crucial for making and sustaining appropriate relationships as well as affect-regulation and acquiring a secure and coherent sense of self.
- Children who have not experienced adequate containment and mentalisation in infancy and childhood, in addition to those on the autistic spectrum, are likely to struggle with ToM and therefore develop issues stemming from this in later childhood, adolescence and into adulthood, unless addressed.

Additional Resources

- Fonagy, P., Gergely, G., Jurist, E.L. & Target, M. (2004) *Affect Regulation, Mentalization, and the Development of the Self.* London: Karnac.

Associated Entries

3.18 Bullying
3.22 Self-Esteem
3.26 Neurodiversity: Autism Spectrum Disorder (ASD) & Attention-Deficit Hyperactivity Disorder (ADHD)
4.8 Looked-After Children (LAC)

1.4 Cognitive Development

Cognition is defined as 'all forms of knowing and awareness, such as perceiving, conceiving, remembering, reasoning, judging, imagining, and problem solving' (American Psychological Association, 2020: n.p.) and is considered, along with *affect* and *conation*, as one of the three components of mind.

Key Understandings

The development of cognitive processes in humans is ongoing from prebirth into adulthood. Evidently, a new-born baby does not have the same capacity for cognitive understanding as a child of 3 years or a young person of 17 years. Theorists have tried to identify and explain the various stages through which cognitive development passes on the way towards mature cognitive functioning as well as what might impede or support this progression.

Jean Piaget (1896–1980)

Perhaps the most enduring theory of cognitive development is that developed by Swiss psychologist, Jean Piaget. Having begun his career studying natural history, Piaget moved into psychology and specifically into the field of children's development. While observing babies and children, Piaget discovered that aspects of their behaviour indicated progressive changes in cognitive capacities. These discoveries became Piaget's (1964) stages of cognitive development (see Table 1.2).

Table 1.2 Piaget's stages of cognitive development (1964)

Age	Developmental Stage
Birth–2 years	***Sensorimotor stage*** – infants and babies experience the world through sense and action.
2–6 years	***Preoperational stage*** – young children begin to represent and understand their experiences through words and images.
7–11 years	***Concrete operational stage*** – children are able to think logically about concrete happenings and make analogies between them.
12 years onwards	***Formal operational stage*** – adolescents and young adults are able to consider hypothetical situations and process abstract, non-concrete, thoughts.

According to Piaget's (1964) theory, each stage must be achieved before further progression can occur. For example, at the sensorimotor stage, the world is experienced 'reflectively' rather than through conscious 'thought', and a child at this stage won't have the same understanding of relationships between objects or experiences as at concrete operational stage. Children who are 'concrete operational' are developing language skills for describing objects as well as differentiating between animate and inanimate objects. As subsequent stages are reached, thinking becomes increasingly sophisticated and the capacity to understand abstract and hypothetical ideas develops accordingly. The shift into the formal operational stage is an integral aspect of adolescent development (see entry 1.9, p. 32).

Lev Vygotsky (1896–1934)

A significant contribution to our understanding of cognitive development was made by Russian psychologist, Lev Vygotsky. Vygotsky's understanding of development was more relational than that of Piaget, as demonstrated by his theory of the 'zone of proximal development' (ZPD). Vygotsky argued that if a child was working on a problem and they were supported in this by someone with more advanced competence and understanding, they would be able to develop their skills and achieve success with the task. Vygotsky (1962) viewed the child's own 'self-talk' when engaged in a task as a precursor to engaging with a more expert other who would be able to 'scaffold' the child's learning. This scaffolding might include reminding the child of steps they have already taken or took on a previous occasion, for example 'Remember how you put the square brick in this square hole? Which brick do you think might go in this shape?' Scaffolding might also include praise and reward for a child when completing a task, thus supporting the child's own developing capacity to hold in mind what task they had set out to achieve. Vygotsky argued that 'such *external* and *social* activities are gradually internalized by the child as he comes to regulate his own intellectual activity' (Wood, 1998: 98, original emphasis). The child who experiences such 'scaffolding' will be secure enough to attempt further challenges and tasks, having experienced themselves as supported in this appropriately by others. Similar to theories of mentalisation (Fonagy et al., 2004) and attachment theory, this relational understanding of cognitive development further exemplifies how a child's early social and relational experiences can significantly impact development. Entry 1.11 (p. 43) considers the implications of developmental processes on counselling and the therapeutic relationship.

Summary

- Cognitive development is a process that lasts throughout childhood and into adolescence.
- The way a child thinks and conceptualises depends on the developmental phase they have reached.
- Cognitive development is considered to be relational by some theorists.
- A child's capacity for cognition will affect the therapeutic process, including confidentiality and consent, and the type of therapeutic intervention selected.

Additional Resources

- Wood, D. (1998) *How Children Think and Learn* (2nd edition). Oxford: Blackwell.

Associated Entries

1.3 Theory of Mind
1.5 Attachment Theory
1.8 Neurobiological Development
1.11 Developmental Implications for Counselling
2.9 Confidentiality & Consent
3.3 Play-Based Interventions

1.5 Attachment Theory

Attachment theory, developed by psychologist John Bowlby in the post-war period of the 1950s, takes as its primary focus the particular types of relational attachment developed during infancy, and the implications if this do not occur. Bowlby (1988) was appointed by the World Health Organisation in 1949 to report on the needs of homeless children, resulting in the 1951 publication of *Maternal Care and Mental Health*. In this publication, Bowlby reviewed the data regarding the impact of separation from a secure caregiver on the mental health and wellbeing of children. This was the beginning of his attempt at understanding the nature of the attachment process in humans and its implications for development and, subsequently, the therapeutic relationship (Bowlby, 1988).

Key Understandings

Bowlby's research into attachment behaviour in both human and other species led to a number of understandings. Bowlby (1988: 27) defined attachment behaviour as 'any form of behaviour that results in a person attaining or maintaining proximity to some other clearly identified individual who is conceived as better able to cope with the world'. Bowlby noted that while such attachment behaviour was most clearly identified in early life, it could be seen throughout the lifecycle, particularly in situations which cause stress or distress to an individual or group, such as a crisis.

In his consideration of attachment in infancy and early childhood, Bowlby (1973) notes that, in order to form a secure attachment, the infant needs a caregiver who is psychologically, physically and emotionally available. The responses of the caregiver, whether attuned or not, lead to the development in the infant of an 'internal working model' (IWM) (Bowlby, 1973), which influences how they experience self and other in later life. These IWMs form the basis for the child's strategy for coping with the world as they encounter it, and can continue to be influential into adolescence and throughout adulthood. For example, an infant whose expressions of sadness or upset lead to rejection by their caregiver may develop an IWM that painful feelings must be supressed in order to maintain proximity. This IWM may continue to influence them as they develop, leading to issues such as self-harm or addiction in adolescence as the individual finds themselves increasingly trying to cope with emotional experiences which they have no internal resources to cope with (see entry 3.10, p. 174).

Ainsworth and the 'Strange Situation' Test

While working alongside Bowlby, psychologist Mary Ainsworth developed a classification of infant attachment strategy patterns. The test from which these classifications are derived is the 'Strange Situation' (Ainsworth et al., 1978).

The test, carried out in laboratory conditions, consists of a series of actions and interactions involving a parent, a child of around 12–18 months and a stranger. The actions of participants are observed at various stages of the test:

1. A parent and child play together in a room.
2. A stranger enters and tries to engage the child.
3. The mother leaves room.
4. The mother returns after a brief interval and the stranger leaves.
5. The mother then leaves the child again after a short time.
6. The stranger enters and engages with the child again, comforting them if needed.
7. The mother returns.

After carrying out this test a number of times on mother and child pairs, Ainsworth (1985) and her team arrived at three categories of attachment behaviour. These were:

'**Secure attachment**', where the children responded with appropriate calm while the mother was present and distress when she left, indicating secure attachment.

'**Insecure anxious/avoidant**', where the child tended to maintain their behaviour across all interactions and showed no distress and was avoidant when mother returned.

'**Insecure anxious/resistant or anxious/ambivalent**', where the child tended to be wary of the stranger and upset by the separations. They appeared ambivalent on the return of the mother, both wanting to be close to her as well as angry and difficult to comfort.

As well as observing and recording the responses of the child, Ainsworth also observed the mothers and their responses. From this, an understanding of the kind of parental behaviour which contributes to certain attachment behaviours began to develop.

A further classification of 'insecure-disorganised', describing the confused and dysregulated responses of traumatised or abused children, was identified by Main and Solomon (1986).

Understanding attachment behaviour and classifications of attachment can be a useful tool for counsellors and psychotherapists. Bowlby's (1988) view was that the therapist acts as 'secure base' for the client, from which they explore difficult and painful experiences. However, given that some young clients may have IWMs which leave them anxious, avoidant, ambivalent or traumatised with regards to those in a position of 'caregiver', it may not be a straightforward process to develop trust in their therapist or the therapeutic process.

The following case example illustrates where this might be the case.

Case Example: Rosie (counsellor) and Luka

Luka has been referred for counselling at school. He has recently arrived at the school having been removed from his biological mother's home after reports that he and his siblings were suffering significant neglect. His teacher has noticed that Luka is isolated in class and finds it difficult to come back into the classroom after break and lunchtime.

Counselling is arranged and Rosie, the school counsellor, goes to collect him at his appointed time. When she arrives, Luka refuses to come with her and backs himself into a corner by a bookcase. Rosie tells him that it's OK not to come but that she will be back to see him at the same time next week.

The following week Rosie takes some slime and a dinosaur from the therapy room and goes to Luka's classroom. Again, he refuses to come and hides behind the bookcase. While the class continue with their lesson, Rosie sits quietly beside the bookcase and begins to play with the slime. She uses the dinosaur toy to explain quietly something about what happens in the counselling play-room and says she understands that Luka has had a lot of difficult things to deal with lately and that she hopes he might come and play next week in case that might make him feel better.

The next week Rosie takes the dinosaur and the slime again, but finds that Luka is ready to come to the playroom for his session.

In this example, Rosie attempts to build trust with Luka before beginning therapy proper. Luka's IWM at this point does not allow him to go with a relative stranger into an unknown situation. Rosie allows empathic attunement with Luka's experience to direct her response. She demonstrates understanding and acceptance of his behaviour by not pushing him to come, but also by not punishing him for not being able to come immediately and by continuing to try to build rapport with him as a precursor to building a therapeutic relationship.

This kind of empathic response can be valuable for the therapist attempting to develop a therapeutic relationship with a child who is anxious or ambivalent about trusting adults.

There are many other implications of attachment theory for the therapeutic relationship, which it is beyond the scope of this entry to cover in depth. Please see the additional resources for more detail regarding this fascinating area of theory and practice.

Summary

- Attachment theory was developed by John Bowlby and is based on his observations of attachment in infancy.
- Mary Ainsworth developed the 'Strange Situation' test, which led to the classification of attachment patterns. These classifications can have implications for developing the therapeutic relationship.
- Attachment theory has many applications in the field of child and family support.

Additional Resources

- Bowlby, J.M. (1997) *Attachment Vol 1.* London: Pimlico.
- Bowlby, J.M. (1997) *Separation: Anxiety & Anger Vol 2.* London: Pimlico.
- Bowlby, J.M. (1997) *Loss Vol 3.* London: Pimlico.
- Crittenden, P. (2015) *Raising Parents: Attachment, Representation and Treatment.* London: Routledge.
- Gerhardt, S. (2015) *Why Love Matters: How Affection Shapes a Baby's Brain* (2nd edition). Hove: Routledge.
- Howe, D. (2005) *Child Abuse and Neglect: Attachment, Development and Intervention.* London: Macmillan.
- Sunderland, M. (2016) *The Science of Parenting* (2nd edition). London: Dorling-Kindersley.

Associated Entries

2.4 Building Rapport
3.10 Working with Risk
3.21 Bereavement & Loss
4.7 Refugee Communities
4.8 Looked-After Children (LAC)

1.6 Object Relations Theory

Psychoanalytic theory places infant and childhood experiences at the root of adult neurosis and disturbance. Freud (1905/1953) suggested that the mind could be understood in terms of these early experiences and that by using an analytic technique to encourage regression, these could be retrieved from the unconscious and worked through by the conscious mind.

Psychoanalytic theories of development, and in particular those of object relations theory, provide important underpinnings for an integrative approach to therapy with children and young people. By understanding the developing mind of the child in terms of their earliest interactions and relational experiences, we can form effective hypotheses for current presenting difficulties and decide on effective strategies for therapy. In this entry we explore the fundamentals of object relations theory as a foundation for the integration of psychodynamic understandings and techniques, as demonstrated in later entries.

Key Understandings

Object relations theory is a psychoanalytic theory of the mind. It developed out of Freud's (1905/1953) original 'drive' or 'instinct' theory, which focused on the internal, or *intrapsychic*, mechanisms of development. This theory posits that the infant is instinctively driven towards certain behaviours, with the aim of effectively discharging and achieving tensions and achieving satisfaction of the drive, i.e. an early sexual drive is expressed orally and will seek satisfaction through sucking on the mother's breast or a substitute. In Freud's (1923/1961) 'structural model' of the psyche, the mind is divided into three 'parts': the id, ego and superego. The id is characterised as the seat of the instinctual sexual drives. Where these are in conflict with other aspects of functioning, they are repressed and become incorporated by the unconscious, where they are kept from conscious awareness by mechanisms of defence (Bateman & Holmes, 1995: 76).

The post-Freudian pioneers of object relations theory, while often keen to assert the importance of drive theory and the *intrapsychic*, were also interested in an individual's *interpersonal* relationship with the external world and its inhabitants.

Melanie Klein

Melanie Klein was one of the first psychoanalysts to take an interest in understanding the mind of an infant from birth. Her view was that the earliest experiences of the infant were the most significant in the formation of the structure of the personality (Klein, 1946). Unlike Anna Freud, who placed emphasis on the external environment of the child (A. Freud, 1965), Klein was most interested in the intrapsychic experiences of the infant and how they relate to the 'object'. In the psychoanalytic context, the term 'object' means:

> That towards which action or desire is directed; that which the subject requires in order to achieve instinctual satisfaction; that to which the subject relates himself ... objects are nearly always persons, parts of persons, or symbols of one or another. (Rycroft, 1968)

In this respect, the object is not a 'thing' as we might commonly understand the term, but 'object' to the individual's 'subject'.

Klein saw object relations as existing from the very beginning of life, beginning with 'the mother's breast which to the child becomes split into a good (gratifying) and bad (frustrating) breast' (Klein, 1946: 293). This is how the infant copes with early experiences of both satisfaction and frustration of their needs. This process of 'splitting' forms the basis for the primary mechanism – the 'paranoid-schizoid' defence. Until the infant can cope with both good and bad stemming from one object, they must keep them separate via this defence. Klein suggests that any 'bad' experienced by the infant would be *projected* back into the object. The infant takes in or *introjects* the parts of the caregiver or their actions which make him feel good, and rejects or *projects* the badness or the frustrating aspects back into the object. In this way the ego maintains a sense of 'goodness' within and 'badness' without, thus maintaining equilibrium by protecting the self from the anxiety that would otherwise be provoked by intolerable internal 'badness'. This mechanism can be seen in pathological narcissism in adults where their own 'bad' qualities are projected into others, allowing them to remain 'good', in their own mind at least.

Klein and Bion

Klein extended these primitive defence mechanisms into her concept of *projective identification* (Klein, 1946: 299). This is the process by which the 'bad', or intolerable, is evacuated into the other via *projection* but in a way that is received relationally by the other. Here the mechanism shifts from being one which is almost entirely intrapsychic, i.e. occurring as a mental process in the mind of the individual, to something relational, that is, occurring between two separate people with independent psyches.

A good example of this occurs in abusive relationships, including bullying. Here, one person can be seen as *projecting* their 'badness' (for example, an experience of intolerable vulnerability) into another who somehow comes to represent that 'badness'. This is then *identified* with by the other, who takes up the projection and sees themselves as 'bad'. When children involved in bullying at school are referred for counselling it is often as easy to identify vulnerability in the perpetrator as in the victim. Due to the configurations of their own internal objects, the victim can be seen as taking ownership of the rejected 'badness' of the perpetrator, who in turn is unable to cope with the anxiety provoked by their internal world and has to manage it via projection (see entry 3.18, p. 206).

Wilfred Bion, a Tavistock Clinic psychoanalyst who was himself analysed by Klein, further developed the concept of projective identification and added to it his own concept of *containment.* This concept is central to understanding some of the relational aspects of development, and of the therapeutic process. Bion identified a distinction between 'normal' and 'pathological' projective identification (Bott-Spillius, 1992). In Bion's (1962) relational conceptualisation of the process, 'normal' projective identification is the infant's attempt to be known in his mother's mind, rather than a defensive process. If the caregiver

> is capable of understanding and accepting the feelings without her own balance being too disturbed, she can 'contain' the feelings and behave in a way towards her infant that makes the difficult feelings more acceptable to him. He can then take them back into himself in a form that he can manage better. (Bott-Spillius, 1992: 61)

This experience of 'containment' facilitates a sense for the infant that emotional experiences can be received and understood by another, allowing the *introjection* of 'an object that is capable of bearing and allaying anxiety' (Bateman & Holmes, 1995: 40).

Bion (1962) saw containment as occurring when the caregiver is able to enter a state of 'reverie' as she experiences psychological contact with her infant and is able to think about them. This idea of reverie has echoes in Freud's 'free-floating attention' as well as in Rogers' (1959) core condition that the therapist and client be 'in psychological contact'. It also echoes Bowlby's emotionally and psychologically available caregiver. Without the experience of this 'reverie', the infant may be left without the sense that experience can be thought about, or that pain and frustration can be ameliorated by love and connection with another.

Research into mentalising (Fonagy et al., 2004) suggests that when children don't have sufficient experience of being thought about in this way within the mind of another (see entry 1.3, p. 9), this affects their sense of self and their capacity for regulation. For example, children of highly anxious parents may have experienced their feelings as dangerously overwhelming for their caregivers and therefore internalise a sense of being 'too much' or needing to repress significant parts of themselves in order to be able to maintain connection to another.

Donald Winnicott

Donald Winnicott was a British paediatrician and psychoanalyst who further developed the field of object relations. In his theory of transitional objects and phenomena, Winnicott (1971) tracks a shift in early development from projection to 'real' relationships with objects, which can also be perceived and related to as subjects in their own right. Winnicott theorised that infants enter a transitional phase in their object relations as they encounter and make sense of what is inside and outside them as well as what is beyond their control and what is within it: 'The transitional object is never under magical control like the internal object, nor is it outside of control as the real mother is' (Winnicott, 1971: 13).

Winnicott (1971) extends this idea into the concept of the 'good enough mother', who allows herself to become real and separate in the mind of the developing infant through her gradual 'failures' in satisfying their demands. Mirroring Klein's (1946) 'depressive position', this process of gradual disillusionment enables the infant to tolerate frustration and for 'objects to become real, that is to say hated as well as loved' (Winnicott, 1971: 14). Winnicott makes clear in his writing that *disillusionment* must not occur before the *illusion* that allows the infant to imagine the breast as all-giving and perfectly adapted to his needs. This is the 'basic trust' that Erikson (1950) also views as being essential for healthy functioning in later life.

Anna Freud

Anna Freud trained as a psychoanalyst in Vienna before moving to London after the outbreak of the Second World War and establishing the Hampstead Nurseries. Here she worked therapeutically with children, many of whom had experienced trauma and loss due to the war. This context encouraged Freud to focus on both the intrapsychic world of the child as well as their external environment. If a child was experiencing displacement due to the Blitz or had lost a parent or their entire family, Freud saw that this could not be ignored. She maintained the view that 'The child analyst who interprets exclusively in terms of the inner world is in danger of missing out on his patient's reporting activity concerning his – at the time equally important – environmental circumstances' (A. Freud, 1965: 51), while also acknowledging that these external factors 'achieve their pathological significance by way of internalized libidinal and ego attributes' (1965: 52). In other words, it is the child's internal world that will influence how they respond and what meaning they make of external circumstances.

Summary

- Object relations theory developed out of Freud's classical drive or instinct theory.
- Melanie Klein viewed the first object relation to be that between infant and breast.
- The infant's psyche uses mechanisms of defence to project 'bad' into the object, thus relieving internal anxiety and maintain a sense of 'goodness' within. Klein called this a 'schizoid defence'.
- Bion's theory of containment looks at the relational processes between the mother and infant, rather than focusing solely on the intrapsychic functions within the infant.
- Winnicott traced the development of object relations as the child develops the capacity to relate to separate beings in his or her environment.
- Object relations theory provides a useful tool for examining and understanding the way clients respond to their experiences and relationships with others.

Additional Resources

- Anderson, R. (ed.) (1991) *Clinical Lectures on Klein and Bion*. London: Routledge.
- Winnicott, D.W. (1969) 'The Use of an Object', *International Journal of Psycho-Analysis*, 50: 711–716.
- Winnicott, D.W. (1971) *Playing and Reality*. London: Tavistock Publications.

Associated Entries

1.3 Theory of Mind
2.2 Core Relationship Components
3.7 Working with Emotions
3.14 Trauma & Abuse
3.18 Bullying
4.8 Looked-After Children (LAC)

1.7 Humanistic Theories of Development

Humanistic psychotherapy, as pioneered by Carl Rogers, has been fundamental in helping practitioners develop the relational therapeutic skills required for effective therapeutic relationships. Here we explore Rogers' (1959) theory of human development, which underpins the humanistic understanding of the roots of psychological disturbance and the practice of humanistic and integrative therapy.

Key Understandings

American psychologist Carl Rogers was the pioneer of humanistic or person-centred psychotherapy. Rogers' work developed from his experience of working with children and families in the USA in the 1930s using the prevailing psychoanalytic techniques of the time. Rogers (1959) was frustrated by these methods, which he felt to be dogmatic and ineffective in the treatment of the individual. Rogers' response was to develop a theory of psychotherapy which placed the client and the therapeutic relationship at the heart of the therapeutic endeavour:

> If I can provide a certain type of relationship, the other person will discover within himself the capacity to use that relationship for growth, and change and personal development will occur. (Rogers, 1961: 33)

'The Soil of the Theory' (Rogers, 1959)

In developing the basis for his approach, Rogers turned to humanistic philosophy and psychology, along with a phenomenological epistemology which takes an optimistic view of life, suggesting that all organisms, given the correct conditions, will attempt to move in the direction of growth, or actualisation. This idea can be linked to Abraham Maslow and his 'hierarchy of needs' model (Maslow, 1943), which suggests that as long as basic needs for food and security are in place, humans automatically move in the direction of higher goals, including the ultimate goal of self-actualisation.

The phenomenological view suggests we can best understand human existence by understanding how *individuals* experience the world. In Rogers' (1959) phenomenological formulation, there could be multiple experiences and perceived realities for each person, no matter how similar the conditions they found themselves in, and the phenomenological reality or lived experience of the individual client is paramount in the therapeutic endeavour. This is reflected in the British Association for Counselling and Psychotherapy's (BACP) (2019) Competence Framework, which suggests that practitioners working with children and young people must be able to 'grasp the client's perspective and "world view"' (BACP, 2019) in order to provide an effective therapeutic relationship. The following exercise is a way of connecting with this experiencing in the present moment.

Experiential Exercise

Either alone or with a partner, focus on what you are feeling and experiencing in this moment, using the following prompts if you wish:

I am feeling...
I am aware of...
I am noticing in my body...
I am sensing...

If working with another, take a few minutes to discuss your experiences.

In 1959, Rogers published an extended framework outlining his 'Theory of Personality and Development'. For Rogers, human life begins with the infant in an undifferentiated state where there is no defined sense of 'me' or 'not me'. This means there is no pre-existing core sense of self or external objective reality. Rogers describes the infant as beginning to have 'self-experiences' when 'a portion of the individual's *experience* becomes differentiated and *symbolized* in an *awareness* of being, *awareness* of functioning' (Rogers, 1959: 223, original emphasis). Out of this gradual sense of being, comes awareness of self, then other and a sense of relationship *with* the other. Like many others writing about human development at the time, including psychoanalysts such as Winnicott (1960) and attachment theorist Bowlby (1973), Rogers indicates that the quality of the relationship with this early 'other' has a huge impact on the development of the individual, particularly in the development of their 'self-concept' (Rogers, 1959). It is from this self-concept that individuals encounter the world and make further connections and relationships. This also provides the first point of potential conflict between what Rogers formulates as the 'organismic valuing principle' and external 'conditions of worth' imposed by those the infant is dependent upon and in contact with, primarily the parents/carers. Through such interactions, the infant learns whether or not he is given approval for his behaviour by these important figures through observing his 'mother's face, gestures, and other ambiguous signs' (Rogers, 1959: 226).

In his 'nineteen propositions', Rogers (1951: 482) outlines his understanding of the human organism as having 'one basic tendency and striving – to actualize, maintain and enhance the experiencing organism'. He describes how this 'striving' is affected in various ways by the human organism's environment and how these experiences are perceived and assimilated into the self-concept. The individual may change their behaviour in order to please or obtain positive regard from someone significant. The 'conditions of worth' imposed on the infant by an external source interfere with the positive organismic flow of development, potentially creating psychological disturbance in childhood, adolescence and beyond.

The following exercise can be used to explore your own experience of 'conditions of worth'.

Exercise

Consider the following questions and write down your answers or explore them with a partner:

- Are you aware of any conditions of worth you experienced while growing up?
- Did you encounter any other conditions of worth as an adolescent or young adult?
- What impact do you think these conditions had on your development?
- Do they still have an impact on your choices or behaviour now?

In the light of this understanding of human development and the roots of psychological disturbance, Rogers' (1951) theory of psychotherapy posited that if the right kind of 'conditions' were in place in the therapeutic relationship, the client would experience themselves as valued, accepted and understood, and therefore be able to reconnect with their organismic valuing principle and move towards actualisation.

Summary

- Humanistic theory takes a positive view of the organism as seeking growth towards actualisation.
- In Rogers' view, the human infant needs optimal relational conditions in order to be able to achieve an organismic flow towards growth and the development of a healthy self-concept.

- Where infants come into contact with 'conditions of worth' imposed by caregivers or significant others, they are removed from the organismic valuing principle and may experience psychological disturbance in later life.
- Humanistic psychotherapy provides the relational conditions to allow the individual to experience themselves as prized without the imposition of conditions of worth.

Additional Resources

- Rogers, C.R. (1951) *Client-Centred Therapy: Its Current Practice, Implications and Theory*. London: Constable.
- Rogers, C.R. (1961) *On Becoming a Person: A Therapist's View of Psychotherapy*. London: Constable.

Associated Entries

2.2 Core Relationship Components
3.3 Play-Based Interventions
3.7 Working with Emotions
3.16 Identity
3.22 Self-Esteem

1.8 Neurobiological Development

Psychotherapeutic interest in neuroscience has increased greatly since the 1990s (Music, 2017), largely due to advances in magnetic-resonance imaging (MRI) technology. Understanding the complexity of the human brain, its development and the implications this has for human existence is a key part of how we understand other aspects of development. Therapists have been fascinated by the insights provided by new research into early neurological development and interpersonal neurobiology as well as the relevance of these insights for the therapeutic relationship (Wilkinson, 2006; Gerhardt, 2015).

Key Understandings

Neurobiological development

The brain is a highly complex organ with over 100 billion brain cells. The brain's developmental journey begins when the foetus is around three weeks old (Cohen, 2017). The brain grows more *in utero* than other parts of the body, which is why babies' heads are so large relative to their bodies. However, at around two-thirds of its full-grown size and functionality, the organ is still premature at birth. Connections linking different areas of the brain, allowing it to function fully, are not present at this point. According to Cohen (2017: 15):

> As the baby feels, moves and perceives, these connections are created. From the outset, heredity and environment interact. The baby's individual experiences create particular pathways and connections between particular cells.

This represents a view of the brain as experience expectant and dependent for its development. The relatively few connections at birth and the pruning process which begins soon afterwards are what allow humans the flexibility to adapt efficiently to different environments, as demonstrated by attachment theory (see entry 1.5, p. 16). This malleability of the brain is described as *neuroplasticity*, and while the majority of growth in connections occur in the first three years of the child's life, developments continue throughout the lifespan and particularly during adolescence and puberty.

Interpersonal neurobiology

'Interpersonal neurobiology' is a term describing aspects of brain development occurring through relationship with others. Gerhardt (2015) draws our attention to the presence of 'mirror neurons' in the infant brain, suggesting that these indicate a capacity to understand the actions of others or to connect with their emotional experience:

> The mirror neurons in these areas automatically fire up when they [the baby] observe [or hear] other people doing things. For example, the sight of someone in terrible pain is likely to make us flinch, or the sound of people laughing happily can make us feel mildly light-hearted. (Gerhardt, 2015: 56)

Having identified the orbitofrontal cortex as the most evolutionarily sophisticated part of the brain in humans, Gerhardt suggests that normal development of this region is unlikely if the individual baby is not in receipt of 'appropriate one-to-one social experience with a caring adult' (2015: 56), and that stressful experiences during this developmental period can make it more difficult to establish connections between this cortex and the *amygdala*, which is part of the primitive area of the brain governing primal fear responses. Without connections between the orbital cortex and other areas of the brain, Gerhardt argues, 'the pre-frontal cortex cannot do a good job of holding back the amygdala's fearful responses ... in fact, poor amygdala-prefrontal connectivity is significantly correlated with both depression and anxiety' (2014: 62).

The baby is dependent on others for development of this orbitofrontal cortex, and without appropriate social contact in the first three years of life, significant difficulties with functioning will arise. Babies find contact with humans, such as smiling and gazing, pleasurable and recognise when another is gaining pleasure from interacting with them. Between 6 and 12 months, there is a growth in synaptic connections as the baby is at its most social and finding the most pleasure in interactions with its parents and significant others. The 'social brain' develops during the first year, leading on to the development in the second year of life of verbal skills and processing. There is the possibility for the expression as well as the experience of feelings as the brain becomes more left brain-dominated and increasingly stable (Gerhardt, 2015). This is succeeded by the development of the *dorsolateral prefrontal cortex*, which is where we are able to *think* about our *thoughts*. It is also the site of our working memory.

The Adolescent Brain

A further 'sensitive time' in terms of neurological development occurs during adolescence. As we will see in entry 1.9 (p. 32), puberty heralds rapid development across all spheres of physical, emotional and social development, and the brain has a vital role to play in these changes. Schore identifies adolescence as a stage 'second only to the neonatal period in terms of both rapid biopsychosocial growth as well as changing environmental characteristics and demands' (Schore, 2003). MRI scans show dynamic changes in the brain's neurochemistry, fibre architecture and tissue composition (Bava & Tapert, 2010) as well as in volume and white and grey matter (Casey et al., 2008). Bava and Tapert (2010) suggest these changes are 'linked with more sophisticated social cognitive functioning and emotional processing, useful for navigating an increasingly complex psychosocial environment' (2010: 398). These changes in structure, while linked to the need to adapt for impending adulthood, are also implicated in an increase in risky behaviours in adolescents, and the potential for addiction, self-harm and other issues often associated with this developmental phase (Casey et al., 2008; Bava & Tapert, 2010; Hawton et al., 2012) (see entries 1.9, p. 32 and 3.10, p. 174).

While this is a brief explanation of what is known about neurobiological development, it allows us to begin to understand more clearly the important processes that infants and children go through neurologically, how dependent they are on their relational experiences with others for this development and what problems may arise when these early experiences are less than ideal.

Summary

- The brain is premature at birth and goes through several phases of development during infancy, childhood and adolescence.
- Many of these developments are shaped by relational and environmental experiences.
- Neurobiological development can have significant implications for capacity for affect-regulation and cognitive development.

Additional Resources

- Gerhardt, S. (2015) *Why Love Matters: How Affection Shapes a Baby's Brain* (2nd edition). Hove: Routledge.
- Music, G. (2017) *Nurturing Natures: Attachment and Children's Emotional, Sociocultural and Brain Development.* London: Routledge.

Associated Entries

1.3 Theory of Mind
1.4 Cognitive Development
1.5 Attachment Theory
1.9 Puberty & the Adolescent Transition
1.11 Developmental Implications for Counselling
3.10 Working with Risk

1.9 Puberty & the Adolescent Transition

The early entries in this part of the book have focused mainly on the first months and years of life, exploring the impact of early relational experiences on various aspects of child development. Developmental progression from birth to toddlerhood is rapid, as the pre-verbal new-born becomes the older baby, seeking out and learning from social engagement as well as developing attachment strategies. Then the developing child becomes able to utilise language to communicate wants and desires as well as use their body with advancing skills to complete important tasks.

Key Understandings

Latency and middle childhood

From approximately 5–11 years (middle childhood), children enter a relatively settled period in terms of development as many enter formal education, leading to increased knowledge and understanding, the development of social relationships, and rapidly increasing physical competence. By 5 years-old, the brain is 90% developed and primed to engage with whatever learning opportunities the environment offers.

In many societies it is the education system which reflects the current view of development, as demands on children to take in complex information increases as they move up through the school. In UK society, the biggest transition faced by young people, since starting school at 4 or 5 years of age, is the move to secondary school around the age of 11 or 12 years. It could be seen as no accident that this transition occurs around the time of puberty when children begin the journey from childhood into young adulthood.

Adolescence

'Adolescence' is a word derived from the Latin *adolescere*, meaning 'to grow up' (www.etymonline.com/word/adolescent), and is defined as 'the period of life when a child develops into an adult: the period from puberty to maturity, terminating legally at the age of majority' (www.merriamwebster.com/dictionary/adolescence). To understand adolescence fully we need to consider it from a number of perspectives. Every individual experience of this phase will be formed by various factors, including: environment, early experiences and culture. Adolescence is a lengthy developmental period, potentially lasting from around 10–24 years of age. Due to the significance of the young person's cultural and environmental context on this process, it is arguably as much culturally as biologically determined.

Pubertal processes include significant growth of the brain (see entry 1.8, p. 29), leading to advances in cognitive capacity as well as the ability to process complex emotions. Piaget (1964) characterised this as the 'formal operations' stage, when the individual begins to think and handle abstract and hypothetical concepts in more sophisticated ways. This change in cognition is significant in terms of confidentiality and consent in the therapeutic relationship (see entry 2.9, p. 84).

Socially, the adolescent relies less on their parents and peer relationships become increasingly significant. Alongside this change, romantic bonds are hoped for and possibly formed, and sexual relationships may begin for the first time. Adolescents who have experienced deficits in early relational experiences may be vulnerable during this time, for example, if they attempt to meet their unmet infantile needs through adolescent sexual relationships (see entries 3.10, p. 174 and 3.15, p. 195).

The Onset of Puberty

The term 'puberty' is derived from the Latin *pubertatem*, meaning 'age of maturity, manhood' (www.etymonline.com/word/puberty), but the term is commonly used to describe the biological processes which drive the dramatic transition from childhood to adulthood, rather than the point of arrival itself.

Puberty brings changes across genders as bodies and minds develop in preparation for adulthood. These changes occur at a different rate for male and females and for individuals of both genders. Puberty generally takes place over 5–7 years, with hormonal changes becoming significant around 10 years for girls and 12 years in boys (Tanner, 1989).

There are five key areas of change at puberty:

1. Accelerated skeletal growth.
2. Increases and/or redistribution of body fat and muscle tissue.
3. Development of the circulatory and respiratory systems, and thus increased strength and endurance.
4. Maturation of secondary sexual characteristics and reproductive organs.
5. Changes in hormonal/endocrinal systems which regulate and coordinate other pubertal events (Archibald et al., 2006).

According to Susman and Rogol (2004: 15):

> Puberty is one of the most profound biological and social transitions in the life span. It begins with subtle changes in brain-neuroendocrine processes,

hormone concentrations, and physical characteristics and culminates in reproductive maturity.

The universal changes which add up to the process described as *puberty* will naturally take a different course and operate to a different timescale for each individual. This in itself can prove challenges, and there is evidence to suggest that the chronological age at which pubertal events occur, such as first menstruation for girls and voices breaking for boys, can be significant in terms of whether these events have a negative impact on the individual (Steinberg & Morris, 2001; Mendle et al., 2007; Mendle & Ferrero, 2012). For example, a girl whose periods begin before she feels ready to cope with impending adulthood may develop eating issues as her psyche attempts to 'stop the clock' on puberty and return her to the place of safety represented by pre-pubescent childhood.

Individuals experience puberty in their own, unique way. Their experience is dependent on a number of factors, such as cultural narratives regarding adolescence and adulthood, early relational experiences, conscious and unconscious feelings about adulthood, etc. Fonagy et al. (2004: 318) suggest that puberty 'might trigger emotional upheaval. Which biological events might do so could be quite idiosyncratic, depending to a degree on what particular changes represent to the adolescent'. Integrative therapy can hold a space for exploration of the individual experience of adolescence in order to make meaning of it for the young person on a developmental path towards adulthood.

In addition to biological, cognitive and physiological changes taking place during puberty, adolescence is a time of intense change in terms of interpersonal relationships. The most significant transition involves the adolescent's relationship with parents and family. The majority of young people gradually separate from their parents as they move through this phase and develop a separate identity and sense of self (see entries 3.16, p. 199 and 3.20, p. 214).

Psychoanalyst Erik Erikson (1968) described this search for identity as the central task for adolescence, as young people transition from reliance on their family for their identity to being able to form one of their own, suited for the adult world into which they are moving. Young people who come for therapy at this time often find establishing this identity problematic, for various reasons. For example, a young man who has not had an opportunity to engage with his own desires and motivation, but follows a path to university laid out for him by his parents, may struggle when he gets there and eventually drop out, not really knowing why he has not been able to manage this transition.

Young people need a rich variety of experiences to help them develop a sense of themselves and their capabilities. For Erikson (1950), the adolescent mind was a 'mind of the moratorium', which needed space and time away from the limitations of childhood but protection from the demands of full adulthood for this sense of self to develop fully. For many young people growing up in modern society, this space is hard to find. Even the relative safety of time spent studying at university is overshadowed by the threat of student debt as well as the challenges of finding housing and making a way in the world after graduation. In this respect, therapy provides a space in which young people can explore identity as well as fears and anxieties about adulthood, without needing to definitely know who they are or what they believe. The therapeutic relationship provides this 'holding' via the core relationship components, including unconditional positive regard (see entry 2.2, p. 51) for the young person's process as they develop. This requires a particular approach from the therapist, who must free themselves of 'memory and desire' (Bion, 1967), freeing the young person from the imposition of further conditions of worth.

Environmental and systemic factors, such as family or cultural expectations of adolescents, socio-economic factors, and the way a particular society supports or impedes the transition to adulthood will all affect individual development. These will be explored in more depth in subsequent entries.

Summary

- Puberty heralds the biological, psychological, social and emotional processes which drive the transition from childhood to adulthood.
- The adolescent phase is a unique experience for all individuals and is affected by various factors, including early relational experiences, environmental and cultural factors.
- Adolescence sees the individual separating from parents and family, with peer relationships becoming increasingly significant. This can lead to vulnerability for some young people.
- Identity formation is a key process for adolescence as the young person individuates in preparation for adulthood. Counselling offers a 'holding space' for the young person as they resolve issues which may impede appropriate development.

Additional Resources

- Lerner, R.M. & Steinberg, L.D. (eds) (2004) *Handbook of Adolescent Psychology* (2nd edition). London: Wiley.
- Steinberg, L.D. (2017) *Adolescence*. New York: McGraw-Hill.

Associated Entries

1.8 Neurobiological Development
1.10 Environmental & Systemic Factors
1.11 Developmental Implications for Counselling
2.2 Core Relationship Components
3.5 Therapeutic 'Chat'
3.16 Identity
3.17 Sexuality & Gender Identity

1.10 Environmental & Systemic Factors

So far entries have focused on the development of the individual child, considering the impact of early relational experiences with primary caregiver(s). However, human development does not take place only in dyads, and, even if that could be argued, dyads themselves do not exist in a vacuum. Therefore, in order to fully understand development we must look beyond infant and caregiver and consider wider influences, including family, community, culture and socio-economic and political factors.

Key Understandings

Anna Freud (1965) was one of the earliest child psychoanalysts to highlight the importance of the child's environmental context. In a paper comparing child and adult analysis, she suggests that rather than focusing exclusively on the inner world of the client, the child analyst must bear 'witness to the powerful influence of the environment', going on to say: 'The child analyst who interprets exclusively in terms of the inner world is in danger of missing out on his patient's reporting activity concerning his – at the time – equally important environmental circumstances' (A. Freud, 1965: 50–51). Anna Freud, who began her career working with children in London during the Second World War, was keenly aware of how environmental circumstances affected her young clients.

Around the same time, the Russian-American psychologist Urie Bronfenbrenner took a similar view that development needed to be understood from not simply one individual-oriented perspective, but rather as 'a theory of environmental interconnections and their impact on the forces directly affecting psychological growth' (Bronfenbrenner, 1979: 8), through which the developing child can be understood as part of an ecology of influential factors.

In its simplest formulation, an ecological approach is one that acknowledges that all interactions between a child and their environment influence their development (Aldgate, 2006). Bronfenbrenner first developed ecological systems theory in the 1970s and continued to refine it until his death in 2005. His bio-ecological model was intended to provide 'a conceptual framework for studying human development in context' (Ferguson & Evans, 2019: 144) and to be used as a basis to facilitate rigorous research into human development, partly in order to develop services aimed at improving outcome for children and families most vulnerable to the negative impact of environmental factors.

Such factors include poverty, racial inequality and discrimination as well as the intersections between them (Velez & Spencer, 2018).

Bronfenbrenner (1979) outlined his theory through the image of a set of nested Russian dolls. The innermost doll represents the individual child and their immediate environment, the next represents the child's immediate setting and includes their relationship to another setting, for example the child's relationship with school is influenced by the connection between home and school. The next doll represents settings which the child may never actually experience directly but which influence their development, for example the parent's workplace. The next doll is one which influences the previous layer, such as the wider culture, which in turn impacts the family 'routines and rituals' (Fiese et al., 2002). The last layer is that of 'time', whether that is the immediate moment in which development occurs or previous eras and epochs which may have occurred long before the individual child was born but which are still part of his or her ecological system. Examples of this would include children raised in families which have experienced intergenerational trauma, such as the holocaust, or historic racial inequality and abuse (Hall, 2011; Dashorst et al., 2019). Bronfenbrenner used the terms 'micro-', 'meso-', 'exo-', 'macro-' and 'chrono-system' to describe the layers. The interactive nature of these ecological layers was key to Bronfenbrenner's theory. In his formulation, there is a constant dynamic and often mutual developmental interaction between each part of the connected system. This begins from the outset with the initial dyad, and Bronfenbrenner (1979: 5) suggests that 'if one member of the pair undergoes a process of development, the other does also'. Bronfenbrenner (1979: 5) suggests that the dyad's capacity to:

> serve as an effective context for human development is crucially dependent on the presence and participation of third parties, such as spouses, relatives, friends and neighbors. If such third parties are absent, or if they play a disruptive rather than a supportive role, the developmental process, considered as a system, breaks down; like a three-legged stool, it is more easily upset if one leg is broken, or shorter than the others.

In these simple terms, Bronfenbrenner conveys the importance and complexity of understanding the relationship of environment on development.

Arguably the most significant developmental influence on an individual is their immediate family, as demonstrated by the first of Bronfenbrenner's nested Russian dolls. In the ecological model, we are invited to consider the family not only as an individual system of its own, but as part of the wider community and culture, influenced by the particular time and context in which it has itself developed. The ecological view of the family considers the dynamic processes at play for all its members, rather than simply linear or uni-directional ones, for example knowledge is imparted to the child by its elders. Rather, 'The child is at the center of her own development, but is also part of a larger system of individuals who are at the center of their own development, and they mutually impact each other's developmental processes over time' (Ferguson & Evans, 2019: 148).

Ecological theorists from a range of disciplines, including anthropology and sociology as well as psychology, have engaged in scientific studies of the family, many focusing on the importance of 'routines and rituals' (Fiese et al., 2002) for family functioning and successful adaptation to challenging events or circumstances. Family routines are argued to provide coherence and predictability to family life (Reiss, 1981), giving members a sense of something consistent and trustworthy. Fiese et al. (2002: 382) argue that routines and rituals, such as family mealtimes, performance of chores around the home, or family celebrations such as birthdays, holidays etc. 'highlight the intersection between individual- and family-level factors'. By examining family life from this perspective, we see how family life influences the development of the individual child, but also how the perspectives and characteristics of an individual can affect the way the family as a whole continues to function. An example of this would be if a child growing up in a meat-eating family decided to become a vegetarian. Other family members might be influenced by this decision to also stop eating meat, thus having a significant influence on family rituals and routines around food consumption.

Observing family routine and ritual is also useful for assessing the impact of various life events on family and individual functioning. For example, life with a new-born baby tends to cause disruption to established family routine. This may impact older siblings who struggle when this occurs. As children grow, family routines such as bedtime can become areas of family life which offer opportunity for negotiation as a child asks to go to bed later, perhaps because they have become aware of their friends doing this and they want similar privileges. This is another straightforward example of the ecological view where, as a child develops their own friendships and perhaps begins to spend more time with other families and experiences other routines and rituals, these have an impact on their own families' routines and rituals. In adolescence, research suggests that the individual begins to place less emphasis on family routine and ritual and more on those of their peer group, in line with other aspects of separation and individuation during adolescence (Fiese et al., 2002: 384). This can have significant implications for young people growing up in families of minority cultures who are influenced by the majority culture of their peers (see entry 2.11, p. 93).

Disruption to family routines may also be an early indicator of the presence of stress in the system (Steinglass et al., 1987). For example, during divorce and separation, family rituals around birthday and Christmas may be disrupted, causing distress for the children and adults alike (see entry 3.20, p. 214).

Family routine and ritual, and therefore development, are also affected by experiences of economic hardship. In terms of socio-economic factors such as poverty, Ferguson and Evans (2019: 151) suggest that 'no measurable factor has as significant an impact on both individual development and the successful functioning of family systems as poverty', describing parents who have grown up in poverty as experiencing 'poorer health and a less efficient stress response'. They go on to state: 'All of these factors intersect to create a very different macrosystem for children growing up in low-income homes and neighborhoods than those who do not' (2019: 152). One study suggests child poverty in the UK has increased sharply since 2011, resulting in 3.9 million children living in poverty at that time and predicting an increase of another 50% of those numbers by 2020 (McCall, 2016: 747). The report found children growing up in poverty had a one-in-three chance of developing a mental health issue by the age of 11, compared to a one-in-ten chance for those who had not experienced persistent poverty. The ecological model facilitates an understanding of the multiple risk factors which poverty can cause to the health, wellbeing and functioning of both individual children and the family system itself. Poverty may not only impact the child immediately, but can influence development through 'proximal' processes within the local community, schools and the wider education system, as well as in the general socio-political environment. For example, after the financial crash of 2008 and the resulting recession, the UK government introduced a fiscal policy of austerity measures intended to reduce the government's budget deficit. These measures included a cut of approximately £30 billion to welfare payments, housing subsidies and social services in the UK (Mueller, 2019). For those children growing up while this policy was in operation, there will have been a significant impact on their development, similar to that experienced by those growing up where there is high unemployment or, as in 2020, a global pandemic, which will have an ongoing impact on the physical and economic health of nations around the globe. The direct economic impact of the pandemic will most likely be felt by the poorest in society (Vesoulis, 2020), and again, a bio-ecological model such as Bronfenbrenner's provides a method of unpacking the layers of impact that this is likely to have on individual and family development. Ferguson and Evans (2019) cite research suggesting that families experiencing poverty are less able to maintain regular family routines and rituals. They may be more likely to be exposed to chaos, higher levels of relocation from home and/or school as well as more family disruption and turmoil (Ferguson & Evans, 2019: 155). This disruption is likely to impact the child's ability to engage and learn at school and may ultimately alter the capacity to regulate and manage stress (see entry 1.8, p. 29). This chaos and disruption to regular family routine may also be experienced by children growing up in families where there is parental substance misuse, mental health issues or chronic illness or disability.

In the ecological model, culture as an influencing factor is situated at the macro-system level. However, cultural influence filters down to all parts of the system as an influence on the family's beliefs, values, parenting styles, routine and rituals, access to education as well as on whether more emphasis and importance is placed on the needs of the individual members or on the group as a whole. This is illustrated by two reports cited by Fiese et al. (2002) which examined cultural differences through conversations at family mealtimes. One study found that Japanese-American families were more likely to discuss group activities and shared experiences at dinner, while 'Caucasian American families were more likely to focus on the child's activities and individual experiences' (Fiese et al., 2002: 384). Cultural differences such as these will have a significant impact on the development of the individual, on their self-concept and on their own views and perceptions regarding themselves and their place in society. It is vital that counsellors are aware of these factors and can take them into consideration when working with individuals who have a different cultural background from themselves (see entry 2.11, p. 93). Understanding the impact of culture on development is a key aspect of cultural competence in therapeutic work with children and young people (Kirkbride, 2018a).

Exploring an ecological systems model of development offers practitioners a means of understanding their client and their worldview through a number of different layers. This is intended to enhance understanding and provide an opportunity for the development of empathic responses and unconditional positive regard as well as facilitating the client's own sense of themselves and why they function in the way they do.

Use the following exercise to explore your own ecological developmental system.

Exercise

Draw a series of concentric circles to represent the layers of Bronfenbrenner's ecological systems model. Fill these in for different phases in your own development.

- What were the 'immediate' factors impacting your caregivers? These might include redundancy or unemployment, bereavement, migration to another country, etc.
- What were the broader cultural or socio-political factors? Did you grow up during a time of political upheaval? Did you belong to a minority culture? How did this impact the other levels of your development?

Consider how your development would have been affected had these factors absent or if others were present.

- Would you be the same person you are today?
- If not, how might you have been different?

Repeat this exercise after two weeks, two months, a year, etc., and notice the changes – subtle and extreme – which take place in your ecology. Consider the impact of these on your wellbeing and sense of self.

Summary

- Development is influenced by factors beyond the primary caregiving relationship.
- Environmental factors can be viewed through an ecological systems lens which offers insight into intersecting factors, including culture, socio-economic conditions as well as family 'routines and rituals'.
- Understanding of the influence of these factors can assist therapists in understanding the 'whole' child.

Additional Resources

- Bronfenbrenner, U. (1979) *The Ecology of Human Development: Experiments by Nature and Design*. Cambridge, MA: Harvard University Press.
- Lago, C. (ed.) (2011) *The Handbook of Transcultural Counselling and Psychotherapy*. Maidenhead: McGraw-Hill/Open University Press.

Associated Entries

2.2 Core Relationship Components
2.11 Cultural Competence
3.20 Family Breakdown & Instability

1.11 Developmental Implications for Counselling

The developmental stage a child or young person has reached has implications for many aspects of the therapeutic process (see entry 1.1, p. 3). These include establishing and sustaining the therapeutic alliance, which is a vital factor in providing positive therapeutic outcomes for children and young people.

Key Understandings

In all therapeutic work, therapists benefit from an understanding of human development, including factors contributing to psychological and emotional difficulties in later life. In work with children and young people, developmental understanding plays a pivotal role in the therapeutic process, with practitioners required to gain a sense of the client's developmental capacity in order to work effectively. For example, the way an 8-year-old client will experience the death of a parent will be different from an 11- or 15-year-old. We can also say that the way this experience is perceived by one 8-year-old might differ significantly from another 8-year-old, and that this difference might be due in part to their developmental capacity for understanding death, or to other factors such as differences in terms of how the death impacted their family system. Developmental differences such as these will also manifest in the therapeutic process. For example, if one of the 8-year-olds has had the opportunity to develop secure attachments in early relationships and has a well-developed capacity to play and to symbolise, they might respond quickly to a therapeutic play-based intervention where they can build a good therapeutic alliance with their counsellor and begin to work through feelings via play and metaphor. They may have a good experience of counselling that enables them to feel confident to return when they perhaps need to revisit the grieving process as an older child or adolescent. Alternatively, the 8-year-old may have experienced trauma and difficulties in early relationships. They may find it harder to form a working alliance with their counsellor, who they might feel mistrust of initially. They may find it harder to play and to symbolise, to trust that it is OK to experience and express feelings, and that these can be worked through relationally. In this case, the early stages of counselling will probably focus on aiding the child in building trust in the therapeutic relationship prior to beginning any work on the loss or the grieving process itself. This is not to say that only one of these children is an appropriate referral for counselling, only that this is an example of the importance of considering developmental stage and capacity when beginning therapeutic work. The provision of the core relationship conditions (for example, see entry 2.2, p. 51) needs to be considered with respect to developmental stage or the particular phase the client is currently encountering. For example, there needs to be an understanding of, and even empathic connection to, where a child or young person is developmentally if the client is to experience interventions as empathic. Often child and adolescent clients perceive their issues as less important than those of 'grown-ups'. The capacity to demonstrate empathy in a manner that allows the client to experience the attempt to understand the problem from their perspective is vital, rather than conveying the message that they will feel differently when they are older and can see things from an adult perspective.

Contracting is an area in which an understanding of developmental capacity is crucial, particularly with regards to consent and confidentiality (see entry 2.9, p. 84). Consent can be complex to negotiate as it centres around seemingly arbitrary concepts, such as 'capacity to consent' and 'sufficient understanding'. Navigating these areas of practice will be greatly aided by a broad knowledge of development and the factors determining what a child or young person is capable of in these respects.

The role taken by parents in their child's therapy will differ depending on factors including developmental stage, the context of therapy and the presenting issue being worked with, rather than being dictated simply by chronological age (see entry 2.12, p. 97). According to Anna Freud (1965: 43):

> Some of the most lively controversies concerning the specificity of child analysis are related to the question of whether and how far parents should be included in the therapeutic process. Although this is overtly a technical point, the issue at stake is a theoretical one, namely, the decision whether and from which point onward a child should cease to be considered as a product of and dependent on his family and should be given the status of a separate entity, a psychic structure in its own right.

As we will see throughout this book, the consideration of whether or to what extent a child is a 'separate entity' provides much of the tension in therapeutic work, as well as for the developing child themselves as they grapple with their own understanding of the journey from childhood through adolescence, and onto adulthood, including the tricky developmental tasks of separation and individuation.

Working therapeutically with children and adolescents requires flexibility and understanding of how developmental experiences and capacity affects the therapeutic process from the earliest stages of contracting, through establishing the therapeutic relationship, and onto choice of intervention and the therapeutic work itself, and including the termination process. While this requirement presents some complex challenges, it also offers the opportunity to develop a deep engagement with the processes of human development, its universalities and its unique unfolding in every individual life and journey.

Summary

- Understanding developmental experiences provides insight into the client and their issues.
- Understanding developmental capacity allows deeper engagement with the client 'where they are' in the present moment.
- Developmental capacity has implications for all aspects of the therapeutic process with children and young people, including capacity to consent, cognitive capabilities, the therapeutic relationship and endings.

Additional Resources

- Freud, A. (1965) 'The relations between child analysis and adult development', in *The Writings of Anna Freud. Vol. VI: Normality and Pathology in Childhood: Assessments of Development.* New York: International Universities Press.

Associated Entries

2.2 Core Relationship Components
2.5 Contracting
2.8 Risk Assessment & Safeguarding
2.9 Confidentiality & Consent
3.3 Play-Based Interventions
3.5 Therapeutic 'Chat'
3.14 Trauma & Abuse
3.26 Neurodiversity: Autism Spectrum Disorder (ASD) & Attention-Deficit Hyperactivity Disorder (ADHD)
4.7 Refugee Communities
4.8 Looked-After Children (LAC)

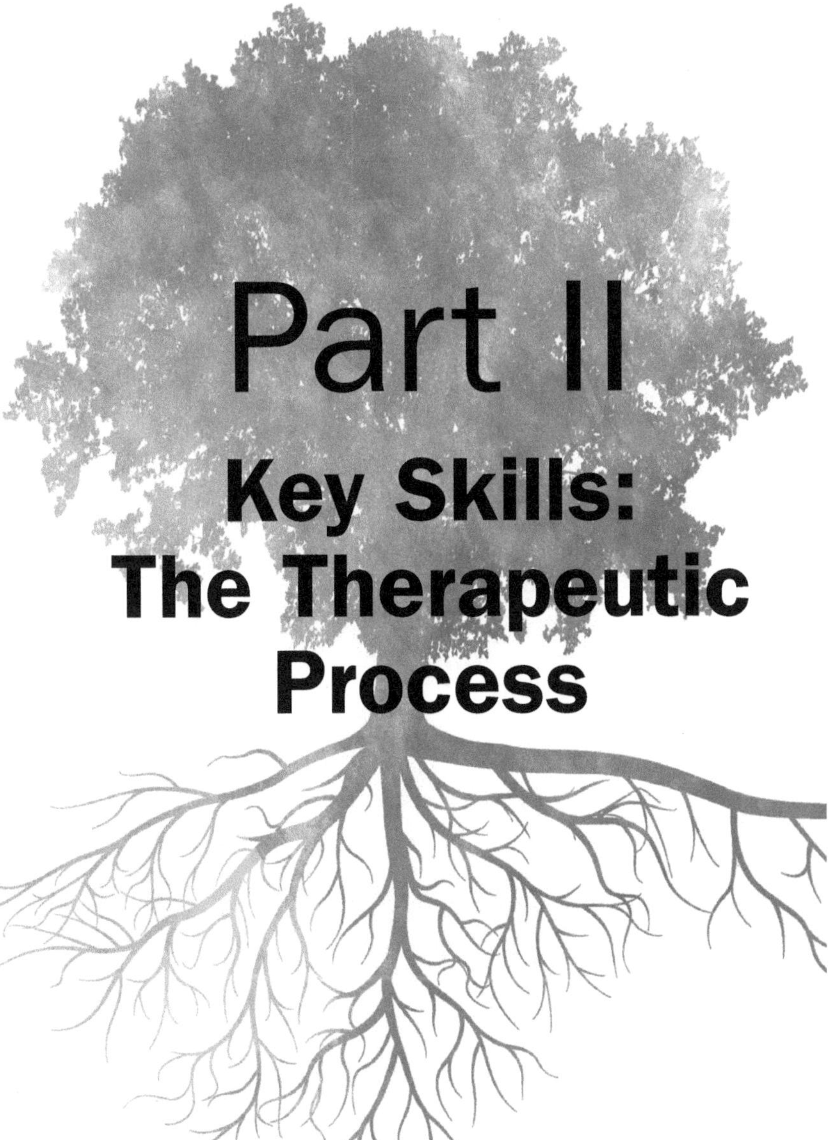

Part II

Key Skills: The Therapeutic Process

2.1 Introduction: Core Principles of Integrative Therapy with Children, Young People & Families

Part II of this book focuses on the central element of the therapeutic process – the therapeutic alliance or relationship. Establishing a solid working therapeutic alliance enables the client to explore and articulate their experience, leading to a progression towards health and relief from their difficulties. Research demonstrates that it is the quality of this relationship, rather than the theoretical approach employed, which has the most impact on therapeutic outcome (Wampold & Imel, 2015), and further research suggests that the emotional bond between client and therapist may be even more vital in work with adolescents (Sommers-Flanagan & Bequette, 2013).

Part I explored key elements of child and adolescent development, offering a secure base of knowledge and understanding to support progression into the therapeutic relationship and process. As noted in entry 1.11 (p. 43), a child or young person's development can have significant implications for the therapeutic relationship, and we will explore some of those in more depth in this part of the book.

Before the work of deconstructing and examining the therapeutic relationship and process begins, it is important to establish some core principles for integrative practice with children and adolescents.

The concept of integrative therapeutic practice is rooted in ideas which emerged from philosophical movements of the nineteenth century, such as existentialism and phenomenology. These movements place emphasis on the *perceiver* of the object rather than on the *object* itself. This makes the view of the perceiver of an object or experience paramount and therefore, in terms of therapy, there can be no simple or objective 'truth'. Truth arises from the experience of the phenomenon in the mind and body of the experiencer. The counsellor and client therefore co-create a relationship with the intention that the therapist uses their skills and understandings in the service of the client's progress towards their own understanding of psychological health and wellbeing as it relates to them individually.

In counselling with children and adolescents, this process is made a little more complex by the developmental factors discussed previously. For example, young children will have a different relationship with their symptoms and issues from that of their parents, and the degree to which a child or young person is able to view themselves and their mind or body objectively will depend on the developmental stage they have reached. This means that the therapist may have to integrate parent or family work into individual work with the client. This kind of integration involves paying close attention to a number of factors in order to ensure that the integrity of the therapeutic relationship with the client is maintained (see entry 2.12, p. 97).

Other entries in Part II explore the therapeutic alliance and relationship, looking closely at the relationship conditions and how these can be integrated with skills and understanding from a range of perspectives in order to provide effective therapeutic interventions. We will break down the component parts of the therapeutic process and examine specific aspects, including contracting, confidentiality, risk assessment, etc., while considering ways of integrating them with relationship skills and developmental understanding to ensure that interventions and approaches are effectively tailored for individual clients. We explore cultural competence, looking at the ways in which, for example, a client or counsellor's cultural background can impact the therapeutic process, and how this can best be understood and any negative impact ameliorated. Towards the end of this part we consider the wellbeing of the practitioner themselves and consider ways of ensuring that clinical supervision is used effectively and that sufficient networks for support are available to support those working in this often-challenging branch of therapeutic practice.

Offering children and adolescents a therapeutic relationship within which they feel safe enough to unburden or explore their struggles, allowing them to develop and move forward, can be rewarding. As counsellors and psychotherapists in this field, it is vital that we take responsibility for ensuring that what we offer is rooted in the understanding that this relationship is a powerful tool to be handled with great skill and care. The intention for these next entries is that they will offer support in developing and utilising these skills in practice.

2.2 Core Relationship Components

The core conditions of the 'therapist-offered' relationship – congruence, unconditional positive regard and empathy – are taken from Rogers' (1961) theory of humanistic psychotherapy (see entry 1.7, p. 25). These components make up the 'certain type of relationship' that Rogers describes, within which 'the other person will discover within himself the capacity to use that relationship for growth' (1961: 33). This entry considers these components and outlines the key skills required to establish a therapeutic relationship to facilitate growth towards actualisation.

Key Understanding: Congruence

The first relationship condition mentioned by Rogers (1959) is that of congruence. Rogers viewed the main difference between the two participants in therapy to be that one person 'is in a state of *incongruence*, being *vulnerable,* or *anxious*', while the other, 'whom we shall term the therapist, is *congruent* in the *relationship*' (1959: 213). In this context, congruence means that the person's ideal state – the state they would like to be in – is consistent with their core sense of self. We might call this 'feeling comfortable in your own skin'. The term 'genuineness' is sometimes used in place of congruence to describe an attitude where the therapist is able to 'be themselves' with the client and is not trying to come across as an 'expert', for example. As Mearns and Thorne (2013: 13) suggest, 'The counsellor who is congruent conveys the message that it is not only permissible but desirable to be oneself'. This is the foundation of the relational approach to therapy. It is the first step towards demonstrating to the client that who they are is fundamentally OK, and this is something to be not only conveyed verbally, but also shown through action and demeanour on the part of the therapist. In work with children and adolescents, this aspect of the relationship is a significant factor not only in building rapport at the outset of the work, but also in sustaining the client's trust in their sense of self, thus encouraging organic growth towards goals and desires. This can be particularly important in work with adolescents going through the phase of identity formation, where they might be full of insecurity about whether they are fundamentally 'OK' as a person (see entry 3.16, p. 199).

Key Skills: Congruence

The following are some ideas about how to cultivate and demonstrate congruence, including what this might look like in practice:

1. Access your own personal therapy or other reflexive activities to assist in developing a congruent sense of self. This is the first step in being able to embody congruence in the therapeutic relationship. It's important to explore specific areas of your core sense of self, such as culture, gender and sexuality, as incongruence or uncertainty in these areas may be experienced negatively by young clients who are themselves struggling with these aspects of self.
2. Try to be as 'genuine' as possible in your approach to the client, while maintaining the boundaries of the therapeutic relationship. This does not mean speaking your mind at any opportunity, inappropriately self-disclosing or being un-boundaried. It means coming from a place of authenticity when interacting with clients. In the following vignette a therapist, Katy, speaks about her experiences of being congruent with clients.

Case Example: Katy (interview)

K: What do I mean by being congruent? I think for me it means that when I'm with a client, even though the professional boundaries are in place, when I respond to them, I'm being me, Katy, and I really feel like I'm being me. I'm not trying to seem like I'm a really good counsellor who knows exactly what they should do. I'm not trying to be 'cool' or pretend I totally understand what they're experiencing. I can be congruent with the fact that I'm different from them, and try to understand the effect this difference might have on the relationship. I'm not sixteen and I'm a white cisgender woman, but I'm curious about what it's like for my client to be where they are now. If they're from a different cultural background to me, or a different gender I'm curious about that difference too and how my difference might be experienced by them. So basically, I'm just sitting with them in the room and trying my best to be present as we look at their problems together and try to understand them.

1. Use language you feel comfortable with and that doesn't feel too, 'counsellor-ish'. Young people are adept at noticing when someone is not being authentic, and this can make them wonder if you're trustworthy. Evidence suggests that young people respond well to candour and 'being real' in the therapeutic relationship, and negatively to insincerity and pretence (Campbell & Simmons, 2011).
2. Bear in mind that the capacity for congruence can take time and work to develop. While training or starting out as a counsellor, it can be challenging

to be fully authentic. The process of developing an identity as a therapist unfolds along with a natural preoccupation with 'getting it right'. Admitting that you are a novice can feel difficult, but it is important to be congruent with this too. One method of developing an understanding of authenticity is to practise. With a partner, role-play being insincere in your conversation as well as being sincere and genuine. This can be a playful way of developing a sense of the difference between the two, while beginning to locate an authentic place from which to meet your clients.

Key Understanding: Unconditional Positive Regard (UPR)

At the centre of humanistic theories of development is the idea that through receipt of unconditional positive regard (UPR) from significant others the infant can develop in accordance with their organismic valuing principle (see entry 1.7, p. 25). Without UPR, the infant is compelled by a need to be loved and approved of to accept 'conditions of worth', imposed by caregivers. This can lead to incongruence and potential psychological disturbance at a later point.

The concept of UPR can be tricky to understand and, in some respects, it is only through practice that we get a full sense of the meaning of offering non-judgemental acceptance to clients in a manner which they are able to receive and make therapeutic use of. UPR is the offering of a relationship in which all aspects of the client's experience are received without judgement. For Rogers (1959: 206), 'To perceive oneself as receiving positive regard is to experience oneself as making a difference in the experiential field of another'. This places UPR firmly in the client's experiencing themselves as positively received, rather than this being something the therapist 'does' to them.

Once UPR is experienced consistently by the client, it allows a sense of genuine trust to be established, allowing the client to trust they will be accepted no matter who they are, and that therefore it is safe to use the therapeutic space to 'play' and discover themselves. Establishing UPR as a core relational condition provides the opportunity for the client to reinstate trust in their own capacity to be self-led and to trust their emotional responses as they develop a congruent sense of self. This can provide vital developmental support for children and young people whose early relational experiences have left them with issues around self-esteem and their likeability as a person (see entry 3.22, p. 222).

Like many of the core relationship conditions, UPR can be challenging to provide in practice, particularly when the client's behaviour is challenging or risky, both within and outside their sessions.

Key Skills: Unconditional Positive Regard (UPR)

1. The key to offering UPR is cultivating an attitude of warmth and non-judgemental acceptance towards your client, as they are, each time you see them. Reflect on your body language, tone of voice and facial expressions as these convey signals to the client about how they are received by you.
2. Make comments which validate your client's experience and feelings in a particular situation, for example:

   - 'You didn't like it when Josh tore the book you were reading. It made you very cross.'
   - 'You found the ski trip quite difficult. You really missed your mum and dad while you were away.'

   These may sound like very basic interventions, but they clearly validate the client's experience and feelings, rather than being dismissive or judgemental, as shown in these alternatives:

   - 'You shouldn't have got so angry when Josh took your book. You upset the rest of the class with your shouting.'
   - 'You were only away for a week. All the other year 9's had a great time on the ski trip. Why couldn't you manage it better?'

   For children and young people whose emotional experiences have been shut down or denied and who have received a message that they are wrong in some way for feeling or experiencing life as they do, the offer of UPR will be beneficial in supporting them in validating their emotional experience and developing a congruent sense of self.
3. Ensure that appropriate distinctions between UPR for the self and the need, where appropriate, to explore responses and challenge behaviour are understood. In the following case study we see a counsellor managing this distinction with his client.

Case Example: Lucius (counsellor) and Hayden

H: (Moving cars around in the sand-tray) I had a bad day yesterday. I was bad in class so Miss made me sit outside so I could think.

L: You're telling me you had a bad day yesterday; you were bad in class and had to sit outside.

H: Yes, it was Josh's fault, though. He took my book in reading time and tore one of the corners. On purpose. I shouted at him to stop and Miss shouted at me.

L: (Using a gentle tone of voice, attempting to convey understanding and acceptance) You didn't like it when Josh tore the book you were reading. It made you very cross.

H: It's my favourite book. The one I showed you in here that time. It's about the pig who can't find his friends.

L: I remember the book; it's a special one for you. No wonder you were cross when Josh tore it.

H: I was cross so I shouted. I didn't know what else to do.

L: It felt like shouting was the only thing you could do.

H: Yes, but that got me into trouble, didn't it? That's why I got sent outside.

L: It was the shouting that got you into trouble.

H: It shouldn't have been me that was in trouble. It should have been Josh. Did I need to shout at Josh? I'm not sure.

L: You're not sure if you needed to shout at Josh. Perhaps you're wondering if there is anything else you could do if that happened again?

In this example we see Lucius offering UPR to Hayden as he explains his experience in class the day before. As he experiences his feelings being received and validated by Lucius – '**No wonder you were cross when Josh tore it**' – space is provided for Hayden's own curiosity about his behaviour, and he begins to wonder if there might be other choices in this kind of situation. He may be picking up from Lucius a sense that his feelings were appropriate and understandable, allowing him to wonder about his action or response to the feeling. Now they can begin to explore this together safely in the therapeutic relationship.

Key Understanding: Empathy

Empathy is inextricably linked to the previous two conditions. We can't really be empathic or empathically attuned to our client if we are not coming from a place of authenticity and unconditional acceptance of the client and their experience. Empathy, in Rogers' (1961) conceptualisation, is a particular kind of understanding of the client and their frame of reference, which can be offered in the form of an empathic response to the client's material.

There is empathy evident in the previous case example where Lucius's response to Hayden – **'I remember the book and I think it's a very special one for you. No wonder you were cross when Josh tore it'** – shows his empathic understanding of how difficult it was for Hayden that Josh was tearing that particular book.

Rogers (1980: 142) saw empathy as integral to making progress in therapy: 'By pointing to the possible meanings in another's experiencing, you help the other to focus on this useful type of referent, to experience the meaning more fully, and to move forward in the experiencing.'

Key Skills: Empathy

1. Offering empathy means staying as close to what the client is communicating as possible. By attempting to empathically attune to the client, we are trying to enter their frame of reference and see things as they do. This means actively listening to their communications, verbal and non-verbal.
2. Empathy means connecting to feelings of which the client may be consciously aware, while also picking up on aspects of their experience which may be on the edge of awareness, that is:

    - 'You are talking a lot about how excited you were to be in the play but I'm wondering if there is also some sadness for you that your mum wasn't able to be there?'

3. Empathic interventions may involve picking up on non-verbal cues, such as body language, facial expressions, tone of voice, etc. In play and art therapy, they may involve empathic understanding of what the child's play or art is communicating:

    - 'You've put those two figures far away from each other in the sand. I wonder if you're feeling like your dad is far away from you at the moment. Like you can't get close to each other.'

4. Empathy can be used to convey a sense of congruence about contradictory aspects of the client's experience:

    - 'I get the sense that even though you are keen to find out more about your biological father and even meet up with him, you're also terrified about what might happen if you do.'

    In this way we convey to the client the acceptability and normality of contradictory or mixed responses to the same thing.

As with the other two relationship conditions explored in this entry, empathy is strongly related to the concept that the client knows what is best for them and which direction to go in. By offering an attitude of empathy we are getting alongside the client and demonstrating trust in their own capacity for growth and development on their own terms.

As these conditions are so essential for an effective therapeutic relationship, it is important that practitioners are aware and congruent regarding problems they experience in offering them. For example, there may be clients whom we struggle to receive positively as well as those whose frame of reference conflicts with our own. These struggles are a natural part of therapeutic work and should be taken to supervision (see entry 2.24, p. 137) and/or personal therapy with the aim of understanding where they are originating from and finding ways to process them in order to be able to work effectively with the client again.

Summary

- The core relationship conditions, when received by the client, facilitate a therapeutic relationship in which growth can occur.
- While these conditions are 'therapist-offered', their effectiveness lies in how they are perceived and received by the client.
- Congruence, unconditional positive regard and empathy, when offered appropriately and received by the client, can provide a sense of trust in the individual, allowing them to trust themselves and their experience of situations.

Additional Resources

- Cooper, M., O'Hara, M., Schmid, P.F. & Bohart, A.C. (eds) (2013) *The Handbook of Person-Centred Psychotherapy and Counselling* (2nd edition). London: Palgrave Macmillan.
- Rogers, C.R. (1961) *On Becoming a Person: A Therapist's View of Psychotherapy*. London: Constable.

Associated Entries

1.7 Humanistic Theories of Development
2.4 Building Rapport
2.14 Developing & Sustaining the Therapeutic Relationship
2.17 Developing Advanced Empathy
2.18 Tracking
3.3 Play-Based Interventions
3.4 Creative-Arts Interventions
3.22 Self-Esteem

2.3 The Therapeutic Frame

'So what's this all about then, Miss? What are we gonna do?'

'My friend came to see you last year and she said all you did was play games and stuff. She said it helped though. Weird!'

'I don't know how this is going to help. How can just talking make stuff better?'

'What are the rules in here? What am I allowed to talk about?'

'Will you tell my teachers what I say to you. Once I told my friend something and then she told Miss Osborne and I cried.'

These are some of the questions that children and young people bring to their first experience of counselling. Even if they can't fully articulate their uncertainty about the strangeness and unfamiliarity of the therapeutic relationship, it's important to be aware of them. After all, this is likely to be a very different encounter from any they have previously had with an adult outside their immediate circle. In order for the client to feel safe in the relationship, it's important that both they and us have a sense of what 'therapy' is all about and why it might be helpful for them to engage with it.

So how do we as practitioners understand the therapeutic frame in counselling with children and young people and, more importantly perhaps, how do we communicate this framework to our clients in a manner which will enable them to feel as secure as possible about entering the therapeutic process?

Key Understandings

First, it's important to understand what we mean by the term 'therapeutic frame'. The word 'frame' denotes something that surrounds or contains contents. It is part of the whole, but is separate from those contents. In art, the frame is part of what we see when we look at a painting in a gallery, but it is not the painting itself. In psychotherapy, the frame consists of aspects of the process which need to be established before the therapy itself – the meeting of a counsellor and client – can take place. Once these components, such as referral, contracting, confidentiality, etc., have been established in the minds of both therapist and client, then the therapeutic process can begin from a foundation of trust and understanding for both parties.

In her book examining the frame in adult psychotherapy, Gray (2013: 7) outlines the following components:

> ...a private setting in which therapist and client meet; fixed times and duration for the sessions; vacation breaks which are clearly stated by the therapist; a set fee for all sessions reserved; and an internal concept on the part of the therapist that whatever is talked about is not talked about with anyone outside of the therapeutic relationship.

The frame consists of practical elements, which may be largely unchanging no matter who the client is, and other, less tangible aspects, such as confidentiality. Counsellors should always bear in mind that some of the concepts may be a little abstract for the client to understand. This is why the frame needs to be discussed in a developmentally appropriate way that ensures both parties really understand the terms used. For example, terms used in contracting for confidentiality, such as 'safe' and 'danger', are somewhat subjective and open to interpretation and different clients may have very different understandings and experiences of 'safety' and 'danger'.

Once the 'rules' of the therapeutic process have been agreed, there are two main implications: one is that a degree of security and trust will have been established; the other is that the therapist will gain insight into the client through their responses to and behaviour in relation to the frame. Do they arrive for their session on time? Perhaps they struggle to leave when their time is up, or always take holidays just before the therapist takes their break. When placed alongside client material or presenting issues, these actions can often tell us a great deal about the client and what they may be struggling with.

The elements that Gray (2013) describes are as much part of work with younger clients as they are with adults. For example, in therapeutic work where arts and play materials are used, it may be necessary to establish 'rules' or limits from the beginning regarding how these are managed (see entry 2.6, p. 72). Children and adolescents are unlikely to feel safe enough to freely express themselves through play or art in a session if they are not clear about what the rules are regarding the materials. Are they 'allowed' to mix the colours of the Play-Doh? How much paper can they use in one session? Establishing these elements of the frame can be particularly important for counsellors working in schools where the 'rules' of the *classroom* regarding play and art are likely to be different from those of the *therapy room*. Here the frame helps both client and counsellor to understand the difference between what they are doing together, compared to the rest of the child's day. The following case examples demonstrate a counsellor establishing the frame for therapy with a 5-year-old client in a primary school.

Case Example: Casey (counsellor) and Hamid

C: So, Hamid, we have 40 minutes in here this morning. (Casey takes the toy clock and shows H the hands and where they will move to by the end of the session)

H: I can tell time, Casey. When the big hand is there it's time for us to finish. Will you take me back to my classroom then?

C: Yes, we'll go back together.

H: OK.

C: As you can see, there are some things in here that you can play and draw with, or make something. You can use whatever you like, but if there's anything that's not allowed, I'll let you know. I also need to tell you that I won't speak about anything that you do in here or anything that you and I talk about with anyone else unless I was ever concerned that you might not be safe. Then we'd need to talk to someone else about that. Does that make sense?

H: Yes. I'd like to do painting first. Do you have any aprons, Casey? I need to always wear an apron my mum says so I don't get my uniform in a mess.

In this example we see Casey establishing the frame. Casey explains the length of the session, introducing the materials that can be used as well as the idea that there are some limits around what can be done with the materials. Casey introduces and explains the confidential nature of the counselling relationship. These elements are covered in a developmentally appropriate manner, taking into account Hamid's ability to understand concepts such as time and confidentiality. Having established the frame, Casey is in a position to observe with curiosity how Hamid responds to it. For example, his request for an apron and comments about his mum not wanting him to get messy may prove significant when placed alongside other aspects of the referral or presentation in the session. The practitioner must hold these observations in mind without immediately interpreting or jumping to conclusions about them. Rather, they can be considered as part of a developing hypothesis or formulation for the work.

The following case example shows how useful the frame can be in a situation where confidentiality needs to be broken in therapy. Katya is a 13-year-old girl suspected of being in a sexual relationship with an older male.

Case Example: Martha (counsellor) and Katya

M: So Katya, do you remember at the start of our sessions when we talked about confidentiality and what would happen if I was concerned that you were at risk of harm from yourself or another?

K: (agitated and tearful) Yes, but I don't want you to say anything. I'm fine. I wish I'd kept my mouth shut now.

M: I understand this is upsetting for you and I'll do what I can to support you in thinking about what's happening, but we had an agreement that I would break confidentiality if I was concerned you were in danger and I have those concerns right now.

In this case example, Martha is able to refer back to the confidentiality agreement established as part of the frame at the beginning of the therapeutic relationship between herself and Katya. As established at the start of this entry, the frame exists as part of the work but is separate from the content of the therapy. It may be deeply worrying for Katya at the moment that confidentiality will be broken, but equally, this was the agreement that she made with Martha at the beginning of their work. The frame could be referred to in a similar manner if the issue was about time-keeping or missing sessions. It is the responsibility of the therapist to hold the frame in mind and maintain the boundaries of the therapeutic relationship, even when this is uncomfortable or difficult.

Summary

- The therapeutic frame consists of aspects of the process which need to be established prior to therapy beginning and maintained consistently throughout the therapeutic process.
- The frame consists of elements such as: the contract; the time, place and frequency of sessions; breaks and holidays, etc.
- The way a child or young person responds to the frame can offer insight into their ways of relating or experiencing boundaries outside therapy.
- Changes or breaks in the frame may cause anxiety for some young clients who require consistency to feel secure in the therapeutic relationship.

Additional Resources

- MindEd – www.minded.org.uk: 412-018 *Establishing a Therapeutic Alliance.*
- Gray, A. (2013) *An Introduction to the Therapeutic Frame.* London: Routledge.

Associated Entries

2.2 Core Relationship Components
2.5 Contracting
2.6 Limit-Setting
2.9 Confidentiality & Consent

2.4 Building Rapport

Building rapport is an essential component of the therapeutic alliance, regardless of therapeutic modality. In this entry we consider the key skills required to develop rapport with a range of child and adolescent clients.

Key Understandings

Building rapport is an essential component of the therapeutic alliance, regardless of therapeutic modality. Much of our contemporary understanding of the therapeutic alliance has come from the work of psychologist and psychotherapist Edward Bordin. Bordin's (1979) major contribution was a paper which outlined a 'pan-theoretical' understanding of the components of the working alliance. For Bordin, the working alliance was 'one of the keys, if not *the* key of the change process' (1979: 252, original emphasis). Bordin saw the alliance as having three features: 'an agreement on goals, an assignment of tasks or a series of tasks, and the development of bonds' (1979: 253). Building the therapeutic alliance is a vital component of therapeutic work with children and young people. However, this is not always a straightforward process. Developmental factors, such as adverse childhood experiences or an adolescent's increasing move towards relationships with peers rather than with adults, can complicate the process. Gender, ethnic and cultural differences also need to be acknowledged and potentially explored if effective alliances are to be formed and sustained throughout the work. Child and adolescent practitioners also have to work with the additional complication of the need to develop multiple alliances with others, such as parents, carers, teachers and other professionals in the service of providing effective therapy for their client.

In her early work with children, Anna Freud (1974) was clear that the need to establish a rapport was one of the ways that classical psychoanalysis needed to be modified for work with younger clients. Freud (1974) suggested that an 'affectionate attachment' should be established before therapeutic work could begin. Her view was that this would ameliorate some of the developmental factors which made therapeutic work with children and young people somewhat different and more complex than work with adults. Freud (1974: 6) articulates these factors as 'everything which seems indispensable in the case of the adult: insight into illness, voluntary decision, and the wish to be cured'. Freud called this modification to the classical method the 'preparatory period' (1974: 7) and stated that this initial phase was separate from the therapeutic process itself.

This process could vary in duration depending on the needs of the child. There is a strong sense from her writing that this process should not be hurried but given the time necessary to ensure that the alliance is sufficiently established for therapy to begin.

There is plenty of research to suggest that the 'bond' (Bordin, 1979) component of the alliance holds even more significance in work with children and adolescents than with adults (Constantino et al., 2010: Sommers-Flanagan & Bequette, 2013). Sommers-Flanagan and Bequette suggest, in line with Anna Freud's original concept of the preparatory period, that '[w]hen working with adolescents the emotional bond may determine whether task collaboration and goal consensus are possible' (2013: 16). Practitioners working with adolescents may need to develop a range of skills for building rapport with a group who are developmentally inclined to trust peers rather than adult 'authority figures'. Useful skills in this respect include:

- Exhibiting genuine non-judgemental curiosity about the young person and their interests.
- Using an appropriate degree of humour and/or playful interactions.
- Demonstrating congruence and unconditional positive regard.
- Exhibiting respect for a young person's developmental stage and validating their capacity for autonomy.
- Providing a sense of warmth and acceptance in the relationship.

Children and young people can sense that things they value and are interested in are often not held in similar esteem by adults. Therapists who are willing to suspend their 'grown-up' view of children's games, and young people's interest in TV or social media are likely to be more able to build rapport with their client at the outset of the therapeutic process (see entry 3.5, p. 154). However, this needs to be balanced against any incongruent attempt on the therapist's part to be something they are not, that is, a young person themselves. Clients are not necessarily looking for a therapist who is the same as them, but for one who is willing to try to understand them and to get alongside and see the world from their perspective while remaining mindful of their relative difference.

The following case example shows a counsellor attempting to build rapport with an 11-year-old client they are meeting for the first time.

Case Example: Meera (counsellor) and Pawel

M: Pawel, now we've talked about what these sessions are about, it would be great if you would tell me something about yourself.

P: Like what? What do you want to know?

M: Well, anything really. What do you like doing when you're not at school?
P: Mostly I play out with my brothers and our friends from the estate. We play football all the time. But when we're not outside I like playing on my X-Box.
M: Oh cool, what do you play?
P: Mostly *Call of Duty*. You probably wouldn't like it cos there's shooting and stuff.
M: I might not like it, but I'm really interested in hearing what you like doing. It helps me get to know you a bit better and that might make it easier for us to work on the goals we talked about at the beginning.

In this example, by displaying genuine interest in the client's world, Meera establishes the idea that even though she and Pawel might have different likes and dislikes, as he suggests, she is interested in hearing about his world.

Building rapport is not always as straightforward as this example suggests. Some children and young people struggle to form relational bonds with others, possibly due to trauma or conditions affecting the capacity for social connections, such as Autistic Spectrum Disorder (ASD) (see entry 3.26, p. 239). Roth (2014) notes that difficulties in the development of mutual attention and joint gaze in infancy can predict problems for clients in forming and sustaining therapeutic alliances. As part of the assessment process, counsellors can consider the needs of a particular client and how best to establish the relationship with them. For some, the frame will be particularly important in this respect. If the practitioner can demonstrate a firm commitment to keeping the boundaries of the session consistent and reliable, it may be possible to begin to develop a sense of trust in the therapist and the process. Some clients may prefer to avoid direct eye contact with the therapist, needing to focus on toys or activities which bring them into a level of contact that they can tolerate. What is most important in this respect is to be client-led, follow cues and allow rapport to be built at a pace which suits the needs of the client rather than those of others, such as the school or a parent.

Culture, gender and sexual orientation may need to be acknowledged and explored during the rapport-building phase, especially with older children and adolescents. Yon et al. (2018) emphasise the importance of the counsellor's awareness of their cultural positioning as well as an understanding of their client's cultural background. Developing cultural awareness offers the therapist an understanding of how they may be perceived by the client as well as potential insights into the client's interpersonal relating style, for example, 'hierarchical vs. collaborative, collectivist vs. Individualistic' (Yon et al., 2018: 182) (see entry 2.11, p. 93).

Key Skills

1. Put time and effort into building a rapport with the client before trying to begin the therapeutic work itself.
2. Offer warmth and genuine interest in young clients; ensure they know you are pleased to see them.
3. Be curious about the client, their world, their interests, their likes and dislikes.
4. Demonstrate an attitude of acceptance and positive regard.
5. Be aware of and curious about your cultural positioning in relation to your client. Explore this where appropriate and be mindful of the impact of self-disclosure, and if it is beneficial to building rapport with the client.
6. Cultivate an interest in the cultural background of your client and consider how this might impact on their interpersonal relating style.
7. Be empathically attuned to your client and their developmental capacity for social connections. Modify and adapt your rapport-building skills accordingly, that is, use games or activities and position seating differently where direct eye contact is difficult.
8. Develop your knowledge and understanding of children, young people and their worlds. Inform and educate yourself about young people's interests, such as music, TV, social media, activism, etc. This will help to develop a familiarity with their world which will help to develop rapport.

Summary

- Building rapport is the first stage of developing the bond in the therapeutic alliance.
- Consideration should be given to ways of building rapport with different clients as well as challenges to this.
- Rapport building needs to be undertaken with the core relationship components in mind at all times.

Additional Resources

- Bordin, E.S. (1979) 'The generalizability of the psychoanalytic concept of the working alliance', *Psychotherapy: Theory, Research, and Practice*, 16(3): 252–260.
- Freud, A. (1974) *Introduction to Psychoanalysis: Lectures for Child Analysts and Teachers 1922–1935*. London: The Hogarth Press and the Institute of Psycho-Analysis.

Associated Entries

1.3 Theory of Mind
2.2 Core Relationship Components
2.11 Cultural Competence
2.15 Managing Ruptures in the Therapeutic Alliance
2.21 Self-Disclosure
3.5 Therapeutic 'Chat'

2.5 Contracting

Contracting is an essential component of the therapeutic frame (see entry 2.3, p. 58) and is fundamental for establishing trust in the therapeutic process. In this entry we consider some key understandings and skills for contracting in integrative counselling with children and adolescents.

Key Understandings

The contract consists of those aspects of the therapeutic frame which are negotiated and agreed on collaboratively by client and counsellor in ways appropriate for the age and developmental capacity of the client. The client must be in agreement with the terms of the contract before therapeutic work can commence. For example, if a young person went to see the school counsellor to find out whether sessions are 'completely' confidential and was told that there are circumstances under which confidence may be broken, then they may decide not to go ahead with counselling. In counselling with children and adolescent clients, it is unlikely that 'absolute' confidentiality will be offered (see entry 2.9, p. 84).

Any agreement or consent given must be 'informed' (see entry 2.9, p. 84) in order to support client autonomy in the relationship as far as possible. Depending on the setting and the developmental capacity of the client, some elements of the contract may need to be agreed with third parties, such as parents/carers, teachers, social workers, etc. (see entries 2.12, p. 97 and 2.22, p. 131). This is more likely to be the case in work with younger children and when clients are seen in private practice or agency settings.

Key Skills

The therapeutic contract is an agreement usually created at the beginning of counselling, which establishes a shared understanding of elements such as:

- Time and place of sessions
- Frequency of sessions
- Number of sessions
- Limits and boundaries in the session
- Confidentiality
- Record keeping and GDPR (General Data Protection Regulation) compliance
- Complaints procedure
- Safeguarding policy

- Protocol for missed sessions
    - Any 'paperwork' (e.g. outcome measures) to be used during the course of the therapy
    - Task or goals for therapy
    - How any artwork or material produced in therapy will be stored and disposed of when work ends.

Trainees may also need to contract for additional elements, such as recording sessions or using case material for assessment.

Aspects of the contract which need to be agreed with the client, such as a protocol for missed sessions, confidentiality, limit-setting and boundaries etc., should be established in developmentally appropriate ways. Both creative and verbal means of exploring the contract can be used, as demonstrated in the following case examples.

Case Example: Michael (counsellor) and Frank (6 years)

M: Now we've introduced ourselves, I'd like to tell you a bit about how our sessions will work. We'll be meeting in here at this time (Michael points to the clock on the wall) every week for the next six weeks. I've put six of these big marbles in a jar here, so you can see how many sessions we have left each week. Every week when we finish our time together, we can take one of the marbles out.

F: OK, and when there's one left then that will be the last time I come here?

M: Well, when we have one in the jar it will be half-term and we'll have a break. We'll come back after the break and see whether you'd like to carry on with your sessions then. We can see if they're helping and then decide how many more times we might meet.

F: You can put more marbles in the jar for how many times I'm going to come here after that.

M: Yes, that's right. That's what we'll do.

F: Does it have to be marbles? Could it be army men?

M: You'd like it to be army men?

In this example Michael uses developmentally appropriate methods to explain the number of sessions to Frank, who at age 6 may struggle to understand this in other, less visual ways. Michael moves out of the deliberately contracting part of the conversation into a more process-oriented response to Frank's question about army men. He is curious about what this question means to Frank and may explore this further as an aspect of the therapeutic frame, which could provide information about Frank's internal world and his presenting issue.

In the second example we see contracting with a young person at a different developmental stage.

Case Example: Andi and Ella (12 years)

A: OK, before we get on with things, we need to talk about how many sessions we might have together. What I usually say is why not come for four and then we can talk about how it's going. That way you'll have a good sense of whether this is something you're going to find helpful. If you'd like to continue after that, we can see then how many more we should have before another review. How does that sound?

E: Yeah, that sounds good. But (looking worried)... what if I don't have enough to say? What if I can't think of anything? Won't that be a bit cringy?

A: You're worried you won't have enough to say and that it might feel awkward.

E: Yeah, but then actually I don't really shut up most of the time, so maybe it won't be a problem.

A: You can see that maybe it won't. Maybe we can give it a go and find out. Would that be OK?

E: OK, we can see. That sounds OK.

When we look at this short extract, we can see the contract being agreed and negotiated as they go along. Although Andi takes the lead, suggesting they meet for four sessions initially, this is then considered and responded to by Ella on her own terms. We see Andi giving an empathic response to Ella's expression of concern that she might not have 'enough' to say. Andi might also be registering the word 'enough' and wondering if that has any significance for Ella. While, on one level, contracting is about practicalities and arrangements, it is also part of the therapeutic encounter and therefore close attention should be paid to how negotiations are made.

In entry 2.12 (p. 97) we see how this process works with parents or caregivers when some of the contracting needs to be between the counsellor and a third party due to the context or age/developmental stage of the child or young person.

Summary

- The contract in therapy is agreed between therapist and client, and may involve parents/carers or other professionals, depending on the context and the client.
- The contract consists of agreement regarding key aspects of the therapeutic frame.

- A clear contract is required to provide a secure base from which the therapy can begin.
- Agreeing the contract with children and young people needs to be managed in a way which is appropriate for the age and developmental stage of the client. This is the only way to ensure that agreement is informed.

Additional Resources

- MindEd – www.minded.org.uk: 412-023 *Contracting.*
- Kirkbride, R. (2016a) 'Contracting and establishing the therapeutic frame', in R. Kirkbride, *Counselling Children and Young People in Private Practice: A Practical Guide.* London: Routledge.

Associated Entries

2.6 Limit-Setting
2.9 Confidentiality & Consent
2.10 Outcome & Process Measures
2.12 Working with Parents/Carers

2.6 Limit-Setting

Limit-setting is an important aspect of the therapeutic frame, informed by the core relationship components (see entry 2.2, p. 51). This entry considers the key understandings and skills required for appropriate and therapeutically informed limit-setting with children and adolescents.

Key Understandings

By setting reasonable limits and consistently maintaining them, trust can be established in the therapeutic process. If limits are challenged or the client seeks to overrule them, then maintaining them while attempting to understand the communication becomes part of the therapeutic work itself.

When the client is secure enough in their understanding of what is and is not possible in the therapeutic setting, as well as trusting that the therapist will let them know in an accepting way if they are approaching a limit, they are then empowered to use their space and time in whatever way they choose, within the established limits.

In *Play Therapy*, Axline (1947: 128) outlines the role of limit-setting in non-directive, client-led therapy: 'The therapist establishes only those limitations that are necessary to anchor therapy to the world of reality and to make the child aware of his responsibility in the relationship'. This concept of 'anchoring therapy to the world of reality' is similar to the concept of the therapeutic frame, providing containment for all aspects of the therapeutic process, but it is also connected to external realities, such as time and the physical person of the therapist.

Limits help us to see the symbolism of the child's play, protecting them from the potential pain of carrying out destructive actions that provoke overwhelming guilt or are otherwise unacceptable to the child. By maintaining the symbolic in this way, Axline argues, 'the experience can be looked at objectively, and both the child and the therapist can accept honestly and completely this verbal and symbolic behaviour' (1947: 129). Axline is clear that the child is not to damage the therapist or the space itself. She suggests that the therapist has a role in directing the child to vent aggressive or destructive feelings on suitable play materials. Axline's (1947) play-therapy model is based on the core conditions established by Rogers (1959) for client-centred humanistic therapy (see entries 1.7, p. 25 and 3.3, p. 147), and these boundaries represent the unconditional positive regard for the *person* of the child, while the limitation is placed only on the *behaviour*. Even when a child has 'broken' a limit, Axline acknowledges the challenge inherent in this situation, but suggests that the skilful practitioner will be able to address and contain this behaviour without creating inappropriate feelings of guilt in the child: 'She would not reject the child because he disobeyed her. She would stay right there with her reflection of feelings: "It was important for you to throw it anyway. You wanted to show me that you *would* throw it"' (1947: 129).

Landreth (2012) suggests that setting limits can be a challenge for practitioners who are concerned about how they are perceived by the child. However, the appropriate setting of limits provides children 'with an opportunity to learn self-control, that they have choices, what making choices feels like, and how responsibility feels' (Landreth, 2012: 257).

Key Skills

1. Limits should be 'minimal and enforceable' (Landreth, 2012).
2. Limits should be set as needed rather than as a list at the beginning of the work. Some limits, including that of time or a basic agreement on not hurting the self or the therapist, may need to be set at the start.
3. In line with the core relationship components, the counsellor maintains a belief that the child will choose positive behaviour. Children who experience themselves as respected and accepted will be more likely to comply with reasonable limits on their actions and behaviour (Landreth, 2012).
4. Limits should be established in a calm and matter-of-fact manner, without anxiety; for example, 'In here, the sand stays on the table'.
   Limits should be unambiguous, child-focused and offered in a way that the child can easily grasp; for example, 'In here, you must keep the sand in the tray', or 'I know you want to go out of the playroom to see your friend, but we have ten minutes of our time left (pointing to clock on wall) and then it will be time to leave'.
5. Limits should be based in a clear rationale which has the best interests of the child and the therapy at its core; that is, 'All feelings, desires and wishes of the child are accepted, but not all behaviors are accepted' (Landreth, 2012: 261).

With older clients these limits may also include those around the kind of relationship they will have with their therapist and what the limits of this are. For example, a client might want to 'befriend' their therapist on social media or invite them to see a performance in the school play. It is important to establish the boundaries of the relationship you will have with your clients early in the work in a developmentally appropriate and empathic manner.

Summary

- Limits are an important part of the therapeutic frame, underpinned by the core relationship conditions of empathy, congruence and unconditional positive regard.

- Limits offer the child an opportunity to view themselves as able to make a choice and to consider the possible implications of this.
- Limits should be set responsively, that is, when needed. Some limits may need to be set at the outset of the therapeutic work and some as required by the child's actions in the session.

Additional Resources

- Axline, V. (1947) 'The value of limitations', in V. Axline, *Play Therapy*. New York: Ballantyne.
- Landreth, G. (2012) 'Therapeutic limit setting', in G. Landreth, *Play Therapy: The Art of the Relationship*. London: Routledge.

Associated Entries

1.11 Developmental Implications for Counselling
2.2 Core Relationship Components
2.3 The Therapeutic Frame
3.3 Play-Based interventions
3.4 Creative-Arts Interventions

2.7 Assessment & Integrative Formulation

Conducting a collaborative assessment at the outset lays important groundwork for the therapeutic process. Assessment performs a variety of functions and, when carried out in a collaborative manner, can further add to the secure base of mutual understanding which underlies effective therapy.

Key Understandings

The assessment process has a range of functions:

- Information gathering:
  - Family history – including any major events, such as illness, bereavement, changes to family stability
  - Life history of the client – including information regarding the mother's pregnancy, birth, early years, etc.
  - Current situation – including socio-economic factors affecting the child or the family's wellbeing, or significant relationships in the child or young person's life
  - Cultural background – including information about family belief systems, religious practices, etc., as needed
- Outline of presenting problem:
  - Why are they coming or being referred now?
  - What are the precipitating factors?
  - (With younger children) is the child aware of this issue themselves? How do they feel about it?
  - How long have they had this issue?
- Assessment for risk factors (see entry 2.8, p. 79):
  - Has the child or young person self-harmed or attempted suicide? If so, is this a current or historic issue? Has a close friend or family member attempted or committed suicide?
  - Is the client currently engaged in any risky behaviours or activities, for example, substance misuse, inappropriate sexual behaviours, etc.
  - Is the client at risk of abuse by others?
  - Do the parent/s or carers have significant mental health and/or substance misuse issues?

- To assess developmental stage and capacity to consent (see entry 2.9, p. 84):
    - Assessment of the cognitive capacity
    - Are they 'Gillick' competent? (See entry 2.9, p. 84)
    - Are there any developmental delays or blocks which may impact on the therapeutic relationship or process?

Key Skills

1. Some elements of the assessment, such as information gathering and the articulation of the presenting difficulty, can be carried out via conversation with either the client themselves or with an appropriate adult, such as a parent/carer, teacher or social worker. This may take the form of a 'screening' interview, and is intended to decide early on in if the client is suitable for the intervention on offer. The screening part of the assessment may be carried out face-to-face with the young person or parent/carer, or via questionnaires and forms designed to establish various aspects of the client's functioning and background. For example, if the referral is for counselling in school but the information gathered during the screening process indicates some concern regarding the psychiatric wellbeing of a child or young person, it may be decided at this point to refer on to Child and Adolescent Mental Health Services (CAMHS) (see entries 2.22, p. 131 and 4.4, p. 270). This screening process may also be used in some contexts to decide on the suitability of a client to work with a trainee or inexperienced practitioner (see entry 2.20, p. 124).
2. While the screening part of the assessment is likely to be fixed in terms of format or time-scale (i.e. a one-hour slot or a certain amount of paperwork to be completed), the broader assessment process will be less determined and can often take several sessions to complete. During the course of the initial sessions, various aspects of the client's functioning – their object relations, attachment style, relationship with themselves and others – are gradually revealed via the therapeutic relationship. Some clients may not initially know what they want from their sessions, and while parents and teachers may have clear agendas for the therapy, it may take time to establish what the individual client's therapeutic needs and goals are before therapy can begin. Allowing space for this process to unfold can be tricky in settings where a fixed number of sessions are available. If possible, this should be a consideration when deciding how many sessions to offer.
3. While this collaborative process is underway and the counsellor is finding out more about the client, it may be useful to begin formulating a hypothesis regarding the therapeutic work. Formulations offer insight into the deeper mechanisms underlying presenting issues, help us to gain a full understanding of the current issue in the context of past experiences, give guidance in terms of how to establish an effective therapeutic relationship, and help to clarify which might be the most effective intervention or therapy for a particular client.
4. For integrative practitioners, there are a variety of formulation tools that can be used for this process, and different client presentations may require the skilful

application of these tools. When making a formulation, it is important to remember that these should always be tentative rather than certain, and will most likely need to be revised as the work progresses.

5. A psychodynamic formulation is a hypothesis about the way a person thinks, feels and behaves. It takes unconscious processes into consideration. A psychodynamic formulation is based on a tripartite understanding of the person in the therapeutic encounter:

   - The current situation
   - The transferential situation
   - The impact on the psyche of early and past experiences.

6. There are various tools available to assist us in making a formulation, such as Malan's (1979) 'Triangles of Insight'. These were developed by David Malan, a pioneer of brief psychodynamic psychotherapy, and are used in therapy with children and young people (Abbass et al., 2013; Briggs et al., 2015). The first 'triangle of conflict' offers a straightforward tool for assessing what might be occurring unconsciously in the psyche of the individual, contributing to the presenting difficulty. The second 'triangle of person' looks at the relationships the client has with others and in the room with the therapist. When used together these present an effective way of developing a hypothesis about the client and their process. These formulations are intended to be tentative and to be constantly revised and re-formulated as the work proceeds. For detailed information regarding the 'Triangles of Insight' and their use, see Mander (2000).

   Anna Freud (1965) devised a series of diagnostic criteria for the assessment of normality and pathology in work with children and adolescents. These criteria have been subsequently revised and developed for contemporary practice with children and young people (Davids et al., 2016; Melandri, 2017). This diagnostic profile explores multiple aspects of the child or young person's functioning, including their object relations, sense of self, capacity for play, cognitive development, etc. While these criterial are devised primarily for assessment for psychoanalytic psychotherapy, they indicate important areas for the integrative therapist to be aware of when making a hypothesis regarding the client's current issues in the context of their past, object relations and developmental stage, in order to consider how best to work with individual clients.

   There are also formulation tools developed for use in cognitive-behavioural therapy (CBT) which may also be of use to the integrative practitioner working with children and young people. These will be covered in entry 3.6 (p. 158) on the use of CBT with children and young people.

Summary

- Assessment and formulation provide the foundation for therapeutic work.
- The assessment process begins at the outset of the work but may take several sessions to complete. It may also need to be returned to and revised throughout the therapeutic process.

- Developing a hypothesis or formulation for the therapeutic work can help in developing an effective therapeutic relationship and deciding on the most appropriate intervention for therapy.
- Formulations should be tentative and open to revision where appropriate.
- The process of assessment should be as collaborative as possible and always conducted with the core relationship components in mind (see entry 2.2, p. 51).

Additional Resources

- MindEd – www.minded.org.uk: 412-020 *Areas to Consider in Assessment.*
- Kirkbride, R. (2018a) 'Assessment with young people', in R. Kirkbride, *Counselling Young People: A Practitioner Manual.* London: Sage.
- Mander, G. (2000) *A Psychodynamic Approach to Brief Therapy.* London: Sage.

Associated Entries

1.10 Environmental & Systemic Factors
2.2 Core Relationship Components
2.8 Risk Assessment & Safeguarding
2.9 Confidentiality & Consent

2.8 Risk Assessment & Safeguarding

Assessing for risk is important in all therapeutic work, but particularly so in work with children and adolescents. As vulnerable members of society, children and young people can be at risk both from other people and themselves. These risks and decisions regarding how to respond change depending on the client's developmental capacity and age. Counsellors therefore need to develop a range of resources and skills to navigate this challenging area of practice. In this entry we consider the key understandings and skills required for assessing for risk as part of the general assessment process for therapeutic work with children and young people.

Key Understandings

Before considering how to assess risk we need to understand what is meant by this word. In terms of dictionary definition, Merriam-Webster gives the following:

> **Risk (noun):**
>
> Possibility of loss or injury
> Someone or something that creates or suggests a hazard
>
> **At risk:**
>
> In a state or condition marked by a high level of risk or susceptibility, i.e. patients at *risk* of infection
>
> **Risk (verb):**
>
> To expose to hazard or danger, i.e. *risked* her life
> To incur the risk or danger of, i.e. *risked* breaking his neck
> (merriam-webster.com, accessed 11 December 2019)

To take risks is a normal part of development and means encountering uncertainty. Even a toddler taking their first steps across the living room is taking a risk as they step into the unknown, unsure how far their newly discovered capacity for walking can take them. Adolescents take risks as part of normal development (see entry 3.10, p. 174). In a risk assessment, therefore, the kind of risk that is being assessed is specifically the risk of harm. This harm can be from the self or from another, and by carrying out effective risk assessment with children and young people we are hoping to reduce the impact of harmful behaviours as well as to protect the child from potential trauma and abuse at the hands of others.

'Safeguarding' is a term used to describe any action taken to protect the vulnerable in a situation. In practice, safeguarding means a commitment to:

- Protecting children from maltreatment
- Preventing impairment of children's health or development
- Ensuring that children grow up in circumstances conducive with the provision of safe and effective care
- Taking action to allow all children to have the best outcomes (Department for Education, 2018).

Child protection is one aspect of safeguarding, and it describes those decisions and interventions which are intended to protect children or young people who are determined to be at risk of significant harm.

The definition of significant harm was first articulated in section 31 of the Children Act (1989), which gives the following guidance:

> (9) …
>
> - 'harm' means ill-treatment or the impairment of health or development (including, for example, impairment suffered from seeing or hearing the ill-treatment of another);
> - 'development' means physical, intellectual, emotional, social or behavioural development;
> - 'health' means physical or mental health; and
> - 'ill-treatment' includes sexual abuse and forms of ill-treatment which are not physical
>
> (10) Where the question of whether harm suffered by a child is significant turns on the child's health or development, his health or development shall be compared with that which could reasonably be expected of similar child. (Children Act, 1989, section 31)

While this does not give specifics on what constitutes significant harm in any situation, it does offer a framework for assessment in this respect, which can be useful when considering risk and whether it requires safeguarding action to be taken. The BACP Ethical Framework (2018) highlights the necessity for practitioners to be aware of the law regarding significant or 'serious' harm, and to be prepared to act accordingly when required:

> In exceptional circumstances, the need to safeguard our clients or others from serious harm may require us to override our commitment to making our client's wishes and confidentiality our primary concern. We may need to act in ways that will support any investigations or actions necessary to prevent serious harm to our clients or others. In such circumstances, we will do our best to respect our client's wishes or confidences that do not need to be overridden in order to prevent serious harm. (BACP, 2018: 13)

This articulates the challenge for counsellors regarding safeguarding and the therapeutic relationship. Having invested in developing trust and offering unconditional positive regard to the child or young person, it may be extremely difficult for a counsellor to make the decision to 'override' the client's explicit wish for confidence not to be broken (see entry 2.9, p. 84). This kind of ethical dilemma (see entry 2.20, p. 124) is why it is so important that practitioners are clear with clients from the outset of the work that there are limits to confidentiality, as this provides a secure base to return to in terms of agreement made at the start of the work (see entry 2.5, p. 68).

There is a substantial amount of evidence to show that early intervention when children and young people are at risk of harm from themselves and/or others is of great long-term benefit to those individuals (Stroud et al., 2010). Therapists need to balance this understanding alongside the uncertainty and discomfort of disclosing abuse or harm outside the therapeutic relationship.

Cultural considerations should also be held in mind when working with risk and making safeguarding assessments. This is both in terms of sensitivity to cultural differences as well as the potential to avoid addressing concerns due to the desire to avoid being culturally insensitive or disrespectful. Practitioners need to be aware that language or behaviour that may seem inappropriate in one culture may be the norm in another; for example, arranged marriage is normal and accepted in many communities. Equally, where there are safeguarding concerns, these should be addressed sensitively, even where this may mean challenging cultural or religious practices, for example, in the case of suspected female genital mutilation (FGM) or forced (rather than arranged) marriage (Akilapa & Simkiss, 2012).

Key Skills

In order to work effectively and ethically in this challenging area, practitioners need to develop a set of skills to help them navigate risk and safeguarding.

1. Relationship building: The stronger the working alliance with the client the more you will learn about their world and their experiences. This will also help if/when you need to act on concerns regarding risk.
2. Knowledge base: Develop a solid understanding of the signs of abuse and neglect, especially in work with younger children who may not be able to verbally articulate their experiences, or even understand them as abusive. Use government guidance along with information from charities such as Barnardo's and the NSPCC (see Additional Resources at the end of this entry) to build and develop this knowledge.
3. Be vigilant regarding how the client presents if you suspect they may be at risk. Listen to the verbal content of the session in addition to keeping an eye on non-verbal communication such as eye contact, appearance and body language, as well as communication via play and/or art activities.
4. With older clients, ask questions to find out more about what they are doing or what they are experiencing. If they are self-harming or engaging in risky behaviour

outside the sessions, find out as much as you can about this. A good rapport and working alliance will assist greatly with this process (see entry 2.4, p. 63).

5. Develop a coherent protocol for assessing risk that allows you to gauge:

   i. How likely is it that a harmful/negative event will occur;
   ii. The types of harmful/negative events;
   iii. How soon a harmful/negative event is likely to occur;
   iv. How severe the outcome will be if a harmful/negative event does occur;
   v. The likely mediating impact of any protective factors (BACP, 2019).

6. Use the assessment process to gather information regarding potential risk factors. These might include:

   i. Previous suicide attempt/current suicide plan;
   ii. Social isolation/bullying;
   iii. Self-harm behaviour/ideation, current or historic;
   iv. Psychological/emotional ill-health, i.e. depression/anxiety;
   v. Poor school attendance/lack of employment;
   vi. Loss, i.e. bereavements/relationship break-up;
   vii. Issues with gender identity/sexual orientation;
   viii. Alcohol and drug misuse;
   ix. History of sexual abuse;
   x. Parent/carer with mental illness, current or historical;
   xi. On the 'at risk' register;
   xii. Parent/family member in prison;
   xiii. Age/gender/cultural background.

7. Gather information regarding protective factors as well, in order to make an effective assessment of risk. These might include the following:

   i. Coming for counselling/the quality of the therapeutic alliance;
   ii. Ability to engage in a curious exploration of their inner world, including difficult thoughts and feelings;
   iii. Support of family and/or friends/other agencies;
   iv. Involvement in interests and activities, particularly those which build self-esteem and positive connections with peers and adults;
   v. Capacity to use self-care and coping strategies.

8. Use all available up-to-date resources available to support your risk assessment. Refer to current government and agency guidance with regards to safeguarding and child protection:

   i. *What to Do if You're Worried a Child is Being Abused: Departmental Advice Providing Best Practice Information for Those who Work with Children in Order to Safeguard their Welfare* (Department for Education and Skills (DfES), 2015)
   ii. *Working Together to Safeguard Children: A Guide to Inter-Agency Working to Safeguard and Promote the Welfare of Children* (Department for Education, 2018).
   iii. *Information Sharing: Advice for Practitioners Providing Safeguarding Services to Children, Young People, Parents and Carers* (Department for Education, 2015a).

9. Use your professional support network (see entries 2.23 p. 134 and 2.24 p. 137) to assist you in making difficult decisions around child protection and safeguarding. The primary source of support in this respect should be your clinical supervisor along with the designated safeguarding lead if you are working in a context which has one. Professional support networks can be invaluable in supporting work involving risk. Depending on the context in which the practitioner is used to working, risk can sometimes be hard to pick up if the caseload is particularly complex and risk has become normalised. Conversely, when practice is relatively 'free' of risk presentations, practitioners may experience an anxious desire to 'act' and begin a safeguarding process without considering the possibility of 'holding' the risk temporarily while putting protective factors in place.

Summary

- Assessing for risk of harm is an important aspect of the counselling assessment for work with children and young people.
- The working alliance is an important factor in this kind of assessment.
- It is important to develop a coherent protocol for assessing risk which adheres to agency or statutory guidance.

Additional Resources

- MindEd – www.minded.org.uk: 412-024 *Risk Assessment*.
- Barnado's: www.barnardos.org.uk/what-we-do/protecting-children/sexual-abuse (accessed 12 August 2020).
- NSPCC: www.nspcc.org.uk/what-is-child-abuse/spotting-signs-child-abuse/ (accessed 12 August 2020).

Associated Entries

2.7 Assessment & Integrative Formulations
2.9 Confidentiality & Consent
2.20 Ethical Issues
2.24 Clinical Supervision
3.10 Working with Risk
3.11 Self-Harm
3.14 Trauma & Abuse
3.15 Risky Sexual Behaviour
3.19 Online Risk
4.7 Refugee Communities
4.8 Looked-After Children (LAC)

2.9 Confidentiality & Consent

Confidentiality plays a pivotal role in both therapeutic relationships and the therapeutic change process. In all therapeutic modalities, the primacy of confidentiality is enshrined as a means of building trust between client and counsellor and enabling the free expression of all aspects of the client's experience – thoughts, feelings, beliefs, fears, etc.

In order to be able to express themselves in this way the client must trust that what they speak about in therapy will not be shared, unless necessary to protect them from harm. This principle is not only stated in the contract for therapy but is also upheld in the Human Rights Act 1988, Article 8.

Therapists working with adult clients can generally assume that they have capacity to consent to a confidential therapeutic relationship, that they understand what this means and what the implications of this are for themselves and their therapy. This same assumption cannot be made in therapy with children and adolescents, and therefore practitioners working with this group need to consider *capacity to consent* alongside *confidentiality* when contracting.

Key Understandings

Current law regarding capacity to consent for under 16s is derived from a House of Lords' ruling on the 'Gillick' case (Gillick vs. West Norfolk and Wisbech Area Health Authority 1985) (Kirkbride, 2018a). The Lords' ruling made it clear that children have the right to make independent decisions regarding health care if they have reached a point of sufficient intellectual and emotional capacity to do so. For practitioners working with children and adolescents, the task is to assess whether a client has reached the point where they can consent on their own behalf to counselling and have the right to the contents of their session remaining confidential.

When assessing this capacity to consent there are a series of questions it might be helpful for counsellors to ask themselves:

In general, does the young person understand the question being asked of them? Can the young person:

- appreciate and consider the alternative courses of action open to them?
- weigh up one aspect of the situation against another?
- express a clear personal view on the matter, or are they constantly changing their mind?

In respect of the counselling process, does the young person have a reasonable understanding of:

- what counselling is, how it works, and what it entails?
- what confidentiality means in terms of counselling and what the limits of confidentiality are?
- what if any information will be shared regarding their counselling and how it will be shared?
- how records will be kept and who will have access to these? (Kirkbride, 2018a)

Counsellors need to manage this process in a way which is developmentally appropriate for the individual client in order that clients are giving *informed* consent. UK law generally assumes children aged 12 years and over have the capacity to consent in principle (Department for Education and Skills, 2006), while younger children require parental consent for counselling. This may also be managed differently by various counselling service providers, but it is important for counsellors to be aware of the law in order they can ensure that the legal and ethical rights of the children they are working with are respected at all times.

While confidentiality is integral to building trust in the counselling relationship, establishing the limits in this respect is also vital. This may be challenging for the practitioner who wants to create a 'safe space' for the child or young person by offering 'absolute' confidentiality. However, if eventually confidentiality has to be breached, this can cause more damage to trust and the therapeutic relationship than if limits had been explicitly set out at the beginning of the work.

Key Skills

1. Use developmentally appropriate language with the client. Younger children may be less concerned about the details regarding confidentiality, so it may be enough to let them know:

   'Whatever you say or do in this session is private. I won't talk about it with your parents, teachers, or anyone else unless I need to in order to make sure you're safe. If you want to talk to them about your sessions that's fine. It's your choice.'

   Landreth (2012) suggests that particular care needs to be taken around establishing confidentiality with children who have been sexually abused and who may have been coerced into 'keeping things secret'.
   When parent or teacher reviews take place during therapy with children, it is important to think carefully about how much information can be shared without breaching confidentiality regarding the sessions. Landreth (2012: 304) suggests that an important guideline

> is never to reveal the specifics of what a child has said or done in the playroom unless permitted to do so by a professional code of ethics. A child's exact comments are for the therapist's eyes and ears only and for professional colleagues who are in a consultative role.

Alongside this, it is important to bear in mind that young children may be empowered by being asked what they would like to be shared with parents or teachers, and indeed having input in considering how this will be shared. For example, a child may enjoy producing a piece of art showing how they feel they have progressed during their therapy or even sharing some of the areas they find difficult or distressing that they would like their parent/s to be aware of.

Older children and teenagers may be keener to know exactly how confidential their sessions are. Here it is important to establish the limits so they are informed from the start what will happen if concerns regarding their safety are raised.

2. Ensure that contracting is clear from the beginning of the work regarding:
   - the limits of confidentiality
   - what will happen if you are concerned that the client is at risk of significant harm, either from themselves or another
   - what will happen to any information you pass on regarding the content of a counselling session.

   By ensuring this is clear from the outset and has been presented in a way which the client or their parent/carer has understood, it can then be referred back to if needed. You might say something like:

   > 'Do you remember when we started working together, I said that if I was concerned that you were at risk of harm we might need to discuss that with someone else, so we can make sure you're safe? Well, my sense is we're at that point. How would you feel about me speaking to mum after the session today and letting her know what's been happening when you stay with dad?'

3. Bear in mind that confidentiality applies to anything created by the client in the session as well as spoken content. If using arts and play materials, it is important to establish with the client what will happen to anything they make or draw in a session. If they are to be stored, then it should be clear that these will only be accessed by the counsellor and the client. Artwork should not be displayed on the walls of the playroom, even when this is something the client has requested, as this is a breach of the confidentiality of the session.
4. Breaching confidentiality is rarely an easy choice for a therapist to make and often presents complex ethical dilemmas for the practitioner to resolve (see entry 2.20, p. 124). Bond and Mitchels (2015: 18) have produced a useful list of questions for counsellors to ask themselves when considering breaking confidentiality:

   i. What has the client given me permission to do?
   ii. Does that permission include breaking confidentiality?
   iii. If I break confidentiality, what is likely to happen?
   iv. If I do not break confidentiality, what is likely to happen?

v. Do the likely consequences of not breaking confidentiality include serious harm to the client or others?
vi. Are the likely consequences preventable?
vii. Is there anything I (or anyone else) can do to prevent serious harm?
viii. What steps need to be taken?
ix. How could the client be helped to accept the proposed action?

The decision to break a client's confidentiality should generally be made in consultation with another professional, preferably a clinical supervisor or experienced colleague (see entry 2.24, p. 137).

In entry 2.15 (p. 106), we consider how to manage potential ruptures in the therapeutic relationship when confidentiality is breached against the client's wishes.

Summary

- Confidentiality is a fundamental aspect of the therapeutic process. It is upheld in law and is a basic human right for all individuals.
- With younger children, parent/carer consent will be required. With older children and young people, counsellors can assess whether a child has reached 'Gillick' competency and is able to consent to a confidential counselling relationship.
- Clear contracting around confidentiality can help clarify the limits of this as well as help to manage the process of breaching confidentiality, should this become necessary.
- The decisions to break confidentiality without permission should generally be made after consultation with an appropriate professional, such as a clinical supervisor.

Additional Resources

- MindEd – www.minded.org.uk: 401-0011 *Capacity and Consent.*
- Bond, T. & Mitchels, B. (2015) *Good Practice in Action 014: Breaches in Confidentiality.* Lutterworth: British Association for Counselling and Psychotherapy.
- Daniels, D. & Jenkins, P. (2010) *Therapy with Children: Children's Right's, Confidentiality and the Law* (2nd edition). London: Sage.
- Mitchels, B. (2015) *Good Practice in Action 031: Safeguarding Children and Young People in England and Wales.* Lutterworth: British Association for Counselling and Psychotherapy.
- Mitchels, B. & Bond, T. (2010) *Essential Law for Counsellors and Psychotherapists.* London: Sage.
- Mitchels, B. & Bond, T. (2011) *Legal Issues across Counselling & Psychotherapy Settings: A Guide for Practice.* London: Sage.

Associated Entries

2.5 Contracting
2.12 Working with Parents/Carers
2.13 Record-Keeping & Data Protection
2.15 Managing Ruptures in the Therapeutic Alliance
2.20 Ethical Issues
2.24 Clinical Supervision
3.10 Working with Risk
3.19 Online Risk

2.10 Outcome & Process Measures

Working with outcome and process measures is an integral part of practice with children and adolescents, as demonstrated by their inclusion in the BACP Competence Framework (2019). From national trials investigating efficacy and value for money in counselling, to institutions using measures for counselling and psychotherapy research, data are collected and used in many different ways, offering benefits to both individual clients and the field in general (Midgeley et al., 2017).

Increasingly, counselling services need to prove that interventions are effective, and outcome measures are a proven method of achieving this (McArthur & Cooper, 2018). Process measures provide insight into how the client has experienced their therapist or counselling sessions and whether particular ways of working are more effective than others, providing valuable insight into which interventions are most appropriate for which clients. Duncan et al. (2006) suggest that outcome and process measures also offer young people opportunities to speak about their experience of counselling services. In this entry we explore the key understandings and skills for effective and appropriate use of measures in counselling with children and adolescents.

Key Understandings

In counselling there are two main types of measure: process and outcome. Process measures are designed to gather information about how the client experiences counselling, while outcome measures look for information on changes in distress or functioning as a result of the counselling process. Wheeler and Elliot (2008: 134) suggest three questions as the basis for collecting and measuring data:

1. 'Do clients change over the course of counselling?'
2. 'Is counselling substantially responsible for these changes?'
3. 'What specific aspects of counselling contribute to client change?'

Exercise

Look at Wheeler and Elliot's three questions.

- Can you think of ways to investigate these questions and find some answers?
- What issues might you encounter?
- How can the results be used to benefit counselling?

Various outcome and process measures have been designed and adapted to explore questions such as these in order to enrich practitioner understanding of the therapeutic process.

Outcome measures

Outcome measures include:

- Young Person's Clinical Outcome Measures in Routine Evaluation (YP-CORE)
- Goal-Based Outcome Measures (GBO)
- Strengths and Difficulties Questionnaire (SDQ)

Process measures

Process measures include:

- Child Session Rating Scale (CSRS)

It is beyond the scope of this entry to explore these measures in detail but additional resources for further learning are provided at the end.

Key Skills

While measures are an important and hopefully beneficial part of the counselling process, it is important that care is taken in their delivery so they remain collaborative and supportive of the therapeutic process as a whole. The following skills are intended to support the effective delivery of measures where appropriate:

1. Measures should be carefully embedded in the counselling process and delivered in accordance with the core components of the therapeutic relationship (see entry 2.2, p. 51).

2. When introducing measures, practitioners should use clear, positive language without technical jargon. If the counsellor is negative about the measures (e.g. 'I'm afraid we have to do this or the service won't get any funding'), this is likely to colour the client's attitude towards completing the measures.
3. Explicit and informed consent should be obtained from the client, or parent where applicable, before using measures. Clients should be informed of how data will be used, stored and disposed of (see entry 2.13, p. 101).
4. Counsellors should only use measures they have been trained to deliver and for which the appropriate licence is held. Measures used will vary from organisation to organisation, depending on the kind of information being gathered.
5. Time must be provided for discussion of measures so that results can be effectively integrated into the counselling as a whole, offering the client insights into their process and progress throughout their therapy. This process can then be generalised in order to enable the client to use this insight to respond to events and experiences outside the therapy room as well as once counselling has ended.

Summary

- Measures offer a valuable tool for understanding the process of therapeutic change and for gathering information regarding the efficacy of interventions.
- Process measures provide valuable insight into the therapeutic relationship and how this is experienced and utilised by the client.
- Measures offer the opportunity for services to be developed that meet the needs of children and adolescents.

Additional Resources

- MindEd – www.minded.org.uk: 412-025 *Using Outcome Measures.*
- MindEd – www.minded.org.uk: 412-026 *Using Process Measures.*
- MindEd – www.minded.org.uk: 412-012 *The Evidence for Counselling Children and Young People.*
- Kirkbride, R. (2018a) 'Evaluation and use of measures in counselling young people', in R. Kirkbride, *Counselling Young People: A Practitioner Manual.* London: Sage.
- Law, D. & Wolpert, M. (eds) (2014) *Guide to Using Outcomes and Feedback Tools with Children, Young People and Families.* London: CAMHS Press.
- Midgely, N., Hayes, J. & Cooper, M. (eds) (2017) *Essential Research Findings in Child and Adolescent Counselling and Psychotherapy.* London: British Association for Counselling and Psychotherapy/Sage.

Associated Entries

2.13 Record-keeping & Data-Protection
4.4 Child & Adolescent Mental Health Services (CAMHS)
4.5 Voluntary & Community Sector (CVS) Counselling Services

2.11 Cultural Competence

Culturally competent practice ensures interventions and services are accessible and appropriate for all. Just as we consider the importance of a developmental understanding in integrative counselling for children and adolescents, cultural understanding is similarly vital for the provision of effective therapy.

Cultural competence requires counsellors to be aware of cultural influences in both their own and their client's backgrounds and, in particular, how these can impact the therapeutic relationship and process. In this entry we consider the key understandings for culturally competent practice and the skills required to deliver this therapeutically.

Key Understandings

A fundamental element of the core relationship components (see entry 2.2, p. 51) is the ability to grasp the client's worldview and to see things from their perspective, allowing interventions to come from a place of empathy and unconditional positive regard (UPR). However, there may be impediments to both the offering and experiencing of empathy and unconditional positive regard if issues relating to difference are unacknowledged and unexamined.

How do we understand and experience culture in the counselling relationship? Ideally, this should be in the broadest possible terms. For example, there are relatively straightforward and simply defined areas, such as age, ethnicity, religious background, gender, sexual orientation, disparity in able-ness, etc. Second, there are the experiences of difference held by either counsellor or client. These may be intergenerational or relate to a client's direct experience of the other. Either of these can damage the therapeutic alliance if left unexamined.

The world is in a constant state of flux, meaning that the environment young people are born into and grow up in is different for each generation. More recently, digital technology, smartphones and social media have had a significant impact on children in the developed and developing worlds, setting them somewhat apart from those who grew up before such influences were prevalent (Prensky, 2001; Palfrey & Gasser, 2008). In counselling with children and young people, there is an additional obvious difference in terms of age and developmental stage. Even if the therapist is not much older than their client, they are likely to be at a different stage in terms of the degree to which they are living as an independent adult. In addition, there may be cultural differences, such as gender, sexuality, race, ethnicity and religious beliefs. These represent some of the nine characteristics protected in the UK by the Equality Act (2010). The BACP Ethical Framework (2018: 15) emphasises the need to respect clients by providing services that 'endeavour to demonstrate equality, value diversity and ensure inclusion for all clients' and 'challenge assumptions that any sexual orientation is inherently preferable to any other'. The BACP also give specific guidance to practitioners working with children, suggesting that '[c]areful consideration will be given to working with children and young people that is informed about the current culture and customs that affect parenting/caregiving and how children and young people interact with each other and other significant people in their lives' (BACP, 2018: 16).

Cultural competence requires consideration of identity, for both counsellor and client. Identity consists of a dynamic assessment of who and what we are as well as who and what we are not. How we understand ourselves from this assessment will also resonate in our feelings about ourselves and others. While the core relationship components of unconditional positive regard (UPR), empathy and congruence all indicate a desire to connect with the client's felt experience, Lago and Hirai (2013: 439) suggest that this must also take into account the counsellor's own attitude:

> for example, if the therapist has strongly negative feelings towards the group from which the client hails, how might he or she offer warmth and acceptance? How might the counsellor then manage congruence or transparency in relation to the client?

This suggests the need for therapists to consider the attitudes they hold towards particular groups or identities as well as how the client might perceive and respond to them, either in relation to their own identity or because of previous experiences with members of a particular 'group'. How a person views themselves as a 'cultural being' has a significant impact on the therapeutic relationship, particularly when the participants are from different backgrounds (Courtland & Na, 2011). Awareness of and relationship to identity and culture changes over the life span. A 7-year-old's concept of their race or skin colour will be very different from that of a 17-year-old's. Therefore, developmental stage and the impact of this on culture should also be borne in mind by the practitioner when considering the impact of culture on the therapeutic relationship.

Key Skills

1. Work on exploring and understanding your own identity in respect of the areas outlined above. This may be done through personal therapy, reflective practice,

supervision and activities designed to help develop an objective understanding of areas such as cultural positioning.

2. Take time to develop knowledge-based and interpersonal skills required to work effectively across cultures. Components of cultural competence include:

   i. Awareness and acceptance of cultural difference
   ii. Capacity for cultural awareness
   iii. Understanding the dynamics of difference
   iv. Developing basic knowledge about the child's culture
   v. Adapting practice skills to fit the cultural context of the child and family (Walker, 2005: 57).

   For example, it is important to understand the impact of systematic racism on young people's identity and sense of self and how their formative developmental experiences might be very different from someone of the majority culture. This was evidenced in the 'Black Lives Matter' protests in the UK and elsewhere in 2020 (Iqbal, 2020). Knowledge about how different cultural groups conceptualise psychological and emotional issues is also central to cultural competence, as this will have an impact on formulation and any interventions offered.

3. Be congruent about difference in the relationship. Be open to acknowledging and exploring this non-defensively. For example:

   > 'You asked about my headscarf and I guess you can probably tell I'm from a particular cultural background that might be different from your own. I'd like us to be able to talk about and explore any feelings you may have about this. Hopefully this will help us develop trust and a good connection from the beginning of your counselling.'

   Or

   > 'I wonder how you're feeling about coming to see a male counsellor. Maybe you would have preferred someone different. I'm really happy for us to talk this through if you think it might be an issue for you here.'

4. Be guided by the client in terms of exploring cultural issues. It may not be something they need or want to do. If you feel that there are unacknowledged differences that are impacting the therapeutic alliance, but the client seems unwilling to explore them, this should be taken to supervision for further exploration and attempts at understanding.
5. Be aware that young people may find it hard to acknowledge or discuss areas of their identity, particularly where these are in conflict with the attitudes and beliefs upheld in the client's community, family or peer group. For example, young people may find it difficult to explore issues around sexuality when they fear the possibly serious consequences of coming out as gay.
6. Concentrate on attempting to provide the core relationship components. Be aware of where you encounter blocks in either the provision of these conditions or in the receipt of them by the client. Explore these in supervision or personal therapy, as appropriate.

Summary

- Cultural competence means understanding the role of culture in the accessibility of counselling services for all.
- It's important to develop understanding of where cultural differences might impede the forming of a therapeutic alliance and to take appropriate steps to address this.
- Developing cultural competence and understanding of culture's different from our own allows us to connect with the client where they are, rather than trying to impose something of our own on them. Key to this is a genuine engagement with understanding empathy and UPR and how to develop an authentic connection with the client.

Additional Resources

- Courtland, C.L. & Na, G. (2011) 'Identity development and its impact on the therapy relationship', in C. Lago (ed.), *The Handbook of Transcultural Counselling and Psychotherapy*. Maidenhead: McGraw-Hill/Open University Press.
- Eddo-Lodge, R. (2018) *Why I'm No Longer Talking to White People about Race*. London: Bloomsbury.
- The Equality Act (2010) London: HMSO. Available at: www.legislation.gov.uk/ukpga/2010/15/contents (accessed 5 July 2020).

Associated Entries

1.10 Environmental & Systemic Factors
2.2 Core Relationship Components
2.4 Building rapport
2.15 Managing Ruptures in the Therapeutic Relationship
2.17 Developing Advanced Empathy
3.16 Identity
4.7 Refugee Communities

2.12 Working with Parents/Carers

One of the central differences in therapy with children and adolescents is that they are to some extent dependent on their family, and in particular their parents. While therapy with children does not always involve family members, particularly when it takes place in an educational or youth setting, it is important that practitioners working with this group develop appropriate skills for managing interactions, as appropriate. This entry considers the understanding required to develop appropriate skills for working with parents and carers in child and adolescent counselling.

Key Understandings

Anna Freud (1965) had significant experience of the challenges of involving parents in children's therapy, and also of the benefits to be gained by doing so:

> The child analysts' techniques of dealing with the parents vary widely from the extreme at one end of excluding them from the intimacy of the treatment altogether, to keeping them informed, permitting them to participate in sessions (with the very young), treating or analysing them simultaneously or separately, to the opposite extreme of treating them for the child's disturbance in preference to analysing the child himself. (A. Freud, 1965: 48)

This quote speaks of the developmental and curative factors at play in parental involvement in therapy. Children cannot refer themselves for counselling, explain their issues or symptoms comprehensively, or provide information regarding their early years. For these purposes, parents, or those *in loco parentis*, need to be involved in the referral and information-gathering phases of the assessment process (see entry 2.7, p. 75), particularly with children under 12 years of age. Therefore, the therapist needs to build a positive relationship with parents/carers while remaining mindful that their primary relationship is with the client.

Apart from assessment and review, there are other aspects of the therapeutic relationship where involvement with parents will become necessary. These include the practicalities of therapy and family sessions.

Practicalities

- Children are often dependent on parents to transport them to therapy sessions where these are outside school, i.e. CAMHS and private practice (see entries 4.3, p. 267 and 4.4, p. 270).
- Paying the fee in private practice.
- Supporting the client in attending sessions if they are finding them difficult or would rather be doing something else. Note: this is not the same as forcing a client to attend counselling when they may be making an autonomous decision in this respect.

Family sessions

- Introducing parents or other family members into a counselling session is a complex process requiring careful consideration to ensure it will be of benefit to the client and the therapeutic process. Benefits include enabling the client to express thoughts and feelings they have been exploring in sessions to their family in an environment where they feel safe and which is facilitated by someone they trust (Kirkbride, 2016a).
- Sessions with parents and carers can also take place without the presence of the client, if this is appropriate and agreed with the client. This can offer opportunities for exploring family issues which might be contributing to the client's difficulties but may be more easily discussed without the client being present. It might include the parents' marital or mental health issues.
- The frame and boundaries for family sessions should be contracted separately from the individual counselling contract. This contract needs to include details of how confidentiality will be held by all parties and how and what information will be fed back to the client after the session. Bear in mind, as Marks Mishne (1986: 314) notes, 'the objective in work with parents is to develop their insight into the connections between their problems and those of their child, to thereby enlist their efforts and involvement to help meet the child's evolving developmental needs'.

Key Skills

1. Be clear in initial conversations with parents/carers regarding contracting around confidentiality. Let them know you have a safeguarding policy which they can see and that they will be informed if you have any concerns regarding their child's safety (see entry 2.8, p. 79). Be clear that while they may naturally be interested in what their child has discussed in their session, the child may not feel comfortable with sharing this and their privacy should be respected.

2. With younger children, ensure they are aware of when you will be meeting with their parents/carers and what you will be sharing with them. While it is appropriate to review counselling with the parents of young children, it is still important to respect the children's right to confidentiality.
3. If it seems involving parents could be helpful in work with older clients, ensure that this is well thought through beforehand, including exploring with the young person how they will feel if the session does not go as they would like. Be clear about what they would like you to do in the session and what they are happy for you to share.
4. Keep the therapeutic relationship in mind at all times when involving others in the work. The alliance with the client and their best interests should take priority at all times, even if these are nor supported by the parent. In this respect, involving parents in individual therapy work is different from specific family therapy.
5. If a young person does not want to involve their parents/carers in the work this should be respected, even if the therapist feels it would be beneficial to do so.
6. Be prepared to provide parents and carers with the details of adult, couple or family therapists that they could work with, if this is appropriate. If you feel a parent might benefit from a therapeutic intervention, this should be couched in terms of offering support and not as a criticism of their parenting.
7. While respecting and seeing things from the client's point of view, it may be that therapists develop negative feelings towards the parents/carers. It is important to be able to hold these feelings alongside a respect for the parents in order that the alliance with the parents is not affected and 'splitting' does not occur (see entry 1.6, p. 20). This can be challenging in situations where a significant bond has developed with the client, and should be taken to supervision for assistance with maintaining objectivity. Equally, where parents bring their own sensitive material to the session, practitioners need to hold the tension of how to use this in a way which will be of benefit to the client while also protecting the confidentiality of the parents. Where this becomes complex, it should be explored in supervision.
8. Explore any intentions to involve parents and carers in individual work with your supervisor (see entry 2.24, p. 137). This ensures adequate consideration of the consequences occurs before any planned family sessions.
9. Particular care should be taken in work with families where there are issues around separation, divorce and remarriage. Counsellors will need to explore these cases carefully in supervision before bringing members of the family into the work.
10. Counsellors also need to be sensitive to the cultural background of parents and carers when considering involving them in the therapeutic work (see entry 2.11, p. 93).

Summary

- Parents/carers sometimes need to be involved in therapeutic work with children and adolescents, and while this is not always the case, counsellors need to have the skills to manage this when needed.

- The involvement of parents/carers can vary between frequent involvement when counselling younger children, to infrequent or no involvement at all with adolescent clients in educational settings.
- Parent/carer involvement in the counselling should be considered carefully in order to ensure the best interest of the client is upheld at all times.

Additional Resources

- Kirkbride, R. (2016a) 'Working with parents and families', in R. Kirkbride, *Counselling Children and Young People in Private Practice.* London: Karnac.

Associated Entries

2.3 The Therapeutic Frame
2.9 Confidentiality & Consent
2.24 Clinical Supervision

2.13 Record-Keeping & Data Protection

Record-keeping, note-taking and protecting client data are all aspects of the broader issues of confidentiality and trust in the therapeutic relationship (see entry 2.9, p. 84). They require skill and knowledge on the part of the practitioner in order to ensure that clients' data are managed appropriately throughout the counselling process and beyond.

Key Understandings

Just as counsellors have an ethical and legal duty to maintain client confidentiality in sessions, this is also the case in terms of notes, records, data and any information which is passed on to other agencies or third parties (see entry 2.22, p. 131). Knowledge of the law in this respect needs to be up to date so good practice can be maintained. This is the case whether counselling is taking place in an agency or educational setting, or within private practice, although protocols will need to be adapted for different contexts. Private practitioners should seek guidance from their professional bodies and/or insurance company with regards to expectations for keeping and storing client records, while employed counsellors will need to comply with service requirements in this respect. They should also ensure that what is required by their employer or agency is in compliance with their own ethical framework. Such guidelines will generally hold the needs of the client as paramount in any decision and this should be reflected in practice.

Key Skills

1. Develop and maintain a clear and consistent policy for clients and their families regarding the taking and storing of client records and notes. This policy should be in line with current relevant legislation and written in language which can be understood by all. Where work takes place in a setting with an existing policy, practitioners should familiarise themselves with this and ensure that clients are happy to agree to its contents (see entry 2.5, p. 68).
2. Counsellors should take responsibility for ensuring that notes are kept and stored in a secure manner, preventing any attempt to obtain them or to identify a client or family from anything that has been recorded. In addition, independent practitioners need appropriate protocols regarding email and online security for client

information. Policies should include information on what will happen if there is a data breach at any time.

3. Be aware that under current UK data protection legislation, clients can ask to see any records held on them. UK practitioners should seek clarification from the Information Commissioners Office (ICO) regarding their responsibilities around control and the processing of sensitive data.

Summary

- Record-keeping is an important aspect of a commitment to confidentiality and the protection of sensitive client material.
- Protocols will need to be developed that are in line with current legal and professional guidance. These will be different according to the context and client group being seen (see entry 4.1, p. 263).
- Counsellors should ensure they have followed guidance from the ICO, if appropriate.

Additional Resources

- British Association for Counselling and Psychotherapy (2019) *Good Practice in Action 014 Legal Resources: Managing Confidentiality within the Counselling Professions*. Lutterworth: BACP. Available at: www.bacp.co.uk/media/6305/bacp-managing-confidentiality-legal-resource-gpia014-july2019.pdf (last accessed 15 October 2020).
- Information Commissioners Office (ICO): www.ico.org.uk
- Mitchels, B. & Membrey, D. (2018) 'General data protection regulation (GDPR) and CYP', *BACP Children, Young People and Families Journal*, December.

Associated Entries

2.5 Contracting
2.9 Confidentiality & Consent
2.20 Ethical Issues
2.22 Working with Other Professionals
4.3 Private Practice

2.14 Developing & Sustaining the Therapeutic Relationship

Having established the therapeutic frame, contracted and built rapport with the client, it is now essential to maintain this relationship so it can provide a continuous, dynamic foundation for the therapeutic process. The following group of entries consider the factors involved in the successful development of the therapeutic relationship and process, as well as how to manage when problems or difficulties arise in this respect.

Key Understandings

When working in an integrative and relational way, the relationship is at the heart of the therapeutic process. By continuing to develop the provision of the core relationship components (see entry 2.2, p. 51), trust between client and therapist will increase, facilitating a deeper engagement with the client's experience and with their presenting issue.

When working with children, during this stage of the work their trust in the therapeutic alliance may present as increased confidence in their use of the playroom. Having developed trust that their counsellor will be there reliably when it is time for their session, and experiencing them as consistently present, attentive and curious, they are likely to naturally feel more able to express their feelings and experiences verbally or through play. In this way, more material will be available to be explored and understood, whether directly or via symbolism and metaphor (see entry 3.2, p. 144 and 3.3, p. 147).

With older children and adolescents, this phase will hopefully find them becoming clearer about the structure of the therapeutic relationship as well as its function, and beginning to develop a sense of how they can make use of it to aid them in working through difficult aspects of their experience. As trust in the consistency and reliability of their therapist increases, they too will naturally feel able to express more of their internal feelings and difficult experiences.

During this time practitioners need to maintain their focus on the core conditions and any agreements made during the contracting phase to ensure that consistency and integrity remain at the foundation of the work.

Key Skills

1. Keep the core relationship components at the heart of practice. Be consistently authentic in the relationship, aim to offer empathy and acceptance via the quality of the relationship provided.
2. Be aware that clients vary in the length of time they may take to reach this phase. Relationships take time to develop and this is particularly the case for one which requires considerable trust to be established before it can be utilised by the therapeutic process. Children and young people differ greatly in their capacity to form an alliance (see entry 2.4, p. 63) and this may be further affected by developmental issues and early relational experiences (see entries 1.5, p. 16 and 1.6, p. 20).
3. Be sensitive to changes in the alliance and in the relationship, for example if a client who has previously been relaxed and open becomes increasingly withdrawn or chooses not to come to their session. It may be that something is affecting their connection with you and therefore impeding their trust in the relationship (see entry 2.15, p. 106).
4. Bear in mind that in integrative, relational practice, the counsellor's personal capacity for relationship has a significant impact on the therapeutic alliance (Clarkson, 1995). Personal development activities, such as personal therapy and clinical and peer supervision, as well as activities aimed at supporting development of self-awareness and resilience, are likely to strengthen our capacity to sustain the alliance, even in challenging circumstances.
5. Practitioner self-care is essential for supporting the capacity to sustain and maintain therapeutic alliances (see entry 2.23, p. 134). When counsellors are working with challenging clients, particularly those who have experienced trauma and abuse, they are at risk of compassion fatigue (Figley, 2002) and/or burnout. In such circumstances, they are unlikely to be able to provide the relationship components effectively. Clinical supervision and professional support networks are vital for practitioners working in the field of counselling children and young people.

Summary

- The therapeutic relationship is the foundation of therapeutic work and needs to be attended to throughout the process.
- The core relationship components are central to maintaining the relationship and the role of the counsellor is to develop their capacity for effectively providing these on an ongoing basis.
- Sustaining therapeutic relationships can prove challenging and require additional support from supervision. Taking part in activities which help develop the capacity to provide empathy and compassion, such as meditation and personal therapy can also help develop the capacity to sustain therapeutic relationships and offer the core conditions.

Additional Resources

- MindEd – www.minded.org.uk: 412-031 *Self-Awareness in the Therapeutic Relationship*.

Associated Entries

2.2 Core Relationship Components
2.15 Managing Ruptures in the Therapeutic Alliance
2.23 Self-Care for Counsellors
2.24 Clinical Supervision

2.15 Managing Ruptures in the Therapeutic Alliance

Having established the central functional importance of the therapeutic alliance, it follows that ruptures in the alliance will need to be attended to and, if possible, repaired. In this entry we try to understand how ruptures occur and the skills required to identify and repair them.

Key Understandings

A rupture in the alliance is defined as 'a deterioration in the therapeutic alliance, manifested by a disagreement between the patient and therapist on treatment goals, a lack of collaboration on therapeutic tasks, or a strain in their emotional bond' (Eubanks et al., 2018: 508). Identifying and addressing ruptures in the alliance has been viewed for some time as important in therapy with adults, and indeed by some as central to the process of therapeutic change (Safran & Muran, 2000). With children and adolescents, ruptures are also significant but may manifest differently (Nof et al., 2019). This means different, developmentally-attuned skills to repair ruptures will be required as they occur in the therapeutic process.

In a key paper on an integrative approach to ruptures, Safran and Muran (2000) consider a pan-theoretical model for rupture, closely aligned with Bordin's (1979) conceptualisation of the therapeutic alliance (see entry 2.4, p. 63). They classify some ruptures as related to the task/goal of therapy, and some to the bond between client and therapist. Ruptures are identified as having two main types of expression: confrontation or withdrawal. In some cases, a rupture may be directly identified by the client and fall into the 'confrontation' category, i.e. 'I don't want to come anymore, this is rubbish. What's the point?' Or it may manifest in a less direct way, such as non-attendance or non-engagement in the therapy room, thus falling into the 'withdrawal' category. The client's age, developmental stage and relational behaviour all affect how a rupture manifests in therapy (Nof et al., 2019). Taking Safran and Muran's (2000) ideas on rupture and repair in adult therapy and applying them to work with children, we can view the process of identifying and working with rupture in the alliance as offering the opportunity for a corrective emotional experience. In their model for repair, the therapist offers a non-defensive relational response to the rupture, viewing it as a communication of something significant in the client's experience, rather than as a personal attack on the therapist or on the therapeutic process itself.

Key Skills

1. Be sensitive to signs that a rupture has occurred. Look for changes in the way the client presents where these indicate a negative change in the therapeutic alliance. The form a rupture takes varies according to the client's age, developmental capacity and relational style, but may include a direct confrontation and attack of the therapist or process, for example:

   - 'This is crap, what's the point?'
   - 'It's boring coming here, the toys you have are rubbish'

   Or it may be less direct and confrontational, for example:

   - long silences in the room
   - changing the topic of conversation to something unrelated to the therapy
   - irregular or non-attendance at sessions or wanting to leave before the planned end.

2. If a rupture appears to be task- or goal-related, this can be worked with by ensuring that the client is clear about the purpose of counselling and that they understand, as far as they are able, the therapeutic change process. For example, a counsellor noticing that the client is disengaging from therapy might say:

   - 'It seemed like you didn't want to come to your session when I collected you this week. I wonder how you're feeling about being here and if there's anything we need to think about together.'
   - Or an exchange between client and counsellor might look like:

   Client: (Pushing toys away and folding arms) I don't want to play anything today. It's all stupid.
   Counsellor: You don't want to play; you think it's stupid.
   Client: Yeah, I don't know why I have to come here anyway. No one else in my class comes.
   Counsellor: You're wondering why you have to come here when others don't. That's something we could think about together if you like. I'm hearing you feel you have to come here, like you haven't got any choice about it.
   Client: (Speaking loudly) Actually I do know why I have to come. It's cos my teacher says. I was bad in class yesterday and got ten behaviour points. Miss says I have to come because of that.
   Counsellor: So, it sounds as though you're not here today because you want to be, but because your teacher says you have to be. That sounds really difficult and I'm not surprised you don't feel like playing. I imagine you might have lots of feelings about that. Maybe you feel angry?

Client: (Picking up some of the figures on the table and moving them around) Yes, I feel angry now.

Counsellor: I don't know if you remember, but the first time you came to see me, I said this was somewhere you could express feelings and talk about anything upsetting or difficult. I said whatever came up in here we would try and understand it together.

Client: (Sounding happier) I remember!

Counsellor: Well, that means this space and time is for you. It's important we both understand that. Your teacher may have an idea about why you come and see me, but we've agreed that this time is for you to play or talk about anything you need to so we can help you figure out the things that worry or stress you.

Client: OK, can I play in the sand then?

As shown in the previous example, it's important to ensure the goals of therapy are those of the client and have not been imposed by the therapist, perhaps inadvertently (Safran & Muran, 2000). This is particularly important where others, for example parents and teachers, may have very specific ideas about what the aim of therapy is for a child or young person. Young people may have internalised and identified with the goals or 'conditions of worth' (see entry 1.7, p. 25) imposed by others, and it may take time and careful work with ruptures in the alliance to discover what their goals are.

Counsellors need to manage any personal, emotional response to a rupture so it can be explored with curiosity. In some cases, this will be an internal process of reflection and regulation, potentially taking place in a moment mid-session. Nof et al. (2019) suggest when a therapist becomes aware of a potential rupture they should try to:

- regulate their affect and focus on the rupture that is taking place
- identify the type of rupture
- self-reflect on the underlying message of the rupture.

They urge counsellors to be prepared to 'pause' during the session when a rupture occurs, rather than continuing with the session as though it hadn't happened.

- Ruptures which are not addressed in the session and which are potentially more complex, can be taken to supervision for deeper consideration.
- Ruptures which are bond-related can occur when there is a breach in trust between counsellor and client. This may be for an explicit reason, such as when confidentiality has been broken due to a safeguarding concern. Bond-related ruptures also occur when the client perceives or experiences something in the relationship between them and the counsellor which causes them to experience a break in the bond. As we have already established, the bond between client and counsellor is the foundation of therapy and so it follows that if there is a rupture in this bond, then the therapeutic

process is likely to be impeded until it can be understood and repaired. For example:

Client:	(Head down, hood up – staring at the floor in silence)
Counsellor:	(After about 30 seconds of silence) You're finding it hard to start today.
Client:	(Muffled mmm)
Counsellor:	I'm aware last week was a difficult session for you and I imagine you've got some feelings about what happened. We can talk about it whenever you're ready.
Client:	(Mmm)
Counsellor:	I'd like us to be able to talk about it if that feels helpful for you. I'm ready to hear whatever you've got to say.
Client:	(Looking up briefly) It's all fucked. That's what I've got to say.
Counsellor:	You want me to know it's all fucked.
Client:	Now mum knows what I've been doing, because Mr fucking Fisher rung her up, and basically, I'm not allowed out at all and I'm not allowed even in the bedroom on my own. She's like with me 100 per-cent of the effing time. It's f'd up... Sorry for swearing.
Counsellor:	So there have been repercussions from last week that you're unhappy about. It sounds like life feels really difficult.
Client:	Yeah, it does... I mean, I know it was pretty f'd up before but at least I wasn't being followed around all the time. This is worse. This is 100 per cent worse.

In this example, the counsellor is not defending against the client's anger and disappointment. They don't try to remind or convince the client that they acted for their own good. They make it clear that they are ready to hear whatever the client has to say. In this way an opportunity is provided for the breach or rupture to become part of the therapeutic process. It may be that the bond they had established previous to the breach of confidentiality was enough that there is still some trust between them that can now be built on through the counsellor's careful, empathic attention to the client's experience.

As shown in the previous example, the skills required to repair a rupture, where this is possible, are demonstrated by the counsellor's non-defensive, curious response, and the provision of the core relationship components of empathy, congruence and unconditional positive regard for the client and their experience. Breaking confidentiality is a difficult decision to make and the counsellor may have complex feelings in relation to this. However, these must not be allowed to impede on the therapeutic space, but be taken and discussed in supervision.

Summary

- The process of rupture and repair provides important opportunities for the therapeutic process.

- Therapists need to develop skills to allow them to be closely attuned to the therapeutic relationship, so they are sensitive to potential ruptures as they occur.
- Therapists need to develop the capacity to meet ruptures non-defensively and with curiosity about their meaning.
- Listening empathically to the client's experience and offering unconditional positive regard provides the opportunity to repair the therapeutic alliance and potentially strengthen it as well as offering an experience for the client that difficulties in relationships can be overcome and moved on from.

Additional Resources

- Nof, A., Dolev, T., Leibovich, L., Harel, J. & Zilcha-Mano, S. (2019) 'If you believe that breaking is possible, believe also that fixing is possible: A framework for ruptures and repairs in child psychotherapy. *Research in Psychotherapy: Psychopathology, Process and Outcome*, 22: 45–57.
- Safran, J.D. & Muran, C.J. (2000) 'Resolving therapeutic alliance ruptures: Diversity and integration', *Journal of Clinical Psychology/In Session*, 56: 233–243.

Associated Entries

2.2 Core Relationship Components
2.4 Building Rapport
2.8 Risk Assessment & Safeguarding
2.9 Confidentiality & Consent

2.16 Transference & Countertransference

Transference and countertransference are psychotherapeutic terms derived from psychoanalytic theory and technique. In its simplest form, transference is the process by which we project features of our inner world onto others in our environment, seeing and responding to them at least partially as though they were someone or something from our past. Being able to work with transference is a useful skill for the integrative practitioner to develop, as it can facilitate a deeper understanding of the client's difficulties and their process.

Key Understandings

Freud (1914/1958) was initially dismayed by his findings that a patient's feelings appeared to be transferred onto the analyst, viewing this as potential interference in the treatment. However, over time he became aware that this was a useful phenomenon which could facilitate deeper understanding of the patient's unconscious via their projections of fantasies regarding the analyst. From these discoveries, Freud developed the concept of 'transference neurosis' (Freud, 1914), which might comprise positive or negative transference feelings, potentially linked to the patient's negotiation of the Oedipal crisis.

Melanie Klein and Anna Freud were early child psychotherapists. During their careers they developed and held very different positions regarding the use of transference in work with children and adolescents. Klein considered that the transferential relationship between child and analyst existed from the beginning of analysis and was therefore available for interpretation (Klein, 1926/1975). Anna Freud (1965) considered that, due to the developmental stage of the child and their ongoing 'real' relationship with parents/carers, they were not able to form a transference relationship. She placed more emphasis on working with the child to build rapport (see entry 2.4, p. 63) as well as on the alliance with parents.

While Anna Freud may have been correct in her assumption that the developmental aspects of therapy with children make transference less pronounced than in work with adults, there is still a place for working with these phenomena in contemporary practice. Blake (2008: 351) stresses the value of allowing transference projections: 'The mental setting must enable an open flow of communication, whereby the child's inner world can be projected not only onto the toys and the room, but also onto the therapist.' There is an important distinction between working 'in' the transference and working 'with' transference. Working 'in' the transference is the classic Kleinian approach and requires the therapist to be a 'blank screen', avoiding 'real' relationship as much as possible in order to be available for the child's projections to be received and analysed. Blake (2008: 352) makes the case for a more balanced approach, stating:

> While this blank screen is only a theoretical possibility, it does remind us to aim at a mental setting that will leave open enough space for it to be populated by the child's inner world and not too much of our own. The need for an open space is why the child should not know the therapist socially, or know about his or her personal life.

Countertransference is a widely discussed and debated concept in psychoanalytic literature. Identified by Freud as those feelings the therapist brings from past experiences and transfers onto the analytic situation, it was originally viewed as another potential impediment to analysis. Paula Heimann changed this with her 1950 paper 'On Countertransference', which suggested that the therapist could skilfully use their countertransferential experiences to deepen their understanding of the patient and their unconscious processes. Heimann (1950) argues that the therapist experiencing 'countertransference' may be in receipt of the patient's projections and therefore experiencing their repressed materials, such as pain or anxiety, in a felt way. Countertransference can be complex to work with in practice as it can be difficult to separate out which feelings belong to the client and which are the therapist's own. Personal therapy and clinical supervision are fundamental in exploring this.

Key Skills

1. Transference and countertransference are useful tools for understanding in more depth the root of difficulties for a client.
2. Transference may also be useful when formulating a hypothesis of the client's presenting issues during the assessment phase.
3. In terms of interventions, both transference and countertransference should be used tentatively and carefully:

    - 'I might be wrong, but I'm wondering if you feel angry about mum's new boyfriend speaking to you like that but it's hard to really speak about those feelings...'
    - 'I wonder if when I missed our session last week it reminded you of other times when people have let you down?'

4. Depending on developmental capacity, transference interpretations can be difficult for a child or adolescent to manage. They may even have a shaming or humiliating affect, for example:

   - 'You find it hard to leave at the end of the session, perhaps you want me to give you more time, just as you wish your mother had given you more time when she was rushing to work in the evenings.'

   Blake (2008) suggests such interpretations can be too 'hot' for the child and leave them feeling they have asked for too much – potentially consolidating a pre-existing sense of themselves as too much.

5. Working 'with' the transference: this means 'thinking about it but not directly referring to it...' (Blake, 2008: 455). This is a helpful rule of thumb for the integrative practitioner working with children and adolescents.

Summary

- Transference is the process by which we project our inner world onto others in our environment, seeing and responding to them at least partially as though they were someone or something from our past.
- Countertransference is when feelings are projected from the client's unconscious and are received by the therapist as a felt experience. The therapist may be able to use this to deepen their understanding of and empathic connection to the client's inner world.
- Transference 'interpretations' should generally be avoided in work with children and young people. Working 'with' the transference rather than 'in' it allows the therapist to think about the transference as part of their understanding of the client and their process.

Additional Resources

- Blake, P. (2008) 'Transference and countertransference', in P. Blake, *Child and Adolescent Psychotherapy*. London: Routledge.
- Heimann, P. (1950) 'On Countertransference', *International Journal of Psychoanalysis*, 31: 81–84.

Associated Entries

1.6 Object Relations Theory
2.14 Developing & Sustaining the Therapeutic Relationship
2.17 Developing Advanced Empathy

2.17 Developing Advanced Empathy

As outlined in entry 2.2 (p. 51), the Rogerian (1951) conceptualisation of empathy is of an attitude or way of being in the therapist that is tentatively offered to the client. This attitude offers a deep understanding of the client and their unique frame of reference which, if received by the client, paves the way for therapeutic change. This entry explores some key understandings and skills for the development of this fundamental therapeutic process.

Key Understandings

The term 'advanced empathy' denotes empathic interventions that are intended to communicate a depth of understanding that not only accurately reflects the client's current worldview, but also goes beyond this to expand the client's understanding of themselves. This is accomplished by attending to and possibly verbalising spoken and unspoken material (Garza et al., 2009). The form of empathic interventions varies across different models of therapy and often depends on the developmental capacity of the client. Working at a deeper level requires the development of relational skills through practice and in supervision. As a general rule, empathic interventions need to be rooted in the core relationship components (see entry 2.2, p. 51) and offered tentatively with non-judgemental curiosity.

Key Skills

1. Try making tentative observations of something when observing aspects of play or spoken material that indicate the client is feeling something they are not quite aware of. For example:

   'The dragon's knocked-over the army-man again. He doesn't seem able to get to his feet without being knocked down. I wonder if that's something you've been feeling with your asthma attacks this week? Like you can't get to your feet without something knocking you down again?'

   Or:

   Counsellor: I'm seeing your shoulders lift and your back straighten when you speak about your exam results. I get the sense you feel quite proud of yourself, but that this is hard to admit?

Client: Yes, you're right. I do feel pleased, but I'm scared if I say something it'll mean I'll fail next time and then I'll have been stupid to think I could do OK at something.

Counsellor: Maybe you're afraid if you enjoy your success, you'll feel stupid if you don't do well every time.

Client: I guess I'm protecting myself from disappointment, but how will I ever feel better if I don't let myself notice and feel good when I've done OK?

1. In the second example, the counsellor notices the client's body language and gently connects it with a feeling the client seems unaware of. The client takes this up and articulates their process in respect of avoiding feelings of disappointment and failure, and is able to gain some insight. We see the importance of trust here, with the client clearly feeling secure enough in the therapeutic relationship to discover their fear of acknowledging success.
2. Clients may not always be ready to receive an empathic conjecture or intervention. This is not necessarily because the counsellor has got it 'wrong', but may occur when the client is not ready to accept their feelings or thoughts. As empathic conjectures are offered tentatively, they can be offered and withdrawn as necessary. It is important not to be 'pushy' when feeling that you've observed or understood something the client will find useful. The work is always client-led and considers the age, developmental level and readiness of the child. Be aware of transference in the relationship (see entry 2.16, p. 111), as this can affect the client's capacity to accept an empathic intervention.
3. Skills in advanced empathy are strengthened by listening and observation skills. The more we are able to listen to the client's choice of words, tone of voice, content of spoken material, and observe their play or body-language, the better our capacity to connect with the client on a deep level, enhancing the therapeutic process and deepening the client's understanding of themselves.

Summary

- Advanced empathic attunement and interventions allow a deeper connection with the client, potentially facilitating insight and awareness.
- Empathic conjectures and interventions should be made tentatively and in the spirit of curiosity rather than from a sense of 'knowing' something the client doesn't about themselves.
- Clients can only receive and use empathic interventions when they are ready.

Additional Resources

- MindEd – www.minded.org.uk: 412-028 *Communicating Empathy.*

Associated Entries

2.2 Core Relationship Components
2.14 Developing & Sustaining the Therapeutic Relationship
2.16 Transference & Countertransference

2.18 Tracking

The term 'tracking' in counselling describes the process of staying close in the moment to the client's words, actions, body language, tone of voice, etc., trying to pick up on their thoughts and feelings in the here-and-now of the session. Tracking is a form of empathy. In order to effectively track the client's process, there must be an empathic connection or emotional bond between counsellor and client. This entry explores tracking and the skills required for this therapeutic process.

Key Understandings

In integrative therapy with children and adolescents, tracking means paying close attention to all aspects of the client's presentation. Landreth (2012: 189) urges: 'Listen to the child with your eyes as well as your ears.' Appropriately delivered tracking comments demonstrate an interest in and close attention to the client.

During early stages of a play-based session, while the client is settling in, a counsellor might make tracking comments to demonstrate their engagement with the client, for example:

- 'You're looking around the room, wondering what to play with.'
- 'You've emptied out the bricks. Looking through them. Ah, you've found the castle brick and you're putting it in the centre of the sandbox.'

Landreth (2012: 217) suggests that tracking comments such as these 'put into words what the therapist sees and observes the child doing and thus validate the child'. Tracking comments demonstrate that it is the client and what they are doing, feeling or thinking that is to be attended to in the therapeutic process.

Tracking the client and following their lead is also a means of conveying unconditional positive regard (UPR) (see entry 2.2, p. 51), as it demonstrates confidence that the client knows best and will progress in a positive direction if facilitated by the therapeutic relationship. This can be particularly important in work with older children and adolescents, who may be used to adults taking a dismissive or judgemental view of their actions or feelings. When tracking is done well it mirrors and scaffolds the child's process and helps the development of self-awareness and a sense of coherent internal dialogue. This relates to Vygotsky's (1962) theories of scaffolding and the 'zone of proximal development' (see entry 1.4, p. 13). For example:

- 'I notice you've spoken quite a bit today about your friendship with Maisie. I wonder if you're showing us how much her dishonesty has bothered you.'

Or:

Client: I've watched loads of TV this week. It's been brilliant. I've binged about three seasons of stuff on Netflix.

Counsellor: You've watched loads of TV and you've enjoyed it.

In the first example, the counsellor tracks a theme running through the session and uses this as the basis for an empathic conjecture. In the second, the counsellor reflects the content of the client's statement and validates the feeling they have expressed without any judgement.

Key Skills

1. Use terms such as 'I'm noticing you are...' or 'I'm noticing you have...' when reflecting content in order to demonstrate engagement with the client.
2. Ensure tracking comments are rooted in the core conditions of empathy, congruence and UPR. This should ensure that comments are perceived as caring and interested rather than scrutinising and judgemental.
3. Offer tracking comments sparingly, so clients don't feel self-conscious.
4. Be careful not to allow tracking comments to be robotic rather than open and curious.

Summary

- Tracking is a method of observing the client as they move through the session.
- Tracking should involve listening and observing the client and then using observations as the basis for intervention or empathic conjecture, as appropriate.
- Comments should be made sparingly so the client doesn't feel scrutinised or impinged upon by the counsellor.

Additional Resources

- Landreth, G. (2012) 'Characteristics of facilitative responses', in G. Landreth, *Play Therapy: The Art of the Relationship*. London: Routledge.
- Rogers, C.R. (1951) *Client-Centred Therapy*. London: Constable.

Associated Entries

2.2 Core Relationship Components
2.17 Developing Advanced Empathy
3.3 Play-Based Interventions
3.7 Working with Emotions

2.19 Endings

The ability to bring counselling to a close, or to manage unplanned endings, is important for all therapists, and working with children and adolescents brings its own challenges and requirements in this respect. The nature of therapy with this group, with its natural focus on developmental stage, as well as the context in which therapy occurs, bring implications for endings which counsellors need to be able to work with flexibly in order to ensure that counselling is productive and client-led throughout. This entry focuses on the key understandings and skills required to manage a variety of endings in counselling with children and adolescents.

Key Understandings

The writing so far in this part of the book has focused on establishing and sustaining effective therapeutic relationships. Bringing counselling to a close and ending this relationship is a central aspect of the therapeutic process and one that needs to be in the therapist's awareness from the outset:

> The therapist visualises the child at a point in time when obstacles to growth are removed and the child progresses to a state of interdependent and healthy functioning. The therapist sees the end as the real beginning for the child. Ironically, the goal of therapy is to end therapy. (Ray, 2018: 233)

This is the moment when the goal of therapy is deemed to have been met, and any changes made or insights gained have been 'worked through', consolidated and internalised by the client in a way that means counselling doesn't need to continue. Winnicott (1969: 712) sums this up, saying: 'We all hope our patients will finish with us and forget us, and that they will find living itself to be the therapy that makes sense.' In terms of understanding ending, this would seem to be linked closely to an understanding of the function of therapy, that is, what is it for, and how do we know when it has served its purpose?

With time-limited counselling, the ending needs to be a focus from the beginning so that pragmatic decisions can be made regarding what can reasonably be achieved in the given timeframe. Coren (1996) discusses the case for time-limited counselling as the treatment of choice for certain groups, such as young people. He suggests that in order for time-limited work to be effective, a focus for the work needs to be agreed early on, and both therapist and client need to be motivated and enthusiastic regarding working in this way. One of the early pioneers of brief psychodynamic therapy,

David Malan, proposed the need to maintain a 'dynamic' focus throughout brief work and to pay 'selective attention and selective neglect' (Mander, 2000: 38) to content in order to maintain the focus on the explicit task of the therapy. Briggs et al. (2015) have developed a time-limited psychodynamic intervention specifically aimed at addressing concerns about engaging adolescents in therapy and the need to make effective relational contact with the client. They suggest that 'for some adolescents, even a short-term therapy can be experienced as entrapping, whilst for others, any hint of a thought of an ending can be experienced as an abandonment or an affront to the developing adult ego' (Briggs et al., 2015: 315–316). This emphasises the importance of taking into account the client's history in terms of ending and termination. It is worth noting that for some clients, success at meeting their goals in therapy can be tinged with anxiety or painful feelings if it means letting go of an important person and relationship.

Key Skills

Planned endings

1. In open-ended therapy, look for signs that the work may be coming to an end (see entry 2.18, p. 117). There may be evidence in behaviour around the frame or in how engaged the client is in the session that indicate they are coming to the end. Use empathic conjecture (see entry 2.17, p. 114) to work with this: 'I'm noticing that you've had much less to say in your last couple of sessions. I wonder if you've been thinking about whether you might be ready to end your counselling?'
2. Be aware that moving towards an ending is likely to bring up new material. Even if the client is ready to end and move on, adequate space must be provided for exploring thoughts and feelings that emerge when the end is in sight. Saying goodbye may bring up memories in the client of other 'endings', and when enough time is allowed, these can be explored in the light of insights and understandings the client has gained during therapy. For example: 'I think I'll feel sad when we finish next week, but I'm going to take my drawings and look at them whenever I want to remember our sessions. I'm going to keep them with the box of memories of mum that we made in here.'
3. Allow space where appropriate to review the counselling from the client's perspective. Artwork might be looked through, or different aspects of the process spoken about, allowing the client to reflect on how things have changed for them.
4. Explore any feelings of anxiety the client may have about ending counselling. Try to help them to work with these as they arise, rather than dismissing them or moving quickly to focus on something positive. For example: 'I think you're showing me something really important about how frightening it feels for you to let go of something you've experienced as trustworthy and reliable. Let's try to stay with those feelings and unpack them a bit.'

5. Be aware of your feelings and thoughts about endings and saying goodbye. Notice whether this is something you feel uncomfortable about and like to avoid if possible. If you find it hard to stay open to feelings around endings, then your clients are likely to notice and it may block them from expressing difficult feelings of their own. This is something to work on in therapy and in supervision in an empathic and non-judgemental way.

Unplanned endings

Not all endings in therapy are planned and therapists working with children and adolescents require skills to manage unplanned endings. Unplanned endings come in various forms. The following are suggestions for how to manage unplanned endings:

1. The client may decide to end before the agreed time, or they may simply stop coming to sessions. This is more likely to be the case in work with adolescents where they have increased agency and autonomy. Equally, a younger child may decide they don't want further sessions. In these cases, it is important to respect the autonomy of the client in choosing whether or not to attend, but also to encourage them to talk thorough any issues they may be experiencing in relation to the sessions, or to consider whether there is anything else they might find useful if counselling is not what they want at this time.
2. An image I find helpful when working with endings with children and adolescents is that of a picnic. Counselling is represented by the food on the blanket. Some clients come and sit and eat for a while, finding things they enjoy and find nutritious. Once they're finished, they might stay and chat and say goodbye, or they might simply wander off to play with friends having taken in enough to sustain them for a while.
3. Make sure you 'leave the door open'. When a client ends, even if they do so abruptly or as a result of a rupture in the therapeutic relationship, it's important they are aware that they can return to counselling in the future, should they need to. Communications need to be clear and non-judgemental regarding the client's choice to end, informing them that services are available in the future, even if it won't be you that they see. This helps to ensure young people feel positive about returning to counselling, knowing this is a choice they can make for themselves rather than to please someone else or to fulfil a need for the counsellor in some way (see point 3).
4. Be prepared to work with your own feelings around rejection, abandonment and loss. When a client leaves without a 'proper ending' this can bring up feelings for us as practitioners. These feelings are human and there's no need to judge ourselves for having them. However, if left unexamined and outside awareness, they can impact on our capacity to work with endings and hold a non-judgemental space for the client and their process.

Summary

- Endings are an important part of the therapeutic process, marking the beginning of the post-therapy phase.
- Planned endings offer opportunities to work through material and feelings raised by the prospect of termination as well as for consolidation of therapeutic progress.
- Unplanned endings occur for many reasons in counselling with children and adolescents. Client autonomy should be respected and a non-judgemental approach offered where the ending is abrupt or unexpected.

Additional Resources

- MindEd – www.minded.org.uk: 412-043 *Concluding Counselling*.

Associated Entries

2.3 The Therapeutic Frame
2.5 Contracting
2.15 Managing Ruptures in the Therapeutic Alliance

2.20 Ethical Issues

Ethical practice is rooted in knowledge and understanding of ethical principles and frameworks, and in the capacity to establish and sustain a living relationship between these principles and the complex realities of clinical practice. This dynamic connection between professional identity, knowledge and practice is one which continues to develop throughout our therapeutic careers as we encounter new situations and dilemmas in the work and learn new approaches to benefit the client and potentially the field at large. An ethically competent therapist needs to hold a balance between therapeutic exploration of all aspects of the client's process alongside the need to mitigate harm and hold their best interest at the centre of the endeavour.

Key Understandings

A concern often expressed by counsellors is that working with children and adolescents will confront them with challenging ethical dilemmas, and there is certainly some truth in this. Daniels and Jenkins (2010: 53) suggest the vulnerability of younger clients creates a 'greater need for ethical vigilance on the part of the therapist'.

Ethical issues can arise in many areas of practice, such as contracting (see entry 2.5, p. 68), risk assessment and safeguarding (see entry 2.8, p. 79), confidentiality and consent (see entry 2.9, p. 84), third-party involvement (see entries 2.12, p. 97 and 2.22, p. 131), working within the limits of practitioner competence (see entry 2.24, p. 137), and managing the boundaries of the therapeutic relationship. In this entry we consider the skills required to work effectively and therapeutically with ethical dilemmas, as we follow one case example through this process.

Key Skills

1. Developing an understanding of the ethical principles underpinning counselling with children and adolescents

The BACP *Competence Framework for Therapeutic Work with Children and Young People* (2019: 10) includes the following: 'Knowledge of, and ability to operate within, professional and ethical guidelines.' The framework outline a series of ethical principles similar to those found in the BACP's *Ethical Framework for the Counselling Professions* (2018).

1. An ability to draw on knowledge that ethical practice is informed by a number of key principles:

   i. confidentiality and consent
   ii. that counsellors should respect clients' rights to be autonomous and self-directed
   iii. that counsellors act in the best interests of clients in order to promote their wellbeing
   iv. that counsellors should strive to mitigate any harm being caused to the client
   v. that counsellors are committed to the fair and impartial treatment of all clients and the provision of equitable services
   vi. that counsellors take steps to enhance their personal and professional wellbeing in order to maintain personal effectiveness

2. An ability to draw on knowledge that therapeutic work may confront counsellors with conflicts of ethical principles and in such circumstances clinical supervision should be used to resolve these.

(BACP, 2019: 10)

While these principles provide a solid foundation for ethical practice, there are areas of clinical practice, as highlighted by point ii, where ethical principles come into conflict with one another, presenting the counsellor with a 'real-time' ethical dilemma. The following case example outlines such a conflict.

Case Example: Beth (counsellor) and Lukas

Beth is a qualified counsellor working in a youth counselling service with Lukas, who is 14. Lukas has experienced bouts of moderate anxiety and agoraphobia since losing his mum to breast cancer a year ago. During the session, Lukas tells Beth he's been spending time with some older boys on his estate and that he's been feeling better. He says that they've been giving him 'jobs' to do and he has some responsibility now. When Beth asks him what these 'jobs' are, Lukas shrugs and says 'Just stuff. You know. But I'm getting out and about now. That's good, isn't it, Beth?' Beth suspects the boys Lukas is referring to are involved with supplying drugs and she's concerned that Lukas may be vulnerable to being groomed. However, she can see from Lukas's perspective that he is engaging with peers for the first time since his mother's death and this is leading to positive feelings for him. She would like the opportunity to explore this further in the therapeutic work.

Questions to explore

- What would you do in Beth's position?
- What are the guiding ethical principles here?
- How would your response differ if Lukas...
  - ...was 18 years old?
  - ...was 10 years old?
  - ...had learning difficulties?

In this dilemma, the principle of respecting clients' rights to be autonomous and to act in their best interest comes into potential conflict with the principle of striving to mitigate harm to the client. This is a typical example of ethical conflicts in practice. There is no 'correct' answer as there is no straightforward means of determining what course of action will be in Lukas's best interests in mitigating potential harm; and it is likely to be difficult to manage this alongside the principle of allowing Lukas, as a vulnerable 14-year-old, to be absolutely self-directing.

2. Take ethical issues to clinical supervision for discussion

It's important that practitioners, no matter how experienced, consult others when managing ethical dilemmas. One of the roles for clinical supervision is the therapeutic consideration of such issues, and this should be the primary place of consultation for most practitioners working with children and adolescents (see entry 2.24, p. 137).

Case Example: Beth and Lukas

Beth is concerned Lukas may be at risk of harm if he continues to hang out with this group of boys, but she is also mindful of needing to maintain the therapeutic relationship and work on the underlying issues that make Lukas potentially vulnerable. As she has a good relationship with Lukas and he attends sessions consistently, she decides to maintain confidentiality at this point but to take the issue to supervision the next day (points iii. acting in the best interest of the client, and iv. mitigating harm).

Beth and her supervisor consider the issues in the context of Lukas's presenting concerns and her supervisor agrees that there is the potential to work on the self-esteem issues which may be at the root of Lukas's vulnerability. She also suggests that they look at the agency guidelines for safeguarding vulnerable clients.

---

3. Consult agency protocols and legal frameworks where appropriate

As discussed in entry 2.8 (p. 79), counsellors should ensure they are aware of relevant guidelines and criteria regarding client work at their agency or nationally, where appropriate.

Case Example: Beth and Lukas

After supervision, Beth goes online to look at the safeguarding guidelines for the youth counselling centre. She finds information on reporting safeguarding issues where there is concern regarding vulnerable young people. The guidelines advise staff who are concerned for a young person's wellbeing to raise these confidentially with the designated safeguarding lead, who is also the centre manager and a qualified youth worker and counsellor. Beth shares her concerns and the manager agrees that, at present, they can keep an eye on the situation, but that if more information is forthcoming, indicating that Lukas is at significant risk of harm, they will need to consider further actions.

Questions to explore

- How do you imagine Beth feels having discussed the case with her supervisor and the centre manager?
- What other courses of action could have been chosen?
  What do you imagine the results would be?

---

4. Seek sources of support with ethical issues

In addition to the processes described above, there are other places for counsellors to seek support and guidance with ethical dilemmas. Professional bodies all have codes of ethics and provide support for practitioners facing ethical dilemmas. The BACP has established a dedicated 'ethics hub' and ethics consultant for practitioners working with children and young people. See the additional resources section for more information.

5. Work within limits of competence

The BACP Competence Framework identifies a requirement for counsellors to 'recognise the boundaries of their own competence and not attempt to practise an intervention for which they do not have the appropriate training or (where applicable) specialist qualification' (BACP, 2019: 11). Working outside our competence is likely to bring us into conflict with the ethical principles of mitigating harm to clients and acting in their best interests. This is of particular relevance to newly-qualified counsellors as well as those in training. Counsellors who are asked to take on clients or to work in ways they do not feel adequately trained or qualified for should seek advice from their professional body before proceeding.

Summary

- Counselling children and adolescents sometimes raises conflicts in protecting the therapeutic relationship versus keeping the client safe from harm.
- There is support in the form of ethical frameworks and guidelines. Counsellors need to be aware of the ethical principles underpinning therapeutic work and to ensure they understand how these relate to practice.
- Dilemmas should be considered in collaboration with supervisors, professional bodies, insurance providers and appropriate colleagues in order to ensure decisions are carefully considered before any action is taken.

Additional Resources

- BACP Ethics Hub: www.bacp.co.uk/events-and-resources/ethics-and-standards/ethics-hub
- BACP *Good Practice in Action* resources: www.bacp.co.uk/events-and-resources/ethics-and-standards/good-practice-in-action
- Bond, T. (2015) *Standards and Ethics for Counselling in Action* (4th edition). London: Sage/British Association for Counselling and Psychotherapy.
- Daniels, D. & Jenkins, P. (2010) *Therapy with Children: Children's Rights, Confidentiality and the Law* (2nd edition). London: Sage.

Associated Entries

2.8 Risk Assessment & Safeguarding
2.9 Confidentiality & Consent
2.15 Managing Ruptures in the Therapeutic Alliance
2.24 Clinical Supervision
3.10 Working with Risk

2.21 Self-Disclosure

Self-disclosure has long been a point of difference between psychodynamic and humanistic modalities. One of the analytic principles established by Freud (1912/1958) was that of therapist neutrality, minimising any 'real relationship' between the person of the therapist and the patient, enabling transferential material to be available for interpretation. Humanistic and Integrative approaches take the view that therapist self-disclosure can be used as a tool to strengthen congruence as well as reduce the power imbalance between the counsellor and client. However, these approaches largely relate to work with adults and assume a particular developmental position, which is unlikely to be paralleled in work with children and adolescents. Therefore, an alternative understanding and skill-set are required when considering an integrative approach to therapist self-disclosure with children and adolescent clients.

Key Understandings

Self-disclosure can take several forms. For example:

Direct statements regarding the therapist's personal life or thoughts and views, for example: 'I was also sexually assaulted when I was 16 and, while it was a difficult thing to experience, I am still here today', or 'I'm a massive Liverpool fan too. I try to get to every home match'.

Indirect personal revelations picked up on in or outside the session, either in a public space or online, for example: the therapist's online recovery blog, which they keep under a pseudonym but which is linked to their Twitter account, or the client may see their counsellor out in town with their partner and children.

Communications in the session which intentionally reveal the therapist's immediate response to client material, for example: 'When you spoke about the assault, I could see how painful it was and I felt so sad for you'. Knox and Cooper (2015) highlight the difference between comments such as these, which reflect immediacy in the moment, and the sharing of personal information related to life outside the therapy session.

Key Skills

1. Use self-disclosure as a tool to enhance therapy, that is, to support the provision of the core relationship components (see entry 2.2, p. 51): 'I'm hearing that you think

counselling is for weak people who can't cope with their problems. I can tell you I've had a lot of counselling in my life and I don't think of myself as weak. I wonder if we might find any other ways to think about therapy and who it might be useful for?'

2. Use self-disclosure to facilitate the client's use of the therapist to form a new object relation (see entry 1.6, p. 20): 'You've said your parents are dismissive of your desire to be a writer and not go to university straight away. I'd be interested to hear more about your writing and what it means to you. It sounds important.'
3. Carefully consider the impact a disclosure might have on the therapeutic process. For example, a comment such as 'When I was rejected to study medicine I was depressed and felt hopeless for a while, but I soon bounced back and found another direction to go in' might lead to feelings of shame in the client that they have not similarly 'bounced back'.
4. Observe the impact that self-disclosure has on therapy. Does a disclosure lead to the client opening up about their own process a little more or does it seem to create a rupture in the here-and-now process in the session?
5. Self-disclosures should only be made when to do so will be of benefit to the client. They should not be used to work on areas that are unresolved or of interest for the therapist. The process should remain client-centred at all times, for example: 'I've recently lost my mum as well. I know how you feel, it's hard to get out of bed some mornings' or 'I think Liverpool have performed terribly this season. When do you think it'll be time for a new manager?'
6. Be mindful of inadvertent self-disclosures, past and present, that may reveal information about you online, including social media (see additional resources section for more information).

Additional Resources

- Online Therapy Institute – www.onlinetherapyinstitute.com: the Online Therapy Institute's *Ethical Framework for Use of Social Media by Mental Health Professionals* can be found on their website (last accessed 16 April 2020).
- Childnet – www.childnet.com: advice for you as a professional (last accessed 16 April 2020).

Associated Entries

2.4 Building Rapport
2.14 Developing & Sustaining the Therapeutic Relationship

2.22 Working with Other Professionals

The complex needs of some child and adolescent clients means that at times clinical work may involve contact with other professionals. Counsellors need to develop the skills required to work with others, always with the benefit of the client held firmly in mind.

Key Understandings

Working with other agencies and professionals may be required at various points in the therapeutic process. This can occur for a number of reasons, including:

- The client may already have other professionals involved at the point of referral for counselling. These could include their GP, psychiatrist, school nurse, educational psychologist, mental health support worker, etc.
- The need for an onward referral may arise during the course of therapy, including as a response to safeguarding concerns.

Collaboration between professionals can be of significant benefit to clients in ensuring their needs are supported by appropriate services alongside or as an alternative to counselling. It can allow for expertise and knowledge around a particular child or family to be pooled, potentially enhancing the services offered (Kirkbride, 2018a). However, in order for collaboration to be effective and beneficial for the client, counsellors need to work skilfully and with ethical principles in mind at all times.

Key Skills

1. Ensure communications with other agencies and professionals are clear and in line with guidance on information sharing (see entry 2.13, p. 101).
2. Where external agencies make contact regarding a client, be clear what you have permission to discuss before responding to requests for contact or information.
3. If an onward referral is being considered, ensure that this is discussed fully and in a developmentally appropriate way with the client as well as with their family, where appropriate. Make sure the client is aware why the referral is being made and how

this is intended to support their needs. Be clear about what the referral will mean and how it will impact their ongoing counselling. Younger clients may not fully understand why they can't continue with counselling if they have been referred for therapy through the Child and Adolescent Mental Health Services (CAMHS). It is important to explain this in developmentally appropriate language so the client is as fully informed as possible about what will happen next.

4. Gather knowledge about services available for children, adolescents and families nationally and at a local level. This should include local CAMHS and other NHS services as well as non-statutory services offering specialist support in areas such as substance misuse, domestic violence, gang-related activities, sexual health, bereavement services, etc. (see entry 4.4, p. 270).
5. Develop mutually respectful and collaborative relationships with associated services and professionals in the field. Try to develop links with key professionals, such as a child and adolescent psychiatrist, child psychotherapist, etc., who are available for consultation should the need arise. Be aware of the potential for 'splitting' between services where one is seen as 'all good' and the other as 'all bad'. Try to come from a position of understanding that most professionals working with children and adolescents are doing their best to provide services, often under heavy workloads and financial constraints. The more clients see their counsellor engaging with professionals in a friendly and collegial manner, the easier it is likely to be for them to do the same.

Summary

- Therapy with children and adolescents can involve contact with other professionals for a variety of reasons.
- Multi-agency working can be of great benefit to clients and their families. However, ethical principles should be adhered to when communicating with other agencies and the best interests of the client is to be upheld at all times.
- When referring-on or contacting other agencies, the client should be aware of all communications involving them and consent needs to be obtained, where appropriate, before any action is taken.

Additional Resources

- Department for Education (2015a) *Information Sharing: Advice for Practitioners Providing Safeguarding Services to Children, Young People, Parents and Carers*. London: HMSO.
- Department for Education (2015b) *Working Together to Safeguard Children: A Guide to Inter-agency Working to Safeguard and Promote the Welfare of Children*. London: HMSO.

Associated Entries

2.8 Risk Assessment & Safeguarding
2.9 Confidentiality & Consent
2.13 Record-Keeping & Data Protection

2.23 Self-Care for Counsellors

The integrative relational approach to counselling relies heavily on the therapist's capacity to make use of their self in the work. Professional musicians devote a considerable amount of time and resources to caring for and protecting their instrument so that it is in the best condition possible when it's time to play. As therapists, we are the instrument or 'tool of our trade' and it is crucial we look after ourselves, just as a violinist would their Stradivarius.

Key Understandings

Working as a therapist, especially with vulnerable children and adolescents, can have an emotional and psychological impact on the practitioner. Figley (2002) coined the term 'compassion fatigue' to describe a condition experienced by professionals listening to clients' traumatic experiences, who subsequently have the potential to develop symptoms of secondary post-traumatic stress disorder, leading to 'burn-out'.

Work with children and adolescents brings us into contact with high-levels of distress in clients as well as in others such as parents and teachers. There may be pressure to magically 'fix' problems that have developed over long periods of time and which will take more than a few counselling sessions to resolve. Counsellors often put significant pressure on themselves to 'get it right', especially when working with child protection and safeguarding. The BACP's Ethical Framework advises practitioners to take responsibility for 'monitoring and maintaining our own psychological and physical health, particularly that we are sufficiently resilient and resourceful to undertake our work in ways that satisfy professional standards' and for 'keeping a heathy balance between our work and other aspects of our life' (BACP, 2018: 27).

Key Skills

1. Make use of supervision (see entry 2.24, p. 137) for support with challenges in the work, ethical dilemmas, safeguarding, etc. These challenging areas of practice should be shared and not managed alone without support.

2. Develop professional networks to complement clinical supervision. Counselling can be an isolating profession, and peer supervision, support networks and involvement in the wider counselling community provide vital resources for building resilience and surviving the challenges of practice, particularly post-training when there is no longer an institutional framework for regular contact with fellow trainees or faculty.
3. Make use of personal therapy whenever appropriate, for example, when facing personal difficulties or when clinical work raises unresolved issues or is particularly challenging or overwhelming.
4. Seek professional support when facing challenges arising from clinical work. Many practitioners experience problems such as complaints or doubts about how they are dealing with something. It's important to remember that most therapists will have been there or somewhere similar at some point in their career and that professional bodies are there to support members as well as to uphold professional standards.
5. Train appropriately for the area you are practising in and then 'top up' with continuous professional development (CPD) activities. This develops confidence and offers opportunities for networking and building relationships.
6. Engage in fulfilling activities and relationships outside clinical work. Make time for relationships, recreation and practices not directly connected to work as a therapist, but which enhance quality of life.

Summary

- Therapy brings us into contact with difficult experiences, including trauma and loss. In order to continue to offer empathy to clients and space for them to express and articulate their experiences, therapists need to develop skills in self-care.
- Failure to care for the self adequately can lead to compassion fatigue and burn-out. These will negatively impact the therapeutic relationship and process.
- Self-care is an ethical requirement for practising therapists and there are a number of identified routes for practitioners to take in developing their practice in this respect.

Additional Resources

- British Association for Counselling and Psychotherapy (2018) *Good Practice in Action 088: Self-care for the Counselling Professions*. Lutterworth: BACP. Available at: www.bacp.co.uk/media/3939/bacp-self-care-fact-sheet-gpia088-jul18.pdf (last accessed 16 April 2020).

Associated Entries

2.24 Clinical Supervision
3.10 Working with Risk
3.14 Trauma & Abuse
4.7 Refugee Communities
4.8 Looked-After Children (LAC)

2.24 Clinical Supervision

Clinical supervision plays a crucial role in the professional life of the integrative counsellor working with children and adolescents. Many of the entries in Part II have focused on the counsellor's use of self to facilitate the relationship conditions proven to be most effective in facilitating the therapeutic process. Sustaining this effectively and ethically requires professional support. Hawkins and Shohet (2012: 3) reflect on the need for practitioners to be 'continually supported and held in staying open to demands of emotionally relating to a wide range of people and needs. ... Quality work cannot be sustained alone'.

Key Understandings

Regular clinical supervision is a requirement of all professional counselling and psychotherapy bodies. For example, the BACP (2018) requirement for registered, qualified counsellors is for a minimum of 1.5 hours of supervision per month. The BACP's Ethical Framework (2018: 22) states: 'Good supervision is much more than case management. Supervision provides practitioners with regular and ongoing opportunities to reflect in depth about all aspects of their practice in order to work as effectively, safely and ethically as possible.'

Supervision serves a number of important functions for both trainee and qualified therapists, including providing a space for:

- further learning
- reflection and reflexivity regarding all aspects of the therapeutic process
- consideration of ethical issues
- professional support with all aspects of clinical practice
- reflection on professional development needs
- consideration of whether therapeutic work is within the limits of capability, including whether the client needs to be referred-on or other professionals involved (see entry 2.22, p. 131)
- consideration of fitness to practise.

As supervision holds such a significant position in clinical practice, it is crucial that practitioners understand the skills required to make the best use of this resource.

Key Skills

1. **Ensure your supervision is appropriate for all aspects of your clinical practice**. This might mean having more than one supervisor, such as one for play-based work with younger children and another for work with adolescents and young people. If clients are seen in private practice, it will be important to find a supervisor who understands this area rather than someone who only has experience working in agency or educational settings and vice versa.
2. **Take time to develop a solid supervisory relationship with your supervisor**. Research suggests that this is important if supervision is to be effective (Ladany et al., 2013). Just as the therapeutic alliance is central to developing trust between client and counsellor, the same is true for the supervisory alliance. Counsellors need to share all aspects of their practice in supervision and also demonstrate openness regarding difficulties and challenges arising in that relationship. In terms of the Integrative approach, supervision should be collaborative and based on the core relationship components (see entry 2.2, p. 51). When experienced in this way, supervision can support the counsellor in their ability to meet clients where they are, to see things from their perspective and to work in depth.
3. **Use supervision when facing ethical issues and safeguarding concerns**. Ethical issues and potential breaches of confidentiality should be explored fully in supervision before any decisions are made (see entries 2.8, p. 79 and entry 2.20, p. 124). Where counselling takes place in agency or educational settings, it may be that issues are discussed with the safeguarding lead or line manager prior to clinical supervision taking place. Clinical implications should still be explored in clinical supervision as soon as possible.
4. **Take responsibility for how you present your work in supervision.** While some aspects of supervision are the responsibility of the supervisor, as supervisee it is important to be an active participant rather than passive receiver of the supervisor's suggestions. It's important to present work in an open, honest and curious manner and to be ready to explore challenging areas non-defensively with the aim of furthering professional development. Be curious regarding your feelings about particular clients. Take the clients you are struggling with most to supervision, as these are the areas from which you will learn most. If there are clients you are finding it difficult to be fully authentic with or to offer UPR or empathy, then this can be explored in supervision. Used in this way, supervision can assist in uncovering therapeutic 'blind-spots' in order to facilitate the capacity to work at greater depth with clients.
5. **Use supervision to explore the impact of client work**. Supervision is an opportunity to discuss sessions which have an emotional or psychological impact (see entry 2.23, p. 134). Ling et al. (2014: 305) identify supervision as one of a range of 'protective mechanisms' which help therapists working with trauma or challenging clients in providing an opportunity to 'release and lessen the stress and distress of their work'.

6. **Be prepared to challenge or change your supervision if it is not meeting your needs.** For many practitioners, particularly those seeing clients in private practice, their clinical supervisor is their main, if not only, source of ongoing professional support. If you feel your current supervision is not meeting your needs, this will impede your capability to effectively meet the needs of your clients. As therapists, we need to have difficult conversations when necessary and these can be done in a professional manner which supports the needs of the practitioner and is therefore beneficial to their clients.
7. **Explore different kinds of supervision and supervisor.** For many practitioners, individual supervision with a suitably qualified and experienced member of the profession is the primary choice to fulfil supervisory requirements. However, there are other sources of supervision which it may be appropriate for practitioners to try in addition to their primary supervisory support. For example, peer supervision, where a number of practitioners meet together to consider cases and support each other's practice, can be useful, particularly for therapists working in a particular context or with a particular client group. Peer supervision is also a way of gaining experience in supervising clinical work prior to taking on the role in a more formal capacity.

Summary

- Clinical supervision is an integral part of therapeutic practice.
- Supervision offers support with various aspects of the therapeutic process.
- Supervision should be the first place to go with ethical dilemmas and safeguarding concerns.
- Due to the importance of this role, it's important to choose a supervisor carefully.
- Additional supervisory support can be provided by peers and colleagues working in similar contexts.

Additional Resources

- British Association for Counselling and Psychotherapy (2017) *Good Practice in Action, Commonly Asked Questions 054: Introduction to Supervision*. Lutterworth: BACP. Available at: www.bacp.co.uk/ethical_ framework/documents
- British Association for Counselling and Psychotherapy (2018) *Good Practice in Action, Commonly Asked Questions 011: Monitoring the Supervisory Relationship from the Perspective of a Supervisee*. Lutterworth: BACP.
- British Association for Counselling and Psychotherapy (2018) *Good Practice in Action, Commonly Asked Questions 008: How to Choose a Supervisor*. Lutterworth: BACP.

Associated Entries

2.8 Risk Assessment & Safeguarding
2.20 Ethical Issues
2.23 Self-Care for Counsellors

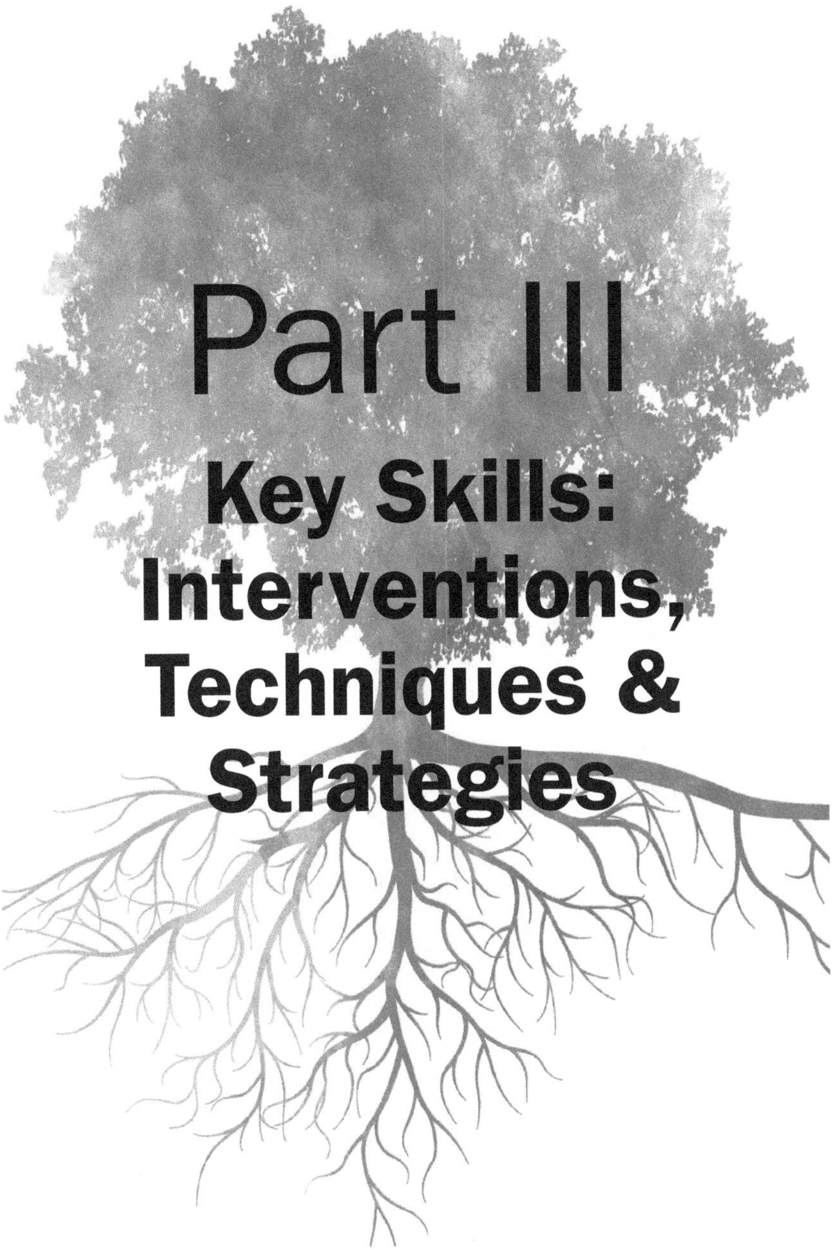

Part III

Key Skills: Interventions, Techniques & Strategies

3.1 Introduction: Skills & Interventions

Part III, with its focus on specific interventions or clinical considerations for work with children and adolescents, has its roots firmly planted in the first two parts of the book. The understanding of developmental processes and environmental factors contained in Part I, along with the exploration of the therapeutic relationship and process in Part II, provide the foundation from which this third part develops. Each area of practice covered in Part III needs to be considered in the context of the therapeutic relationship and the developmental stage the client has reached. Each entry will link back to previous ones where appropriate, as we continue to emphasise and develop our understanding of the dynamic process of therapy, grounding down into the roots before reaching further into the branches of specific skills and interventions.

The first group of entries cover common therapeutic interventions used with children and adolescents, including play-based and creative-arts work, cognitive-behavioural therapy, working with the emotions and use of mindfulness techniques. The second group considers working with risk presentations, both in a general sense and in relation to specific clinical presentations linked to 'risky' behaviours. These include self-harm, substance misuse, sexual behaviour, online risk and bullying. The entries also look at common presenting issues, such as family instability, loss and bereavement. The third group of entries in this part explores issues around psychological and emotional health, including anxiety, depression, psychiatric diagnosis and medication. The final group looks at a range of common presenting issues for young people, including learning disabilities, physical disability and chronic illness. At the end of Part III, we consider the development of resilience for children and young people and how therapeutic interventions might assist with this.

In this part of the book, we will be considering interventions and clinical considerations from a developmental point of view and with the provision of the core relationship components (see entry 2.2, p. 51), therapeutic frame, and ethical and legal frameworks in mind throughout. While interventions and considerations are an extension of core therapeutic skills, counsellors should bear in mind the ethical requirement that they work at all times within the limits of their competence, only using skills they have been adequately trained in, referring-on to other services where necessary (see entry 2.20, p. 124 and 2.22, p. 131).

3.2 Symbol & Metaphor

The following entries focus on the use of a range of creative and play-based therapeutic interventions. These offer an alternative to talking therapies or can be integrated into practice where appropriate to provide interventions which are sensitive to the developmental or other needs of young clients. As an introduction, this entry explores the important role of symbol and metaphor as a foundation for these approaches in child and adolescent counselling.

Key Understandings

The word 'metaphor' has its roots in ancient Greek, and is derived from the word 'metaphora', meaning 'to transfer' (www.etymonline.com/word/metaphor). Similarly, 'symbol' means 'something that stands in for something else'. Symbol and metaphor are both ways of using something to 'stand in' for something else, and for meaning to be 'transferred' between the two. For example, a small pebble placed in the centre of the sand-tray can 'stand in' for many different things, depending on what is being 'transferred' at the time. It could 'be' the client, another person in their life, their depression, their hope, their sense of abandonment… the possibilities are infinite. Once meaning has been transferred onto an object, image or idea, there is the possibility for it to be worked with therapeutically. It can be extended and explored, allowing the imagination to take hold, and facilitate new links and understandings for the client. In these next entries we explore a number of therapeutic applications for symbol and metaphor, including play and creative interventions and 'therapeutic chat' with older clients.

By 'standing in' for another object or meaning, metaphors and symbols provide a useful means of placing distance between the self and the event, person, or feeling the symbol represents. This process has various important therapeutic functions. It can help when the replaced object/event is too raw or difficult for the client to work with directly. It may be that the client has experienced trauma or painful feelings that are too 'hot' to be in direct contact with. Transferring these feelings onto an object or enacting them in play (see entry 3.3, p. 147) allows the potential for the client to approach and retreat from the experience at a pace which is manageable for them.

In entry 1.2 (p. 5), which explored the importance of play for development, we considered the crucial role of the capacity to symbolise as the child grows and becomes more able to use their imagination as a developmental tool. This capacity can be used in numerous ways in therapy to engage the client in a creative exploration and understanding of their experiences and feelings.

Key Skills

The entries on play-based therapy (3.3, p. 147), creative-arts interventions (3.4, p. 151), therapeutic 'chat' (3.5, p. 154) and cognitive-behavioural therapy (CBT) (3.6, p. 158) explore specific ways in which metaphor and symbol can be used in different ways. The following are some general ideas for working with metaphor and symbol which can be applied across all therapeutic interventions:

1. When working with symbols and metaphor, be child- or young person-led where possible. Allow the client to attribute their own meaning to objects, artwork or play. Be curious about what their understanding of the meaning might be. This offers the client encouragement to be curious about their world and its meaning. As Axline (1947: 99) suggests, 'In play, a therapist tentatively reflects on themes and metaphors of the child's play with a goal of helping the child understand himself and his world'.
2. When working 'in the metaphor' with a client, it is important to enter the metaphorical world and stay in it alongside the client as much as possible. If the client is playing with toys in the doll's house, stay focused on what the child is showing via their actions, rather than come out of metaphor and reflect on what the play might be showing. For example, 'You've put the little girl doll outside the house on her own. I wonder if that's how you feel when your family exclude you from their games?'
   While this interpretation may be picking up on an important theme in the child's play, it comes at a point where the play and the meaning are still unfolding for the client. Blake (2008: 292) highlights this in relation to containment:

   > Staying in the metaphor can be effective because it is so containing. By letting the adolescent play in the metaphor, you are not only listening to stories, but also allowing projections to be projected and thus contained, rather than being fed back too quickly in the form of an intervention.

3. Be open to using metaphor and symbol in a variety of ways. As previously stated, metaphor can help a client find 'aesthetic distance' (Cattanach, 1997) between themselves and a difficult experience or feeling. Metaphor can also be used as communication where children don't have the developmental capacity to talk directly and explicitly about difficult thoughts or feelings.
4. Be mindful of those children and young people who are not able to make use of metaphor and symbol. Many children who have experienced trauma, abuse or who have disabilities such as Autistic Spectrum Disorder (ASD) may find it difficult to move out of the concrete meaning of an object into an imaginative and symbolic place (see entries 1.2, p. 5 and 3.26, p. 239).

Summary

- Symbol and metaphor are used to express and explore client material in therapy.
- They are particularly prominent in play-based and creative-arts based interventions.
- Symbol and metaphor provide a means of working through issues at a distance and in ways that are meaningful for the client.

Additional Resources

- MindEd – www.minded.org.uk: 412-034 *Introducing Creative and Symbolic Methods.*
- MindEd – www.minded.org.uk: 412-035 *The Range of Creative and Symbolic Methods.*

Associated Entries

1.2 The Importance of Play
3.3 Play-Based Interventions
3.4 Creative-Arts Interventions
3.5 Therapeutic 'Chat'

3.3 Play-Based Interventions

Play-based therapeutic interventions offer a vital means of working therapeutically with children and adolescents. Play offers a rich opportunity for the expression of emotions and working through therapeutically for those clients for whom this is more effective and accessible than talking therapy. In this entry we consider the key understandings and skills required to use play-based interventions with children and adolescents.

Key Understandings

Play had played a significant role since the beginning of child psychotherapy. Although Freud himself did not work therapeutically with children, and while the psychoanalysts who followed him, such as Hermine Hug-Hellmuth, Melanie Klein and his own daughter Anna Freud, pursued different clinical approaches, they all considered the use of play central to therapeutic work with children (Blake, 2008). Anna Freud, for example, used play to engage with the child and build the therapeutic alliance. Melanie Klein was interested in analysing the child's play in order to understand their unconscious process in the same way as dreams and free association were used in work with adults at the time. Winnicott (1971: 54) was also clear about the fundamental therapeutic function of play, for both therapist and client, asserting that:

> If the therapist cannot play then he is not suitable for the work. If the patient cannot play, then something needs to be done to enable the patient to become able to play, after which psychotherapy may begin. The reason why playing is essential is that it is in playing that the patient is being creative.

While other psychoanalysts interested in the role of play in child-therapy primarily view it as a means for analysing and interpreting the child's psyche, Winnicott is clear that play has a therapeutic function in itself:

> It is good to remember always that playing is itself a therapy. To arrange for children to be able to play is itself a psychotherapy that has immediate and universal application, and it includes the establishment of a positive social attitude towards playing. (Winnicott, 1971: 50)

This is echoed in the work of clinicians who have explored play as a 'therapeutic action' in its own right (Scott, 1998).

Virginia Axline (1947) was the pioneer of non-directive play therapy, founded on the same philosophical approach and principles as Rogers' (1951) client-centred therapy (see entry 1.7, p. 25). In her seminal book, *Play Therapy*, Axline (1947) outlined eight principles for practice which echo those of Rogers (1951), including the need to accept the child as they are, the need to establish a warm and trusting relationship, the need to allow the play to unfold at the child's pace and to maintain a respect that the child can solve their own problems. For Winnicott (1971), this final principle highlighted the value of approaches other than classical psychoanalytic interpretation in play-based interventions:

> A good example of this is the work of Axline (1947) of New York. ... I appreciate Axline's work in a special way because it joins up with the point that I make ... that the significant moment is that at which *the child surprises himself or herself.* It is not the moment of my clever interpretation that is significant. (Winnicott, 1971: 51)

This is an important quotation for those taking an integrative approach as it suggests an important synthesis of psychoanalytic understanding with the core components of client-centred therapy.

Axline's (1947) principles form the basis for most play-based interventions currently used in clinical practice. Evidence suggests that play therapy is effective with a range of clients and presentations (Leblanc & Ritchie, 2001; Bratton, 2010).

Practitioners using play-based interventions work in a variety of settings, which can be viewed on a spectrum from fully-equipped 'playrooms' at one end to a portable case of objects and play materials at the other. In order to facilitate a play-based session, a range of materials are required which can be used in a variety of ways. The following list of suggested equipment and materials is indicative rather than exhaustive:

1. Toys for sensory play: sand-tray, water tray, clay, play-doh, slime, stretchy balls, etc.
2. Toys for projective/symbolic play: doll's house and dolls, various miniature figures (human and animal), and objects, shells, feathers, pebbles, etc.
3. 'Real-life' toys: dressing-up clothes, hats, puppets, swords, medical kits, etc.
4. Equipment for creative activities and expression: paint, pens, stickers, paper, etc. (see entry 3.4, p. 151).

Practitioners using play or other creative interventions will also need to consider these when arranging their schedule of clients to ensure there is enough time between clients to clean and tidy up and to prepare for the next child or young person (Kirkbride, 2016b).

Key Skills

1. Play-based interventions should be founded on the core relationship components of the integrative approach (see entry 2.2, p. 51).
2. Non-directive play-based therapy (NDPB) takes a fundamentally permissive approach, allowing the child freedom to engage with various play activities as they choose, demonstrating respect for their capacity to make choices, enabling them to solve problems or difficulties. However, it is also important to set realistic limits within the play therapy in order to anchor therapy to reality (i.e. while it is OK to play at 'killing' me with the sword, it is not OK to actually hurt me or yourself as there are real-life implications for this behaviour (see entry 2.6, p. 72).
3. Having established the therapeutic relationship and limits for therapy, the focus will be on facilitating play, using active listening and observing in order to track the play (see entry 2.18, p. 117), reflecting and acknowledging the client's actions and choices, making empathic conjectures or statements in an attempt to reflect the emotional content of the play (see entry 2.17, p. 114).
4. When using NDPB interventions, allow the child to enter metaphor and remain there without any pressure to explicitly link the symbolic to reality (see entry 3.2, p. 144).

Summary

- There is a long history of the use of play-based interventions in child and adolescent psychotherapy.
- Play has a range of identified therapeutic functions.
- Non-directive play therapy was developed by Axline (1947) and is based on the principles of client-centred therapy.
- Play-based interventions can be integrated into counselling where they are an appropriate intervention for the client.

Additional Resources

- Axline, V.M. (1947) *Play Therapy*. New York: Ballantine.
- Landreth, G.L. (2012) *Play Therapy: The Art of the Relationship*. London: Routledge.
- Winnicott, D.W. (1971) *Playing and Reality*. London: Tavistock Publications.
- British Association of Play Therapists (BAPT) website: www.bapt.info/play-therapy (last accessed 26 April 2020).

Associated Entries

1.2 The Importance of Play
1.7 Humanistic Theories of Development
2.2 Core Relationship Components
2.6 Limit-Setting
3.4 Creative-Arts Interventions

3.4 Creative-Arts Interventions

Creative-arts interventions are used in a range of therapeutic approaches with children and adolescents. Creative-arts interventions can be used to engage clients in the therapeutic alliance as well as to act as a symbolic means of helping the client experience and express themselves as part of the therapeutic process. In this entry we consider the key understandings and skills for the therapeutic use of creative-arts.

Key Understandings

The previous entry discussed Winnicott's (1971) thoughts regarding the role of play and playfulness, particularly with a view to facilitating creativity as, in his view, 'It is in playing and only in playing that the individual child or adult is able to be creative and to use the whole personality, and it is only in being creative that the individual discovers the self' (1971: 54). Winnicott is speaking here of the fundamental importance of finding ways to facilitate the creative process in the client and the therapeutic relationship, allowing the client to encounter and express themselves safely within the metaphor or symbol of the creative activity (see entry 3.2, p. 144). Malchiodi (2005: 1) suggests the use of creative arts in therapy acknowledges the client's individuality and enhances 'each person's ability to communicate effectively and authentically'. This concept is particularly relevant for the integrative approach to therapy with children and adolescents, where the unique developmental requirements of each client are integral to the provision of the core relationship components.

Key Skills

1. Allow engagement with art materials to be client-led as far as possible. Offer as broad a range of paint, clay, sand, toys and dressing-up materials as is practical and allow the client to engage with whatever they are drawn to, carefully observing and tracking their choices and engagement.
2. Some clients may feel anxious around art materials, perhaps experiencing fears about perfectionism and needing to get something 'right' or to impress. For adolescents, their use may feel like an unwelcome return to the 'babyishness' of childhood, while for others they may support an important regression to an earlier

developmental stage. It can be helpful to consider this in terms of the therapeutic alliance and creating a trusting environment where it might be possible to feel safe enough to experiment and explore through creative expression. Try to ensure that creative work is client-led and not informed by a desire on the part of the therapist, particularly where there is anxiety prior to establishing an effective therapeutic relationship or when 'contact is tenuous' (Pearce & Sewell, 2014).

3. Work collaboratively with the client in thinking about what will happen to any projects or drawings made during sessions. This process can be integrated into the therapeutic process. For example, one client might create a set of drawings symbolising their experiences of abuse which they decide to destroy as part of their grieving process. Young clients may need help in thinking about what to do with their artwork or slime and what it might mean if they take it home.
4. There may be moments in therapeutic work where the tentative introduction of creative materials is particularly appropriate. For example, when the client seems to be struggling to find the words for something they want to express, when they find speaking about themselves and their feelings anxiety-provoking, or when they actively express a preference for non-verbal methods of communication and expression.
5. When responding to what the client draws or presents, use a tentative approach when observing or commenting, rather than interpreting or directing the process. Comments such as 'Could you tell me more about your picture' and 'You've put on the costume you said was for the bully. What does that feel like for you?' offer curiosity and facilitate an opening for the client to explore their work or experience. Comments such as 'You've drawn a pig and a hamster. Is the pig supposed to be your step-dad? Who's the hamster?' or 'I wonder if you need to put a bit more red on that one if it's an angry picture' are less facilitative of the client's process, and more about how the therapist is responding to the work.
6. Try things out yourself. If you are interested in using creative methods therapeutically, try engaging with paint, play or drama yourself and see how it facilitates your own relationship with your inner world.

Summary

- Creative-arts interventions can be used either as stand-alone therapeutic approaches by appropriately trained therapists or integrated into counselling as a means of facilitating creative expression and the therapeutic process.
- Creative-arts interventions should be client-led rather than imposed by the therapist.
- Creative-arts interventions should be underpinned by the core relationship components of the integrative approach.

Additional Resources

- Malchiodi, C. (2005) *Expressive Therapies*. New York: Guilford Press.

Associated Entries

3.2 Symbol & Metaphor
3.3 Play-Based Interventions

3.5 Therapeutic 'Chat'

Therapeutic 'chat' is a method of working 'in the metaphor' with verbal content. The term 'chat' is taken from Blake (2008), but the method may also be familiar to practitioners as 'wittering' or by other related terms. In this entry we consider the role of therapeutic 'chat' and the skills required to use it with clients.

Key Understandings

In therapeutic 'chat', the client is encouraged to talk about whatever they are interested in – skateboarding, music, TV shows, movies, video-games, etc. – while the counsellor attempts to receive and understand the material in both a literal and a symbolic way. In this way, it is possible to work in the metaphor with young people without art or play materials. Blake (2008: 290) suggests this as a way to work with young people who 'give monosyllabic responses to questions about their family, relationships, or concerns, but are willing to "chat" about other issues'.

'Chatting' effectively keeps the conversation in metaphor, maintaining 'aesthetic distance' from difficult feelings. In this way, issues can be identified and explored while maintaining a sense of safety for the young person.

Even when talking about seemingly trivial things like reality TV shows or video-games, the counsellor can gain insight into how the young person thinks and feels about themselves, others and the world in which they find themselves. Engaging with the client in this way, 'on their own territory', is a powerful method of conveying a curious and non-judgemental attitude towards the client. Young clients are often surprised and pleased that their counsellor wants to know about the video-games they play and how they play them, or which contestants in their favourite reality TV show they find themselves most drawn to. This can strengthen the therapeutic alliance and develop trust and connection between counsellor and client (see entry 2.4, p. 63). Just as with play-based interventions, there is no need to come out of the metaphor and make conscious links, although this might be appropriate at some point in the process. Therapeutic 'chat' enables a connection to develop in the therapeutic relationship which is essentially playful and flexible as well as client-centred.

Exercise

With a partner, practise listening to each other speak about something of interest, such as a hobby or TV show. Take turns to listen while holding an outward curiosity about the subject matter along with an inward curiosity about potential meanings. After you have both had a turn, debrief and talk about your experience both as listener and listened to. What did you discover about yourself or your partner you didn't know before?

Key Skills

1. Encourage clients to talk about anything they are interested in or which come to mind. This could be anything from shows they are streaming, video-games, sports, music, etc.
2. Listen to the verbal content using 'evenly-suspended attention' (Freud, 1912/1958). This requires the therapist to 'be open to register cues and patterns of cues. ... This means a concentrated attentiveness to minute particulars and, at the same time, a readiness to see these anew in a freshening of the familiar" (Hobson, 1985: 199). In the following case example, the counsellor uses 'chat' both to build a relationship with the client and to begin to explore material. The client here is an 11-year-old boy whose father has recently died. He is the oldest of four siblings and has been referred to the counsellor as he has been experiencing low-mood and is disengaging from studies at school.

Counsellor: So, you told me you used to enjoy playing football after school every day. Can you tell me more about that?
Client: (slumped in chair with hood up) What d'you wanna know?
Counsellor: You can tell me whatever you like, but how about we start with what position you play in?
Client: (sitting up and looking mildly interested) I'm goalie. It's not as good as being a striker.
Counsellor: You're the goalie. Tell me more about what that means. I guess the goalie stops the other team from scoring, but is there anything else you can tell me?
Client: I have to keep the defence in order. I see a lot of what's going on from where I stand. I need to tell them where they're s'posed to be.
Counsellor: You tell them where they should be on the pitch?
Client: Yeah. They have to listen to me. I'm like the boss of the defence.
Counsellor: You're the boss.
Client: Yeah. It's hard sometimes. Sometimes they don't listen and a striker from the other team gets through and scores.
Counsellor: They get through and score.

Client: Yeah. And then I've failed and let everyone down. That's when I feel like crap and don't wanna play no more. I'd like to be the striker scoring the goals and with everyone telling them how good they are. It winds me up.

Counsellor: It sounds hard. It's a difficult position to play in by the sound of it. There's a lot of responsibility by the sound of it, but not always much celebration.

Here the counsellor stays 'in the metaphor'; using reflection, tracking and then an empathic conjecture to connect with the emotional content of the client's material. It's early in the therapeutic relationship and the counsellor is not sure at the moment how much the client is exploring their own material in the dialogue. They keep the client engaged by staying in a subject they are interested in while keeping track of where the client goes with this subject. This is a way of being outwardly curious by asking exploratory questions, but being inwardly curious at the same time, wondering what to make of how the client is speaking and what they are saying.

3. Be open and curious about the material, but don't be too 'in the know' about the subject. Allow the client to lead: 'I don't know much about that TV show. What can you tell me about it?' or 'I have seen that film, but I'm more interested in hearing what you made of it'.
4. Be aware when it feels safe to explore content in this way and when it doesn't. For example, if the work is with a client who has issues with compulsive gaming (see entry 3.19, p. 210), it may be difficult to explore this without judgement or concern. When working with risk presentations, it is important to maintain a balance between providing a relationship which allows for the exploration of difficult areas and behaviours alongside a need to manage concerns around significant harm to the client. This will be covered in more detail in the entries on risk and risk behaviour (see entry 3.10, p. 174).
5. Be clear about the difference between 'chat' and information gathering and/or risk assessment. For example: 'Tell me more about what happens when you play Fortnite? What's going through your mind?' and 'I'm hearing that you're struggling to sleep when you've been up late gaming. What might be going on there d'you think?'
6. Recognise when your own preferences and prejudices might interfere with your capacity to be open to 'chatting'. Be congruent and admit to yourself if you find football and skateboarding boring, or think *Love Island* is rubbish TV. Try to accept this and bear in mind that what you're listening to is the content of the client's inner world.
7. Hold appropriate boundaries. 'Chat' is about exploring the client's inner landscape; it is not an opportunity for you to talk about how devastated you were when Arsenal beat Liverpool on Saturday.
8. Be attuned to when the conversation feels dull or boring. This may mean the client is defended or too anxious to maintain a connection with their genuine feelings and thoughts. When this occurs, you can gently and empathically ask how they are feeling in that moment.

Summary

- Therapeutic 'chat' is a way of using conversation to work in symbol and metaphor.
- This can be useful in work with adolescents who struggle with talking therapy but don't want to use play or art materials.
- 'Chatting' involves skilfully facilitating a conversation and then listening for clues in the content which may be significant for the therapeutic process.

Additional Resources

- Blake, P. (2008) *Child and Adolescent Psychotherapy*. London: Routledge.

Associated Entries

2.4 Building Rapport
2.18 Tracking
3.2 Symbol & Metaphor

3.6 Cognitive-Behavioural Therapy (CBT)

Cognitive-behavioural therapy (CBT), a 'third-wave' socio-psychological intervention, developed from behavioural and cognitive psychological understandings of the person and the process of therapeutic change. While CBT was originally developed for work with adults, it became increasingly popular among practitioners working with children and adolescents from the 1990s onwards (Stallard, 2018). CBT is listed in the National Institute for Health and Care Excellence (NICE) guidelines as an effective intervention for children and young people with depression (Fuggle et al., 2013).

Key Understandings

CBT takes the view that psychological issues are created and sustained by problematic patterns of cognition and behaviour (Creswell & Waite, 2009). CBT works in collaboration with the client to explore relationships between cognitive, behavioural, emotional and physiological processes as they occur within a particular situation. Interventions are focused on addressing maladaptive patterns in these relationships, potentially freeing the client from problematic experiences and behaviours.

CBT utilises a collaborative approach where the therapist and client work actively together to identify problematic patterns and address them by gradually testing the client's interpretations and beliefs about themselves, their relationships and the world. With children and adolescents, this might take the form of working together as detectives, trying to understand negative thoughts and beliefs which underpin emotional and cognitive experiences of self and other.

CBT offers a 'problem-focused' therapeutic approach for working collaboratively in identifying maladaptive thoughts or feelings at the root of the problem and then employing various techniques to adjust maladaptive cognitions or behaviours. In this respect it differs from the integrative approach broadly proposed by this book, which places the therapeutic relationship as the agent of therapeutic change. CBT does require an effective therapeutic alliance in order for therapy to be effective (Fuggle et al., 2013), but this is not the principal mechanism of change. CBT is used as a stand-alone approach for work with children and adolescents where practitioners have appropriate training and supervision. However, it can also be successfully used as part of an integrative, creative and flexible approach to therapy where CBT techniques are used in a collaborative and child-centred way, founded on a solid therapeutic alliance.

Key to the delivery of CBT is a collaborative approach between therapist and client. Both parties (along with parents where appropriate) need to be able to 'think' together about the client's issues in order to formulate an appropriate treatment plan that will be effective in bringing about therapeutic change. Stallard (2005) emphasises the need for the client to be in a place of readiness to change in order to be able to collaborate with the therapist in this way. He suggests the 'Stages of Change' model (Prochaska et al., 1992) can be used to assess where the client is situated in relation to their issues and whether they are ready to establish goals for their treatment process. In order to be able to benefit from CBT, the client needs to acknowledge the following:

1. There is a difficulty or problem.
2. This problem could be changed.
3. The form of help on offer could bring about this change.
4. That the therapist is able to help the client to develop the skills required to secure this change (Stallard, 2018: 9).

Key Skills

1. **Formulation:** In order to incorporate CBT into an integrative approach, both counsellor and client need a clear understanding of the maladaptive behaviour or cognition they are proposing to work on as well as a formulation which takes into account factors underpinning the problem. Stallard (2005: 3) suggests 'mini-formulations' can be developed which help the client to 'see the connection between a situation and how they behave or between their thoughts and feelings'. Stallard (2005: 4) identifies the 'maintenance formulation' where '*triggering events* are identified and then the resulting *thoughts, feelings and behaviours* [are] tracked'. For example:

Counsellor: So, looking at how you've filled out the diagram, you were on the field after school with some classmates; you thought they were ignoring you and that they don't like you; you felt unhappy; when you arrived home that evening you went to the bathroom and cut the top of your thigh with a scalpel.

Client: Yes, I'm such a twat. Can't believe I did that. It seemed like the only thing I could do at the time.

Counsellor: OK, maybe we can look together at what happens when you have a thought or feeling, and whether there are other ways you could respond to difficult situations that might be better for you.

Formulations can be as simple as the one above or more complex depending on the presentation and therapeutic aim of the intervention.

2. **Methods and interventions:** CBT utilises a range of methods to establish maladaptive patterns in thoughts and behaviours. These include:

    - **Socratic questioning:** This is a method of engaging in a genuinely open and enquiring way, conveying interest in the client's process and in discovering how they think and feel about themselves, others and the world. Through the process of asking a series of open questions, the counsellor is able to support the client's engagement with their thoughts and feelings in a questioning way, uncovering assumptions and rules underpinning problems. For example:

      Counsellor: So what was happening before you hurt yourself with the coke can?
      Client: Daisy and Kaiya were looking at something on Daisy's phone and when I asked if I could look, they turned away from me and started giggling.
      Counsellor: What did it mean to you that that happened?
      Client: That they think I'm stupid and don't want me to be their friend.
      Counsellor: And what does it mean to you that they don't want you to be their friend?
      Client: I'm not sure... (tears forming) I think it means no one will want to be my friend. That I'm stupid and unwanted. My dad didn't want me. I might as well hurt myself, it's what I deserve.
      Counsellor: It sounds like you hit your core belief – that you're unwanted and that made you want to hurt yourself. Is there another way of understanding what happened with your friends?
      Client: Yeah – I suppose they might have just been stupid or mean or something. Or they might have been having a laugh. I just can't see that at the time.
      Counsellor: Your core belief gets triggered sometimes – and that's understandable. Maybe we can work on this to see if we can help you respond differently when something like this happens?
      Client: Yeah – that would be great!

    - **Thought and mood diaries:** These can be a useful way of encouraging older clients to be curious about thoughts and feelings and the relationship of these to their behaviour. Worksheets can be used to provide a structure for recording thoughts and moods as well as the situation in which they occur in between counselling sessions. These can then be used as a basis for further collaborative work.

- **Behavioural experiments:** These can be a useful way of inviting the client to work on assumptions and fears between counselling sessions. The process involves inviting the client to identify an assumption they have and then to design an experiment to test this.
- **Worksheets and exercise:** In addition to thought and mood diaries, a variety of worksheets can be used to support clients in exploring various aspects of their functioning.

Summary

- Originally developed for work with adults, CBT has been successfully adapted for children and adolescents.
- CBT will need to be tailored for the age and developmental capabilities of the client.
- CBT can be used to develop understanding of the relationships between thoughts, feelings and behaviour with a view to empowering the client in managing their problems in more helpful ways.

Additional Resources

- Stallard, P. (2019) *Think Good, Feel Good: A Cognitive Behavioural Therapy Workbook for Children and Young People*. London: John Wiley & Sons.

Associated Entries

1.4 Cognitive Development
1.11 Developmental Implications for Therapy
2.7 Assessment & Integrative Formulation
3.22 Self-Esteem
3.23 Anxiety
3.24 Depression
3.31 Resilience
4.4 Child & Adolescent Mental Health Services (CAMHS)

3.7 Working with Emotions

The capacity to experience, articulate and process emotions effectively has long been viewed as a central feature of the therapeutic change process. In early analytic work with 'Anna O' (Freud, 1926/1959), Freud and Breuer identified 'strangulation of affect' as being at the root of her hysterical symptoms. Freud's view was that as affect was encountered and articulated in analysis – a process he termed 'abreaction' – catharsis would occur, and the patient would be freed of their symptoms. This process continues to be considered central to contemporary psychodynamic therapy (Lane & Garfield, 2005) and is a key feature of other therapeutic approaches, including humanistic, gestalt and emotion-focused therapy (EFT) (Greenberg, 2008). In this entry we explore the process of working therapeutically with emotion and its role in counselling with children and adolescents.

Key Understandings

In order to be able to work with emotions effectively it is important to understand what is meant by the term. Most of us are aware of our emotional responses to our environment, including people we are in contact with, places we encounter, our pleasures and our difficulties. We experience emotional responses on a spectrum from powerful rage to slight irritation, from 'welling up' to sobbing uncontrollably or freezing with fright. Campos et al. (1989: 395) gave a working definition of emotion as 'processes of establishing, maintaining, or disrupting the relations between the person and the internal or external environment'. Emotions serve an important social function, providing information about the social environment in which the individual finds themselves. They also have a functional purpose in supporting effective adaptation to that environment.

Greenberg (2008), in writing about the theoretical basis for EFT, agrees with Freud (1926/1959) and Campos et al. (1989) that emotion is information 'signalling the significance of a situation to a person's wellbeing' (Greenberg, 2008: 49). He goes further to state that, coupled with the view that regulation of affect (or difficulties with this) is often a key motivation for change, 'it has become clear that emotion needs to be focused on, accepted and worked with directly in therapy to promote emotional change (Greenberg, 2008: 49).

For children and adolescents, the capacity to experience and express emotional states is a key aspect of development. Our understanding of this goes back to the infant's early relational experiences of affect-regulation, containment (Bion, 1962) and mentalisation (Fonagy et al., 2004) (see entries 1.3, p. 9 and 1.6, p. 20), through phases of tantrum in early childhood and beyond into the 'sturm und drang' (Hall, 1904) of adolescent emotional lability. If children receive an attuned and flexible response to their emotional states, allowing them to develop the capacity to mentalise both their own and others' state of mind, they are likely to develop the capacity to live spontaneously in relation with their environment; they will be able to trust and be guided by their emotional responses to experience. However, where this has not been the case, emotional responses can be affected in ways which become pathological. Emotion can become blocked as children fear the consequences, both internal and external, of 'knowing' their feelings. Alternatively, children can be under-regulated, constantly 'in' their emotions with no coherent understanding of themselves, simply needing to enact feelings and discharge unwanted emotion onto others or their environment.

If we accept in principle that it is our capacity to think and feel which allows us to use our emotional responses to navigate life and its challenges, then it follows that when children and young people present for counselling, their emotions may well be the key to both the issue itself and the process of therapeutic change. For example, a young person presenting with anxiety and depression following a sexual assault may need to make use of their therapy to connect with a range of complex emotional responses to this experience. By articulating feelings such as anger, shame and sadness in a secure and accepting therapeutic relationship, they may be able to move towards acceptance and an integrated sense of themselves and their experience. Alternatively, a child of 7 years whose parents have separated may need a space in the sand or with art material to explore and express their feelings about this through symbol and metaphor, in order to reach a similar, developmentally appropriate place of understanding and integration.

With this, it's clear that a key task for the therapist working with children and young people is to develop the skills required to help the client to access and articulate their feelings in a way which supports their capacity to work through difficulties and gain a deeper understanding of themselves and their feelings.

Key Skills

1. Working with blocks to accessing and articulating emotions

Under-/over-regulation of emotion. One of the blocks to accessing and working therapeutically with the emotions is under- and over-regulation of affect.

Interventions should be formulated to achieve an optimal level of emotional arousal by helping to contain emotions that are overwhelming and gently encouraging contact with emotions which are being avoided. We will see examples of such interventions later in this entry.

Over-regulation: Clients who are over-regulated may experience difficulty in contacting and expressing emotional states. They may consciously or unconsciously experience feeling states as frightening or overwhelming, and their psyche may be engaged in defending against them for fear that they can't be coped with if experienced. Clients who are over-regulated may have had early experiences of their feelings not being sensitively received by their carer. The carer may have responded to their feelings by becoming over-aroused themselves, in a way which was frightening or disturbing to the child. This results in a defensive structure designed to protect the child from the frightening consequences of expressing emotion, but also has the effect of leaving them estranged from their feelings and unable to respond appropriately to their environment as they develop.

For the over-regulated client, establishing a strong therapeutic alliance (see entry 2.3, p. 58) will be the first step before emotions can be safely explored. Any difficulty articulating emotions will need to be empathically accepted to avoid the danger of the client experiencing shame at their difficulty in 'getting emotions right'.

Techniques such as 'pacing', where emotions are explored at a gradual and slow pace, can be useful when working with over-regulated clients who wish to access and articulate their feelings.

Under-regulation: Clients who are under-regulated are unable to effectively manage their emotional responses except by 'discharging' or 'acting-out' the emotion through action and behaviour. Children may 'be' angry or distressed, rather than be able to articulate and express feelings in more appropriate ways. In school, a teacher might say to a raging child: 'Use your words'. The difficulty for children who have not had their feelings adequately contained or mentalised is that they don't have the capacity to think about their feelings and therefore have not developed the capacity to put them into words.

Therapists working with clients who are under-regulated may need to use calming or grounding techniques at the start of the session in order to be able to work therapeutically. This could mean asking the client to focus on their breathing or the feel of their feet on the floor for a few minutes at the start of the session. Play equipment such as 'stress-balls' or 'Play-Doh' can be useful for helping the client to discharge emotional energy kinetically without damaging themselves or their environment.

2. Accessing and expressing emotions

Methods include helping the client by:

1. Asking them to focus their attention inwards, for example, '*I wonder if you could turn your focus inside and tell me what's happening right now?*'

2. Finding playful or symbolic ways of describing emotions, for example, *'What might that feeling look like if it were a shape or a cartoon character? Can you give it a colour?'* or *'I wonder what that angry feeling smells like?'*
3. Using empathic attunement to identify feelings that are implicit and not yet fully in awareness, for example, *'Big sigh as you talk about dad'* or *'You're biting your nails as you speak about mum – did you notice that?'*
4. Using empathic conjectures. Here empathic understanding helps us to imagine how the young person might be feeling, even though they are struggling to express it. These conjectures are offered tentatively and without defensiveness, giving the young person the freedom to reject or disagree. Often, even if the conjecture is not quite right, the young person can be helped to find a more accurate expression, such as *'You've been talking about some very difficult experiences. I wonder if there might almost be a bit of anger or something around that? Does that fit?'* or *'So you feel as though your emotions are all over the place; it's almost like, what? Somehow ... feeling out of control?'*
5. Focusing the young person's attention on bodily sensations, for example, *'You're saying you feel sad. I wonder if you can describe or show me where you feel that in your body?'*

3. Articulating emotions

Helping the client to articulate feelings might mean:

1. Helping them to find appropriate language to describe feelings, for example, *'What words can we find to describe that feeling? Is it frustration, irritation or maybe rage? There are lots of words to describe anger, let's see if we can find some that work for you.'*
2. Helping them to verbalise key concerns, meanings and memories triggered by an emotional response, for example, *'You've told me you feel sad this morning, and your body language reflects that too. I wonder if there's anything that's come up for you that might be making you feel that way?'*
3. Helping them to identify, name and expand on a range of meanings associated with feelings and emotions, for example, *'Could you say more about that feeling? What does it bring up for you? Is there something it tells us you need or want at the moment?'*
4. Suggesting imagery and metaphor to help the young person to become more aware of, and able to articulate the meaning of their experiences, for example, *'When you talk about what happened yesterday it sounds almost like you were an exploding volcano of feelings.'*

4. Working with confusing or distressing emotions and situations

Helping the client to make sense of difficult situations might mean helping them to:

1. Identify how they were feeling before they encountered the situation, for example, *'You say you don't know why you started panicking in class on Tuesday. Maybe we can take a really close look at what happened. What were you feeling that morning before you went into the classroom?'*
2. Re-imagine the situation, for example, *'Now let's see if you can give me a blow-by-blow account of what happened in the classroom, with as much detail as possible.'*
3. Identify the moment when the reaction was triggered, for example, *'So, it sounds as though you really got anxious when you thought you had got the answer wrong and everyone was laughing at you.'*
4. Explore their reaction to the situation, for example, *'What do you think about how you reacted? How did you feel afterwards?'*
5. Make links between their reactions and the way they construed the situation, for example, *'So when you thought they were laughing at you it made you feel frightened and you started to panic.'*
6. Develop new ways of understanding the situation and their responses to it, for example, *'So what do you make of what happened now? How might you have liked to have responded? What would that look like?'*

Summary

- Emotions are fundamental to our relationship with the world. The articulation and expression of emotion has long been viewed as central to the therapeutic process.
- Clients may present as under- or over-regulated in their emotional life and this can have an impact on behaviour and general functioning.
- Working with emotions therapeutically can support the client in understanding their responses to experience. This can help in developing a capacity for thinking about feelings, enabling an ability to make objective choices regarding actions and decisions.

Additional Resources

- Elliot, R., Watson, J.C., Goldman, R.N. & Greenberg, L. (2003) *Learning Emotion-Focused Therapy: The Process-Experiential Approach to Change.* Washington, DC: American Psychological Association.
- Greenberg, L.S. (2011) *Emotion-Focused Therapy.* London: EDS Publications.

Associated Entries

1.3 Theory of Mind
1.6 Object Relations Theory
1.8 Neurobiological Development
2.2 Core Relationship Components
3.10 Working with Risk

3.8 Mindfulness & Relaxation Techniques

Mindfulness and relaxation techniques can successfully be used to support the therapeutic process with children and adolescents. These techniques have been successfully integrated into CBT approaches (Biegel et al., 2014; Semple & Lee, 2014), but they can also be used as part of an integrative approach to therapy.

Key Understandings

The roots of mindfulness practice are found in Buddhist teachings, and the practice of mindfulness is defined as 'a form of nonjudgemental and nonreactive attention to experiences occurring in the moment, including bodily sensations, cognitions, emotions, and urges, as well as environmental stimuli such as sights, sounds and scents' (Baer, 2014: 3). There are clear parallels between this definition and many aspects of the integrative approach. Mindfulness represents a 'going inwards' with an attitude of open curiosity and non-judgement, which is also key to the therapeutic relationship.

Mindfulness and relaxation techniques can be used in many therapeutic situations. For example:

- When the client is experiencing dysregulation, they may find focusing attention on anchor points such as their feet on the floor, their breath, or any focal point in the room helps to reduce anxiety and panicky feelings.
- Techniques can help the client connect with their own experience, for instance by using exercises that focus on emotions, automatic thoughts, general bodily sensations, etc.
- Techniques can be used in session and can be taught so that clients can use them in between sessions and after sessions have ended.

Key Skills

1. Practitioners wishing to integrate these techniques into practice will benefit greatly from developing their own mindfulness practice (Semple & Lee, 2014). It

is important to access further training before using mindfulness techniques with clients in order to ensure they are used effectively and that any risk is managed appropriately. While these techniques have proven to be very useful for therapeutic purposes, counsellors need further knowledge of their appropriate use, which is beyond the scope of this entry.

2. Techniques include:

   - **Anchoring:** The client is encouraged to focus on one aspect of their experience, such as their breath or their feet on the floor. The aim is to bring them into contact with their body and the stability of their position. This can help clients who experience anxiety or panic. Young people can be guided in using these techniques outside their sessions.
   - **Mindfulness of breathing (MoB):** Similar to 'anchoring', this practice can be used in-session as well as outside. MoB involves finding a comfortable seated position and then focusing on the breath, without attempting to change it. The client is guided by the counsellor to focus on the in and out breath, returning to this focus whenever their mind wanders. Any thoughts arising can be noticed and then 'let go', as attention is returned to the breath. In situations where focusing on the breath is anxiety provoking for the client, for example when they feel panicky, another point can be selected, such as sounds in the room or outside, etc.
   - **Mindful awareness:** As described above, the client can be encouraged to apply 'mindful awareness' to a range of activities both during and outside the session. This might include mindful awareness of eating, walking or performing routine activities, such as cleaning teeth, showering, etc. Once again, the client is encouraged to notice any thoughts, emotions or bodily sensations that arise while they are doing the activity and then to return their attention to what they were focused on previously.
   - **Body scan:** This can be used both in and out of the session and is an excellent relaxation technique for children and adolescents. The client is guided through a scan of their body as they focus on different parts and try to notice tension and allow themselves to relax.

It is important that all the techniques mentioned in this section are used with sensitivity to the particular client and their issues. For example, clients who have been sexually abused may find the body scan technique upsetting, and other clients may find closing their eyes for mindfulness practice uncomfortable or frightening. The use of these techniques should be client-led and never forced on someone unwillingly. Mindfulness and relaxation techniques rely on a secure foundation of trust between counsellor and client, and so should only be used where a solid therapeutic alliance has been established.

Summary

- Mindfulness techniques are rooted in principles of Buddhist philosophy.
- Their therapeutic use is supported by evidence of their efficacy.
- Techniques can be introduced in sessions in order to assist the client in developing the capacity for regulation and calm where they experience symptoms such as anxiety and panic.
- Techniques can be used in session and also independently by the client as needed.

Additional Resources

- Headspace – www.headspace.com: free mindfulness app for adults, children and young people.

Associated Entries

3.6 Cognitive-Behavioural Therapy (CBT)
3.7 Working with Emotions
3.23 Anxiety
3.31 Resilience

3.9 Groups

Therapeutically-focused group-work is a common intervention with children and adolescents. Being part of a therapeutic group can help with feelings of being the only one experiencing a particular issue. Group-work is often popular in schools and CAMHS settings as it allows several children and young people (CYP) to be seen together, which can be helpful when demand for services outstrips provision.

Key Understandings

Group-work with CYP provides more than a way of bringing down waiting-lists. It offers an adaptive approach for addressing shared issues, such as bereavement, disability and illness, family breakdown, bullying, low self-esteem, anxiety, etc. An integrative approach to group-work allows the use of different interventions, such as CBT (see entry 3.6, p. 158), as well as a range of play-based and creative-arts methods (see entries 3.3, p. 147 and 3.4, p. 151). Group-work offers an opportunity for participants to share experiences with others who have gone through something similar as well as to offer and receive help from the group. These benefits, arguably particularly relevant for young people who often feel isolated in their situation, are identified by Yalom and Leszcz (2005) as 'universality' and 'altruism'. Group-work requires careful planning in order to offer an effective therapeutic experience for participants, and practitioners need to bear in mind the age and developmental stage of participants when deciding on their approach.

Key Skills

1. Decide on a clear focus for the group. This might be an area such as self-esteem, bullying, bereavement, etc. This focus or theme forms a basis for the choice of intervention to be used. For example, CBT may be a useful technique for a group with a focus on self-esteem or managing social anxiety, and a group of teenagers who have experienced parental bereavement may benefit from a creative intervention such as using art materials to express and share their experience. Any approach should be tailored to the developmental and intellectual capacity of potential members.
2. Decide on the size and structure of the group. Evidence suggests that groups work best with between five and twelve members, with eight participants being considered the optimal number (Pearce et al., 2018a). Group size also depends on factors

such as demand for space along with practicalities such as the availability of suitable premises and rooms.

3. Explore barriers to participation among potential members. Some young people may feel apprehensive about taking part. The initial interview/assessment for potential group members offers an opportunity to explore such concerns and see how they might best be overcome or managed. When groups take place in school or community settings, young people may have concerns about who else is taking part and whether they will get on or what might happen if they speak about something sensitive in front of them. These are important considerations for the young person and will need to be taken seriously for them to feel safe enough to benefit from the group.
4. When establishing the group, make sure you develop a clear and coherent set of 'ground rules'. These should establish the frame for the group, including what is and is not acceptable behaviour for its members. With older children, the rules can be established collectively, allowing members to feel involved in the process and in taking 'ownership' of their group and how it functions.

Exercise

Design a set of ground rules for a self-esteem group of year 7 pupils in a secondary school.

- How might you go about this process?
- What would be the most important ground rule?
- How would this process be different with a group of year 10s or year 11s?
- Would it be different if this was a group for exam stress or bereavement?

5. Once ground rules are established, ensure the group stays focused and the dynamics are managed effectively so all are included and able to make use of the process. This can be achieved by maintaining the core conditions and setting clear boundaries around respectful interaction and clear communication (Kirkbride, 2018a).
6. Ending the group needs the same consideration as ending in any therapeutic relationship (see entry 2.19, p. 124). The ending is an opportunity for reflection, consolidation of learning, grieving the end of the group and an exploration of feelings about this, such as disappointment or celebration of what has been shared and understood. In settings where group members may see each other after the group has concluded (i.e. in school), it is important to spend some time considering how to manage relationships post-group and how skills can continue to develop once the group has ended.

Summary

- Group work provides the opportunity for young people to meet with others who have shared similar experiences or who struggle with similar issues.
- In order for participants to benefit fully, groups should be well planned and facilitated. Ground rules should be developmentally appropriate and collaboratively devised.
- Ending the group requires careful consideration so participants get maximum benefit from the intervention.

Additional Resources

- Yalom, I.D. & Leszcz, M. (2005) *The Theory and Practice of Group Therapy* (5th edition). New York: Basic Books.

Associated Entries

2.2 Core Relationship Components
2.3 The Therapeutic Frame
2.19 Endings
3.4 Creative-Arts Interventions
3.18 Bullying
3.21 Bereavement & Loss
3.22 Self-Esteem
4.2 Educational Settings
4.4 Child & Adolescent Mental Health Services (CAMHS)

3.10 Working with Risk

This is the first in a series of entries exploring risk presentations. This entry looks generally at the topic of risk, and in subsequent entries specific clinical considerations associated with risk are considered. It can be read in conjunction with the earlier entry on risk assessment (see entry 2.8, p. 79).

Key Understandings

Due to their vulnerability and relative lack of agency, children and adolescents can find themselves at risk of harm from others. Forms of abuse range from physical and sexual to emotional abuse and neglect. Abuse can be perpetuated by people of all genders. Abuse occurs both in real life and online. In addition to being at risk of harm *from others*, children and adolescents may also be at risk of harm from *themselves*. Again, forms of self-harm vary, but include self-injuring behaviours, risky sexual behaviour, substance misuse, disordered eating, and so on (see entry 2.8, p. 79).

Risk-taking is a functional aspect of development, so when we are working with a young person engaged in risky behaviour it's important to understand their behaviour as being potentially functional, rather than immediately assuming behaviour is maladaptive and in need of curtailment. Risk behaviour is often a communication of a deeper sense of dysregulation or incongruence in the self and it is vital that counsellors develop the capacity to work in a way that contains the risk and protects the client while also allowing the communication to be explored therapeutically and understood.

The 'asynchronous' development of the brain during adolescence (see entries 1.8, p. 29 and 1.9, p. 32) has the effect of making the adolescent prone to making decisions based on emotion rather than an objective assessment of the consequences.

Working with risk is a challenging area. Making decisions about safeguarding can be daunting, especially when we can't be certain of the outcome. Taking responsibility for breaking or maintaining confidentiality after a risk disclosure is challenging and painful for all practitioners, no matter how experienced they are. Hearing stories of trauma and abuse can also bring up our own past experiences as well as potentially lead to secondary post-traumatic stress disorder or compassion fatigue (Figley, 2002). Support, including good clinical supervision, is crucial for practitioners working with risk presentations in order to ameliorate some of the potential for negative impact. This is an area where practitioners are ethically required to take responsibility for ensuring they have adequate support for the work they are undertaking (see entry 2.20, p. 124).

Key Skills

1. Develop a solid therapeutic relationship where the client can be received with empathy and unconditional positive regard and non-judgement (see entry 2.2, p. 51). These are key elements of an effective approach to working with risk. If the client feels they will be listened to and accepted, regardless of what they disclose, they are more likely to bring the parts of their experience they are struggling with the most.
2. Set clear boundaries regarding confidentiality. In order to establish and build trust, the client needs to know in advance what you will do if they disclose something that raises concerns about their safety. Forming a clear and realistic contract outlining what will happen if a concern is raised allows both parties to work safely in challenging areas (see entry 2.5, p. 68). The form the contract takes will depend on the context in which the work takes place. For example, there may be different requirements for practitioners working in school regarding disclosure of safeguarding concerns than those working in private practice or CAMHS (see entries 4.3, p. 267 and 4.4, p. 270).
3. Have a clear risk assessment process (see entry 2.8, p. 79). Depending on the age or developmental stage of the client and the presenting issues, this may be done in collaboration with the client themselves or with school staff or parents/carers.
4. Develop a risk management/crisis plan for when risk is identified. This might include elements such as:

   i. Exploring ways to ensure there is adequate support between sessions, over breaks or when therapy comes to an end.
   ii. Developing healthy coping strategies, such as talking to a trusted person outside therapy, activities such as engaging in exercise, walking, drawing, listening to music, etc. This could also include the use of mindfulness and relaxation techniques (see entry 3.8, p. 168).
   iii. Identifying resources for support, for example, helping the client to think about appropriate people to approach if they feel unsafe. With older clients this may become part of the therapeutic process by encouraging the young person to take some degree of responsibility for their wellbeing. In the example below, a counsellor explores this with a 15-year-old client who has been in counselling for about six months. Originally, she was referred because of incidents where she had self-harmed in the classroom in front of other pupils. Having worked through the emotional impact of her parent's separation in her counselling sessions, there have been no further incidents of cutting in the previous month.

Counsellor: You're worried that when mum's boyfriend moves in this weekend you might want to cut yourself again. I wonder if we might explore that together.

Client: I don't know what I'm going to feel and that scares me. We've talked a lot in here about how I used cutting to help me cope with feelings I didn't know how to express. I'm worried that when Ian moves in that's going to happen again. I don't want to do it but I'm scared the urge will take over and I'll end up in the bathroom with my blades.

Counsellor: Could we take some time now to think together about the feelings that might come up and about what you could do to express them. This might help them feel manageable until we meet next week and can talk about it then.

Client: Thinking about it, it's complicated. I wonder if there's a bit of me that's been looking for a reason to cut again. Like an excuse, and this is it. I've got lots of strategies for helping me not to cut that we've talked about in here. I've got my journal and my mood diary. I could talk to mum about how I'm feeling. She's better at listening now and that helps, even though I can tell she's really excited about Ian moving in. I understand why it's happening and I think it will be better. I just hate that it means dad definitely isn't coming back (starts crying).

Counsellor: Something about this feels final and you're grieving for your parents' marriage. These are big feelings, no wonder you're thinking about old strategies. But you're also telling me that you have other resources you can choose from. What do you imagine would be most useful for you to consider?

Client: I'm going to make a playlist of 'up songs' to listen to if I feel crappy. I'll put it on in the morning on Saturday. I've got my meditation app too. I'll do some of that and then maybe go online and chat to whoever's around. I've told Aimee I'm feeling worried about it and she said to call her anytime. I know I can talk to her. She gets it cos she went through it last year with her parents. I think that's why I didn't talk to her before; I thought she had enough on her plate, but she's told me she feels good when I talk to her cos she feels like she can help. Yeah, maybe I'll be OK... until Wednesday when I'm back here anyway!

5. Develop an awareness of protective factors which help to manage the impact of risk. Understanding what these might be for a particular client can help to identify areas to work on with risk presentations. Protective factors include:

   i. **Coming for counselling and the quality of the therapeutic relationship:** This in itself can have a huge impact. Being heard and understood can be effective for clients who are exhibiting signs of distress through risk behaviours.
   ii. **The ability to explore and articulate their inner world, including difficult thoughts and feelings:** The core relationship components are essential for developing relationships where the client is able to speak about areas which are distressing for them. Experiencing these 'unspeakable' thoughts and feelings as accepted by their therapist can help the client to begin to develop a different sense of themselves and their internal world. This relates to Bion's (1962) 'containment' (see entry 1.6, p. 20), where the client, through the

therapeutic relationship and the core components, finds even the most difficult feelings and thoughts can be received and understood by their therapist, allowing them to see themselves as someone who can be accepted as a whole by another.

iii. **Support of family, friends and/or other agencies:** This includes appropriate engagement of parents or other agencies in the therapeutic work (see entries 2.12, p. 97 and 2.22, p. 131).
iv. **Developing interests and activities:** Particularly those which might help to build self-esteem or positive connections with peers and adults.
v. **The capacity to develop and use appropriate self-care and coping strategies:** (see 4b).

6. Develop a self-care and support structure for working with risk. It is important to be aware of the risks of working with risk and to ensure adequate support to manage this, including elements such as:

   i. Clinical supervision for support with making decisions, reviewing outcomes, etc. (see entry 2.24, p. 137).
   ii. A sense of achievement. Figley (2002: 1438) suggests that this can help lower or prevent compassion fatigue, but it requires a 'conscious, rational effort to recognise where the psychotherapist's responsibilities end and the client's responsibilities begin'. Practitioners working with children and adolescents often perceive themselves as being omnipotently responsible for the client's wellbeing, rather than just a small part of that child's life. Similarly, Figley (2002: 1438) writes that the capacity of the therapist to 'disengage' or to 'distance himself or herself from the ongoing misery of the client between sessions' is also significant in terms of compassion fatigue. Again, this can be complex for therapists working with young clients who don't have a great deal of agency or autonomy. Struggles in these areas may be an indication that personal therapy is needed to help resolve conflicts around this issue that may otherwise impact practitioner wellbeing.
   iii. Peer support and supervision. Working with risk is challenging, but building networks with other therapists means we are not alone in managing this. Colleagues also provide insight and resources from their own experience of working with challenging presentations.
   iv. Personal therapy is crucial for processing difficult feelings arising from working with risk, whether or not these are triggered by our past experiences.
   v. Reading, training and continuous professional development (CPD) activities help develop the skills and confidence to work with complex and challenging presentations.
   vi. Self-care activities not connected with therapeutic practice can be vital for protecting us from the impact of working with trauma, abuse and risk.

These skills and understandings form the basis for working with a range of risk presentations and clinical considerations, as will be seen in the following entries.

Summary

- Children and adolescents can be at risk of harm, from self or other.
- Risk is an important part of development. However, risk-taking can be maladaptive and lead to risk of harm.
- Risk behaviours may be a communication of deeper psychological issues. Counselling provides a space for the safe exploration of these issues.
- Counsellors working with risk need to find a balance between exploring issues and maintaining the client's safety from significant harm.
- Risk is a challenging area of practice and counsellors should ensure they are adequately supported so they can work effectively with clients.

Additional Resources

- Kirkbride, R. (2018) 'Walking a tightrope': The dilemmas of working with risky adolescents'. Available on the BACP CPD Hub: www.bacp.co.uk/cpd/cpd-hub/children-young-people-and-families/ (last accessed 22 May 2020).

Associated Entries

2.2 Core Relationship Components
2.5 Contracting
2.8 Risk Assessment & Safeguarding
2.9 Confidentiality & Consent
2.20 Ethical Issues
2.23 Self-Care for Counsellors
2.24 Clinical Supervision
3.11 Self-Harm
3.12 Food & Body Issues
3.15 Risky Sexual Behaviour
3.19 Online Risk
4.7 Refugee Communities
4.8 Looked-After Children (LAC)

3.11 Self-Harm

Acts of deliberate self-harm (DSH) among young people are often a communication of emotional and psychological distress. While they can be anxiety-provoking for adults around the young person, it is the role of the therapist to attempt to facilitate understanding of the communication with the aim of resolving the underlying issues, while also managing risk of harm (see entry 3.10, p. 174). In this entry we explore a contemporary understanding of DSH and consider a range of skills that are useful when working with this presentation.

Key Understandings

Self-harm is taken to mean any act of deliberate harm to the self, including self-injury and self-poisoning. DSH is seen as a major public health issue for adolescents, 'with rates of self-harm being high in the teenage years and suicide being the second most common cause of death in young people worldwide' (Hawton et al., 2012: 2373). Self-harm does not necessarily involve suicidal intent, and the motives for DSH are unique to each person. The majority of DSH is carried out by females, whereas males are most at risk for completed suicide (Hawton et al., 2012). DSH is strongly associated with the onset of puberty and adolescent neuro-development (see entry 1.8, p. 29), and is potentially linked to 'emerging evidence of a period of particular neuro-developmental vulnerability around this time, with increased risk of emotional disorders and risk-taking behaviours. This vulnerability might be associated with particular developments in the cortical brain regions after puberty' (Hawton et al., 2012: 2374).

DSH often provokes strong feelings in those who discover or witness it. For Brady (2016), this may be part of the unconscious need to communicate something the young person is grappling with internally: 'The initially cutting adolescent often shows someone his or her cuts and that person can begin to perform the other "part" of a symbol by seeing that there is an urgent emotional problem at hand' (Brady, 2016: 44). However, self-harm in adolescents is often met with disgust or shock by those who discover the behaviour, or is labelled pejoratively by peers and adults alike as 'attention seeking'. This can affect a young person's willingness to discuss or explore their behaviour in therapy (Saunders et al., 2012). Working with DSH can be challenging for therapists as they try to set their own feelings about DSH aside in order to enter the distressing world of their client with the aim to understand the behaviour, rather than to condemn it as senseless or selfish.

Key Skills

1. When a referral indicates DSH or it emerges in the course of therapeutic work, a risk assessment must be made before beginning therapeutic work (see entry 2.8, p. 79). This allows for a coherent frame and contract around confidentiality to be established (see entry 2.9, p. 84), enabling the relationship to be built on trust between client and counsellor (see entry 3.10, p. 174). Attending to this frame throughout the work and ensuring that it is adequately containing allows therapeutic work on underlying issues to take place.
2. The core relationship components are essential for working with DSH (see entry 2.2, p. 51). The client needs to experience themselves as fully accepted in the relationship in order to begin to be able to do the deep work required to understand DSH and its underlying cause. This may require some work in therapy or supervision for practitioners to ensure they are able to work through any feelings or assumptions which may interfere with the provision of the conditions and therefore with the therapeutic process itself.
3. Therapeutic work with DSH can be supported by using symbol and metaphor in order to help the client to uncover meanings underlying the act (see entry 3.2, p. 144). Offering an attitude of open curiosity regarding the act also conveys to the client an acceptance of the validity of their communication. In the example below, the counsellor is attempting to provide a space for exploring the meaning of one 14-year-old female client's DSH:

   Client: It's not so much about cutting, it's how I feel when I see what I've done. The blood and the break in my skin. It feels like a victory, like I've achieved something.

   Counsellor: You feel you've achieved something. Could you say more about that?

   Client: I've broken something apart and there's this stuff coming out and it's mine, and that feels good... like it needed to happen.

   Counsellor: Like something needed to be broken open... I wonder if you have any thoughts about why that might feel so good for you?

   Client: I don't know...I guess I don't feel able to show what's inside me very often. I used to show mum but that can't happen anymore (the client's mum died when she was 8).

   Counsellor: So maybe this is a way of breaking open and letting something out?

   Here the therapist is able to enter the client's world and try to see their behaviour as having meaning and sense, if only so they can work together to understand it. This is clearly a relationship built on trust. The client feels able to speak openly about her experience of cutting in a way she would not be able to do if she was fearful of being judged or punished for the behaviour.
4. Working with DSH can provoke countertransference feelings in practitioners (see entry 2.16, p. 111), which may be useful when attempting to receive and

understand unconscious communication Brady (2016: 43) writes about a client who picked a scab during a session, allowing her to connect in the transference with his internal experience:

> At this point I could do a piece of psychological work more in tune with his inner world. My horror was homologous to my patient's experience of horror when he felt overexposed to trauma and neglect by his parents and by the fumbling efforts of his replacement caregivers. His action required me to inhabit the negative transference more. It may be that his ripping of the scab was as much a communication to himself as to me as a way of being in touch with himself. However, to begin to be truly emotionally meaningful, such an action requires being seen and known in another's mind.

Brady (2016) emphasises containment (Bion, 1962) (see entry 1.6, p. 20) in work with DSH. If the client's communication can be received and understood in the mind of the therapist, this allows a process of containment which may have been lacking in early relational experiences.

5. Working with emotions is an integral aspect of the approach to working with DSH (see entry 3.7, p. 162). Often young people who self-harm have significant difficulty even connecting with their emotional worlds and therefore struggle greatly to articulate and express them. As seen in the example above, DSH can be a symbolic expression of feeling that cannot be known or expressed directly, and therefore working to facilitate this is an important skill in approaching this area.
6. As with many clinical presentations, acts of DSH may also be a communication of difficulty within a family. In line with family-systems theory, one member of a family may develop a symptom or behaviour which symbolises an unprocessed issue or is a response to a dysfunction within the family. As Brady (2016: 45) suggests, 'The adolescent's impulse to a self-destructive action is often related to a familial inability to grapple with major emotional situations'.
7. Working with DSH is often emotionally challenging for therapists, as they walk the tightrope between risk management and deep therapeutic work. Use of clinical supervision and self-care techniques (see entry 3.10, p. 174) is essential for navigating this difficult issue in a way which is likely to be effective for young clients. DSH provides an opportunity for unresolved relational experiences to be addressed in therapy and it is vital that therapists are able to use all available resources to meet this challenge in practice.

Summary

- Self-harm in children and adolescents is often a bodily expression of underlying emotional and psychological distress.
- Counsellors working with self-harm need to hold a balance between therapeutic exploration of the underlying issues and assessing for risk of significant harm.

- Techniques such as working to express and articulate emotions in a supportive therapeutic relationship can assist in allowing the client to work through underlying issues and let go of the need for DSH.

Additional Resources

- MindEd – www.minded.org.uk: 437-003 *Identifying Self-harm and What to Do.*
- Brady, M.T. (2016) *The Body in Adolescence: Psychic Isolation and Physical Symptoms*. London: Routledge.
- Hawton, K., Rodham, K. & Evans, E. (2006) *By Their Own Young Hand: Deliberate Self-harm and Suicidal Ideas in Adolescents*. London: Jessica Kingsley.

Associated Entries

1.6 Object Relations Theory
2.8 Risk Assessment & Safeguarding
3.7 Working with Emotions
3.10 Working with Risk
3.13 Alcohol & Substance Misuse
3.15 Risky Sexual Behaviour
3.23 Anxiety
3.24 Depression

3.12 Food & Body Issues

Issues around eating and body image are often the reason why someone is referred for counselling. They are most prevalent among adolescents, although disordered eating in younger children does occur (Bryant-Waugh & Lask, 2013). Eating disorders have been defined as presentations 'in which there is an excessive preoccupation with weight or shape, and/or food intake, and accompanied by grossly inadequate, irregular or chaotic food intake' (Bryant-Waugh & Lask, 1995: 13). An integrative approach to these presentations seeks to understand the underlying developmental and psychological causes in order to work effectively to relieve young people of distressing and potentially life-threatening behaviour. This entry explores food and body issues, looking particularly at the skills required to work in this complex and challenging area of practice.

Key Understandings

Feeding is one of our earliest relational experiences, combining the satisfaction of a physical need for nutrition with an intense and complex relational experience. Given the early nature of this experience and its connection with development, it is no wonder that in later life children, adolescents and adults alike experience emotional difficulties in their relationship with food, their bodies and the process of eating. There are several theories regarding the development of eating and body image issues, but it may be most helpful to understand their development as a process of the interaction of a number of factors, including inherited genes, attachment and early relational experiences, as well as cultural and environmental factors (Kirkbride, 2018b).

Issues around body image are also prevalent in children and adolescents and may or may not coincide with disordered eating behaviours. The body enters a period of sustained and significant development during puberty and it can become the recipient of projections of the 'bad', as in body dysmorphia, as well as of fantasies of control and mastery, as in anorexia. The biological trajectory of puberty towards physical and sexual maturation signifies the 'loss' of the childhood body, and this must be mourned if the young person is to successfully 'take ownership' of their adult body, sexuality and identity. While this is a normal biological process, for some this transition provokes conscious and/or unconscious tension along with psychological and emotional distress, potentially emerging in eating and body issues requiring therapeutic intervention. Viewed through a psychodynamic lens, the development of an eating or body disorder during puberty may be an expression of this crisis of separation, sexuality and impending adulthood, as symbolised through the changing body.

In order to formulate interventions for eating issues, we need an understanding of the presentation as well as what the underlying causes might be. While it is beyond the scope of this entry to explore this in full, additional resources are listed at the end of this section.

Counsellors working with vulnerable children and adolescents require the skills to decide when the work can be managed in the therapy room and when there is a safeguarding issue which may require the involvement of other services and/or family members (see entry 2.8, p. 79). As with many risk presentations, this means balancing the need for therapeutic exploration alongside maintaining safety from risk of harm. Due to the complexity of eating and body image disorders, therapeutic work may involve parents/carers and/or other professionals in order to ensure the client's physical wellbeing is supported outside the therapeutic relationship (see entries 2.12, p. 97 and 2.22, p. 131).

A further complexity in work with eating issues is that the nature of the disorder is such that often the client has no conscious desire to be relieved of their symptoms and may in fact fear recovery. One symptom of an eating disorder is phobia of gaining weight or getting fat. The client may fear losing control of restricting food intake, over-exercising and other behaviours that help manage their anxiety, even when this fear places them at risk of significant harm. This can make forming an effective therapeutic alliance challenging from the outset, as there may be no conscious agreement on the 'task' or 'goal' of therapy (Bordin, 1979) (see entry 2.3, p. 58).

Key Skills

1. Risk assessment (see entry 2.8, p. 79) should be undertaken at the beginning of counselling and returned to throughout in order to ensure risk of harm is managed effectively. When significant risk of harm is indicated, for example if weight/size has visibly changed, or if cognitive functioning appears impaired, then breaching confidentiality and involving other professionals must be considered. In moderate to severe cases, practitioners should be in regular contact with other professionals involved in treatment. This will need to be part of the explicit contract between the client and/or parents at the outset of the therapy or introduced as required at a later stage (Kirkbride, 2018b).
2. Alongside risk assessment, the core relationship components (see entry 2.2, p. 51) are central to providing a space to explore and express difficult feelings. The behaviour of those suffering with eating issues often seems alarming and bizarre to observers, and it can be challenging to offer unconditional positive regard (UPR)

or empathy in these circumstances. However, accepting the behaviour as serving a purpose for the client relating to underlying issues, such as unmet relational needs or internal distress and dysregulation, allows for the person to be accepted even when the behaviour is not. Where the client is not ready to work collaboratively on their behaviour, 'Motivational Interviewing' – a technique originally devised by Miller and Rollnick (2012) as a method of working with addiction – can be useful for finding the optimal moment to begin working with the disorder (Kirkbride, 2018b).

3. Eating and body issues can be understood as a defence against frightening or overwhelming internal states (Bruch, 1973). The impulse to control eating and/or weight can provide a way of managing this for the child or young person. As Troupp (2013: 285) observes:

> One could say that in eating disorders, the 'deal' offered by the internal tyrant runs like this: 'If you give me your allegiance and obedience, and don't eat and become thinner and thinner, I will in turn protect you from all difficult emotions and painful thoughts. You will not have to think or feel, as long as you do what I tell you'.

'Externalising' the inner critical voice or 'tyrant' in therapy can be an effective way of encouraging the client to understand their disorder in a different way. This may include naming the inner critical voice or giving it a shape or character. Creative interventions can help to facilitate this process, allowing the client to work with symbol and metaphor in seeing the eating disorder as separate and then looking at how they relate to it (see 3.2, p. 144).

Troupp (2013: 283) suggests three aims of therapeutic work with young people with eating issues:

1. To help the young person understand herself better and develop 'emotional language'.
2. To support the young person's development in terms of individuation, and integration with peers and the social world.
3. To help the young person find ways to communicate her internal states to her parents, in ways that are acceptable to both.

Helping the client to contact and articulate their emotions is therefore central to the process of working with these issues (see entry 3.7, p. 162). As Carr (2006: 808) states:

> Children with eating disorders have difficulty learning how to interpret need-related internal physiological states and develop a coherent sense of self, because their mothers adopt a parenting style in which parental needs for control and compliance take primacy over the child's need for self-expression and autonomy.

As with self-harm (see entry 3.11, p. 179), working with metaphor and symbol can be highly effective in helping the client uncover the meaning of their behaviour, and many clients respond well to creative methods of exploring feelings about their bodies and about becoming an adult.

With regards to the second aim – supporting the young person's development in terms of individuation (Troupp, 2013: 283) – the focus of therapeutic work with eating and body issues is often that of identity formation for the client as they struggle to find a sense of their thoughts, feelings and desires, as well as in helping them recognise their own resources and capability, where they might previously have experienced themselves as overwhelmed relationally by another. Working therapeutically with this requires the skill to see both the wounded child who did not receive what they needed in their early relationships alongside the young person who is developing their own identity. Therapy should focus on the development of appropriate autonomy for the client, while being mindful of any potential ambivalence about what this might mean. As Crisp (1983: 857) warns, recovery may in itself be triggering for some clients, '[a]s puberty is rekindled adolescent turmoil must be recognised and the patient will need intensive support'.

4. As with other risk-related entries, practitioners working with clients experiencing eating and body issues will need to ensure they have the right support to help them engage fully in this challenging and demanding area of practice (see entry 3.10, p. 174).

Exercise

Consider your own relationship with food, eating and your body from childhood, through adolescence, and up to the current time. What do you notice about this relationship? Were there any significant points of change or transition? What might have caused this?

How do you think your own history with this might affect your work with clients experiencing difficulties in this area?

Summary

- Issues with food and body image often manifest during puberty and adolescence due to tension caused by impending adulthood.
- Therapeutic exploration of symptoms and their underlying cause should be balanced alongside the need to protect the client from the potential harm of their behaviour.
- Interventions need to be tailored for the individual client and their situation. This will depend on factors such as the severity of symptoms and the developmental capacity of the client.
- Depending on severity, work with eating disorders often involves working alongside other professionals and family members to support recovery.

Additional Resources

- American Psychiatric Association (2013) *Diagnostic and Statistical Manual of Mental Disorders* (5th edition). Washington, DC: APA.
- Bryant-Waugh, R. & Lask, B. (2013) 'Overview of eating disorders in childhood and adolescence', in R. Bryant-Waugh & B. Lask (eds), *Eating Disorders in Childhood and Adolescence* (4th edition, pp. 33–49). Hove: Routledge.
- Kirkbride, R. (2018b) 'Eating disorders', in S. Pattison & M. Robson (eds), *The Handbook of Counselling Children and Young People* (2nd edition). London: Sage.

Associated Entries

2.8 Risk Assessment & Safeguarding
2.12 Working with Parents/Carers
2.22 Working with Other Professionals
3.2 Symbol & Metaphor
3.7 Working with Emotions
3.10 Working with Risk

3.13 Alcohol & Substance Misuse

Experimentation with drugs and alcohol is an accepted part of adolescent cultural development in much of contemporary Western society and not necessarily pathological or a reason for referral in itself. However, compulsive or harmful use of substances can stem from more complex roots than a desire for rebellion, social pleasure or to 'fit in' with a peer group. Adolescents may be vulnerable to addiction and risk of harm due to sustained and uncontrolled use of substances and it is this, or difficulties resulting from this misuse, which may bring them to therapy.

Exercise

Consider your own experience of drugs and alcohol during adolescence by exploring the following questions:

- Did you use substances or alcohol yourself or were you aware of others' use?
- What was your family or community culture in terms of alcohol and substance use? How do you think this impacted your own attitudes and behaviours?
- What were your perceptions and judgements of your own use/non-use and that of others?

How might your answers to the above questions impact your capacity to work with these issues in young clients? Do you feel able to hold a non-judgemental space for a young person who has issues with alcohol or substance misuse?

Key Understandings

While a 'normal' part of growing up for many adolescents, there are aspects of recreational substance use which raise concerns. If confronted by these concerns, the adolescent may not agree with their teacher or parent that their behaviour is harmful. Substance use can represent an arena for displays of adolescent omnipotence where concern is 'held' by adults, leaving the young person to enjoy their activities with no fear of negative implications.

Reasons for using substances vary as much as the young people using them. It may be that a peer group has a culture centred around or involving drug and alcohol use, or substance use may be an escape from or an attempt to 'self-medicate' the effects of psychological or emotional distress. Integrative counselling can be used to identify and explore underlying issues as well as to provide skills for the young person in managing their behaviour, where appropriate.

Key Skills

1. Building trust and establishing a therapeutic alliance is the foundation for working with substance misuse. It is vital that the client feels they can explore their issues without judgement. A collaborative assessment during the initial stages provides an opportunity for the counsellor to be curious about the whole person of the client, rather than focusing on substance use at the exclusion of other aspects of their life or experience. Levingston and Melrose (2009: 116) emphasise the importance of making sure that the starting point for this is identifying the concerns of the young person in relation to their use, using this to explore 'underlying factors, including what, when, how and why they drink'.
   Contracting should be undertaken to establish appropriate limits to confidentiality so both the client and counsellor clearly understand what can be 'held' in the therapy and what might require a safeguarding response (see entry 3.10, p. 174).
   Mirza and Mirza (2008: 358) propose a model to identify which 'stage' a young person is at in their substance misuse, proceeding from 'non-use' at one end of the continuum, through 'experimental', 'social', 'at-risk' and 'harmful' stages, and ending ultimately with 'substance dependence'.
2. When the referral for therapy is due to substance misuse, or if such issues emerge during the course of counselling, a risk assessment should be conducted to establish whether this is placing the client at risk of significant harm (see entry 2.8, p. 79).
   Risk with drugs and alcohol takes several forms, and these may be combined, increasing vulnerability for some clients (Mirza & Mirza, 2008). For example, risk may arise from:

   i. the substance use in itself, for example, if use of cannabis negatively affects mental health or where there is risk of psychosis from the use of drugs such as amphetamines or crack-cocaine.
   ii. behaviours associated with substance misuse, such as risky sexual behaviours, driving under the influence or general risk from increased vulnerability due to substance-related cognitive impairments.
   iii. young people at risk from grooming for trafficking, including 'county lines', may be coerced into drug use to make them more vulnerable to the traffickers.
   iv. the use of substances during sensitive periods of neurological development, which can cause long-term problems for young people (Bava & Tapert, 2010).
   v. contact with the criminal justice system, whether due to behaviour while intoxicated or because of the illegal nature of possessing and using certain substances.

3. Once limits have been established and risk has been assessed, it will be possible to work therapeutically to help the client explore and understand their relationship with drugs and/or alcohol, as well as to move towards a place where they are able to make choices or use different means to articulate and express their internal processes. 'Motivational Interviewing' (Miller & Rollnick, 2012) can be used to establish where the young person is in terms of their readiness to address the issue.
4. In some cases, involvement with other services, such as CAMHS or local NHS services for young people with substance misuse issues, may be necessary. Such decisions will need to be made in collaboration with the client and family, where appropriate (see entry 2.22, p. 131).

Summary

- **Substance use is a normative part of adolescent social and cultural development for many young people growing up in permissive Western environments.**
- **Substance misuse can place young people at risk of harm from self or other.**
- **Underlying causes for substance misuse can be explored in a secure therapeutic relationship where the core relationship components are provided along with solid boundaries regarding limits of confidentiality.**

Additional Resources

- MindEd – www.minded.org.uk: 410-039 *Substance Misuse.*
- Levingston, B. & Melrose, J. (2009) 'Alcohol and young people', in K. Geldard (ed.), *Practical Interventions for Young People at Risk.* London: Sage.

Associated Entries

1.8 Neurobiological Development
1.10 Environmental & Systemic Factors
2.2 Core Relationship Components
2.8 Risk Assessment & Safeguarding
3.10 Working with Risk
3.15 Risky Sexual Behaviour
3.23 Anxiety
3.24 Depression

3.14 Trauma & Abuse

Therapeutic work with children and young people who have experienced abuse and/or trauma is possibly the most challenging area of practice, but also one where there is much to be gained. Trauma and abuse have a huge impact on children's development and the effects are often continued into adult life (Cashmore & Shackel, 2013). Therapy offers hope that overwhelming and painful experiences can be processed within a facilitating relationship, allowing children and adolescents the opportunity to connect with other aspects of their experience and regain a sense of trust and hope for their future (Cattanach, 2008).

In this entry we explore trauma and abuse and consider ways of working therapeutically with those clients who present for counselling having experienced some form of this. This is a complex area of understanding and practice and it is beyond the scope of this book to explore this area exhaustively. Readers are encouraged to read further and engage in CPD activities to gain further knowledge and skill in this area.

Key Understandings

Cattanach (2008: 13) writes: 'When adults abuse children they steal from them, destroy curiosity, joy in living and learning and in its place leave darkness and fear', powerfully articulating the impact on those who are abused during their vulnerable early years.

The vulnerability of childhood and the need for children to be protected during this time is enshrined worldwide in the UN Convention on the Rights of the Child (United Nations, 1989). In the UK, The Children Act (1989) was fundamental in establishing these rights in UK law and in emphasising the responsibility of parents to ensure that these are not violated and that children are protected from 'significant harm'. The Children Act 1989 defines significant harm as 'ill-treatment or the impairment of health or development', which includes, for example, impairment suffered from seeing or hearing the ill-treatment of another (Children Act, 1989, section 31:9). The UK government has produced a regularly updated set of guidelines for those who are concerned a child might be experiencing abuse or neglect (see additional resources section for more information) (see entry 2.8, p. 79).

The NSPCC (2020) defines child abuse as:

> when a child is intentionally harmed by an adult or another child – it can be over a period of time but can also be a one-off action. It can be physical, sexual or emotional and it can happen in person or online. It can also be a lack of love, care and attention – this is neglect.

Trauma is broadly defined as 'any experience which threatens your life or your body, or any harm which is inflicted on you intentionally' (American Psychiatric Association, 2013: n.p.). Understanding the impact of trauma and abuse on individual children in therapy is complex and requires a willingness on the part of the therapist to enter the world of the abused child and attempt to understand their pain and the impact the abuse has had on their development. This is a challenging task and one that requires a particular set of therapeutic skills. Inevitably, where a child or young person has experienced abuse at the hands of an adult, there will be difficulties in establishing a therapeutic rapport and relationship based on trust and confidence in the process. With some clients, this will be a major task of the therapeutic process and may take a long time to establish, if it happens at all. Children who have experienced abuse may act out or withdraw, they may behave in sexually inappropriate ways with peers and adults, and they may find themselves further excluded by their peer group, reinforcing ideas about their fundamental worthlessness or un-lovableness. These children may struggle to cope in school. It may be difficult for them to concentrate due to hypervigilance, or they may exhibit oppositional or defiant behaviour and frequently find themselves in trouble with authority or excluded from class.

Abuse inevitably involves disempowerment of the victim. Therefore, an important role for therapy is to empower children and young people. Turner-Daly (2018) makes the point that, while it is vital that child abuse is identified and actiontaken to ensure the child's safety, care should also be taken to ensure that therapists do not contribute to abuse becoming part of the child's identity. She cautions: 'Devastating though it may be, we must remember that abuse is an experience, one aspect of a child's life' (Turner-Daly, 2018: 369). In doing so, she reminds us that, as integrative practitioners, we are interested in knowing and understanding the 'whole' person of the client and not simply seeing them through a lens of 'victim' or 'perpetrator'.

Key Skills

1. Working therapeutically with trauma and abuse is challenging and emotionally demanding for the therapist. Figley (2002) writes about the implications of this for compassion fatigue and secondary post-traumatic stress disorder. Before beginning work with clients who have experienced abuse, counsellors should ensure they have an effective support structure in place, including clinical supervision, peer support and appropriate training (see entry 2.23, p. 134). Counsellors need to be mindful of their own experiences of trauma and abuse and ensure they have worked through these thoroughly in their own personal therapy. Failing to do so can have implications for the capacity to fully connect with and hear the

client's experience, where this brings up unprocessed and unwanted feelings in the practitioner.

2. A fundamental therapeutic skill for work in this area is patience. Clients recovering from abusive or traumatic experiences may exhibit a range of emotional, psychological and behavioural difficulties, and counsellors need patience to manage these appropriately in therapy. Clients may struggle with confidentiality if they have previously been asked to keep abuse 'secret', and may not initially feel comfortable spending time alone with a 'strange' adult. Engagement with the client, their family and other professionals may be necessary to develop a therapeutic frame which is reliable and consistent while also being flexible enough to account for the client's needs.
3. A flexible and integrative approach allows the use of a range of interventions, based on the centrality of the therapeutic relationship and the provision of the core relationship components. Ann Cattanach (2008) writes extensively on the successful use of play therapy, based on these components, with abused children (see additional resources for more information).
4. Effective counselling can only take place when the client is safe from current harm and their basic needs are met. Where this is not the case, the counsellor may need to consider safeguarding procedures in order to ensure the client is protected from significant harm (see entry 2.8, p. 79).
5. Counselling is a space for exploring thoughts and feelings in all their complexity, and counsellors need the skills to facilitate this. For example, a child who has been removed from their parents due to neglect may need to express anger and sadness at being away from home, even if their current situation is a considerable improvement on previous circumstances. This requires the counsellor to see things from the perspective of the client as much as possible, rather than with the eyes of an adult with the child's 'best interest' at heart. Turner-Daly (2018: 399) urges therapists to avoid identifying and labelling clients as 'abused children', and to 'balance the negatives with what we know about courage, resilience and survival', allowing both client and counsellor to engage with the therapeutic process with hope for what can be achieved.

Summary

- Trauma and abuse suffered by vulnerable children and adolescents have a significant effect on development, often extending into adulthood.
- Therapy can be used as a method of engaging the client in the process of recovering from their experience.
- Clients who have experienced abuse may struggle with some aspects of the therapeutic relationship and process, and adjustments may be required to accommodate this.
- Interventions based on the core relationship components can assist the client in processing painful experiences and rebuilding trust and hope for their future.

Additional Resources

- MindEd – www.minded.org.uk: 412-09 *Safeguarding Young People and Vulnerable Young Adults*.
- NSPCC (2020) *What is Child Abuse?* Available at: NSPCC.org.uk/what-is-child-abuse (last accessed 1 July 2020).
- Cattanach, A. (2008) *Play Therapy with Abused Children*. London: Jessica Kingsley.
- Department for Education and Skills (DfES) (2006) *What to Do if You're Worried a Child is Being Abused: Departmental Advice Providing Best Practice Information for Those who Work with Children in Order to Safeguard their Welfare*. London: HMSO.
- HM Government (2017) *Child Sexual Exploitation: Definition and Guide for Practitioners*. London: HMSO.
- Turner-Daly, B. (2018) 'Sexual, physical and emotional abuse', in M. Robson & S. Pattinson (eds), *The Handbook of Counselling Children and Young People* (2nd edition). London: Sage.

Associated Entries

2.4 Building Rapport
2.8 Risk Assessment & Safeguarding
2.23 Self-Care for Counsellors
2.24 Clinical Supervision
3.10 Working with Risk
3.19 Online Risk
3.22 Self-Esteem
3.31 Resilience
4.8 Looked-After Children (LAC)

3.15 Risky Sexual Behaviour

As the biological changes of puberty prepare the body for adult sexuality and reproduction, the desire for sexual exploration is a normative aspect of development. Sexual experimentation and romantic attachments play a crucial role in identity formation and sexual development. This experimentation is a form of adolescent 'play', where different sexualities and relational possibilities are explored by young people seeking a 'safe place' relationally as they make their way towards an adult sexual identity. However, sexual behaviour can involve risks for the young person to contend with, including unwanted pregnancy, sexually-transmitted diseases and vulnerability to sexual assault. Risky sexual behaviour is often a cause for concern in adults, who may be more aware than the young person themselves of the consequences of such behaviour.

Exercise

Consider your own sexual and emotional development when answering the following questions:

- What part did your romantic and sexual behaviour during adolescence play in your own development?
- What was expected of you in terms of sexual behaviour during adolescence?
- How did these expectations impact you?

How might your own sexual and emotional experiences impact your capacity to work with young people demonstrating risky sexual behaviour?

Key Understandings

Young people presenting or being referred for counselling may disclose sexual behaviours or abuse requiring a safeguarding intervention, depending on the nature of the disclosure, their age and their developmental capacity (Kirkbride, 2016a). However, risky sexual behaviour may be linked to other factors, such as alcohol and substance use (see entry 3.13, p. 188), low self-esteem and bullying (see entry 3.18, p. 206).

As with the other risk presentations explored in this part of the book (see entry 3.10, p. 174), practitioners must hold a balance between aspects of the client's behaviour which can be explored therapeutically and those requiring a safeguarding response.

Key Skills

1. Build a therapeutic alliance based on the core relationship components and careful contracting. This is the basis for non-judgemental exploration of the behaviour, in order to empower the client to meet their needs for sexual and emotional development without placing themselves at risk.
2. Conduct a collaborative assessment, including an assessment of any risk factors in the presentation (see entry 2.8, p. 79), and develop a clear contract with the client so they are fully informed on the limits of confidentiality. Risk factors include:
   i. sexual behaviours which carry physical as well as psychological risk, for example, unwanted pregnancy or sexually-transmitted diseases.
   ii. vulnerability to sexual abuse or assault, including where young people are groomed for sexual exploitation by others. This can be online or in 'real life'.
   iii. exposure to pornography and graphic imagery of sexual violence (Martellozzo et al., 2016).
   iv. sexual behaviour which is illegal or inappropriate due to the age or capacity of the child or young person. The legal age of consent in the UK is 16 years, and any sexual relationship with a child under the age of 13 is a criminal matter, prosecutable under the Sexual Offences Act (2003).
3. When working with a client who has been sexually assaulted or experienced sexual violence, it is vital to bear in mind the impact of describing verbally what is likely to have been a traumatic experience. The client should be encouraged to talk about their experience of sexual abuse and assault at their own pace and in a way that is appropriate for them. Some clients may feel more comfortable exploring their experience at a distance through art or play (see entry 3.2, p. 144), rather than speaking directly about what happened.
   It is important to ensure the client is given time to process their experience before leaving their counselling session and that thought has been given to how they might manage any feelings which arise afterwards, especially if these are likely to be overwhelming and trigger other behaviours, such as substance use or self-harm, as in the following example.

   Client: This is the first time I've told anyone about what happened to me. I've felt so ashamed and disgusting. Before this, whenever I thought about it, I'd smoke weed and listen to music to get it out of my head.

If that didn't work, I'd burn my arm and then the pain's about something else, isn't it?

Counsellor: And now you've spoken about it with me?

Client: (Crying and reaching for a tissue) Now I feel sad. I feel really sad and I feel like I could cry my way through this whole box of tissues. And I'm scared. I've got to go in a minute (glancing at the clock), and I'm scared how I'm going to feel when I'm at home tonight. What if I can't sleep? What if I see his face again when I close my eyes?

Counsellor: We've got some time so let's have a think about that now. You've made a great step forward in talking about what happened today. You've put words to your experience and that's the beginning of processing what happened so you can live with it more easily than you have been while it's been bottled-up. Let's think together how you can take care of yourself or even let others take care of you until we meet for our next session.

If sexual abuse or assault occurred historically, therapy may involve an exploration of how the client would like to proceed in terms of holding a perpetrator to account. This is a complex matter and should be client-led as far as is possible. Where there is evidence or suspicion that an alleged perpetrator still has access to vulnerable children or young people, this must be taken into account in any safeguarding decisions made.

4. Be mindful of the need for self-care and support when working with issues of sexual behaviour and assault. This can be a sensitive area for many practitioners and it's vital to seek support as needed through supervision, personal therapy and other self-care activities.

Summary

- While sexual expression and experimentation is a normal aspect of adolescent development, some are vulnerable to harm in this area.
- Risky sexual behaviour may be an indication of underlying distress and this needs to be explored in a safe, boundaried therapeutic relationship.
- Clients who have experienced sexual abuse or assault may need support while they develop the resources needed to revisit this in therapy.

Additional Resources

- Department for Education and Skills (DfES) (2006) *What to Do if You're Worried a Child is Being Abused: Departmental Advice Providing Best Practice Information for Those who Work with Children in Order to Safeguard their Welfare*. London: HMSO.
- The Survivors Trust – www.thesurvivorstrust.org.uk: an umbrella organisation for specialist rape and sexual assault services in the UK.

Associated Entries

2.2 Core Relationship Components
2.8 Risk Assessment & Safeguarding
3.2 Symbol & Metaphor
3.7 Working with Emotions
3.10 Working with Risk
3.14 Trauma & Abuse
3.19 Online Risk

3.16 Identity

Identity formation is an area often associated with adolescence and the transition to adulthood. In etymological terms, identity is rooted in the latin word 'idem', meaning 'same' or 'sameness'. Having traced human development from birth, through infancy and childhood, we come now to consider what Anna Freud (1965: 43) described as the central issue of when 'a child should cease to be considered as a product of and dependent on his family and should be given the status of a separate entity, a psychic structure in its own right'. In other words, when and how is a separate identity formed and how might issues around this present for young people within the therapeutic process?

Key Understandings

In his seminal paper, 'The Eight Ages of Man', Erik Erikson (1950) outlines the developmental conflicts to be resolved as we seek a coherent sense of self and place in society. Erikson characterised adolescence as a period of conflict between 'identity' and 'role confusion': the young person in the process of moving away from their primary identification with parents and family seeks 'sameness' and belonging with peers, while also facing the threat of doing this at the cost of their individuality. Young people presenting for counselling often face difficulties arising from conflicts regarding identity. They may present with 'friendship issues', such as difficulties forming appropriate relational bonds with peers. They may struggle to imagine themselves worthy of another's liking or love, and this may affect their capacity to form and sustain relationships with others. As seen in other entries, identity or sense of self can manifest in bullying (see entry 3.18, p. 206), risky sexual behaviour or gang membership, as young people seek relational experiences to scaffold a sense of self which has not been able to fully develop due to early relational experiences, and which subsequently leave the young person vulnerable to risk. For some, the search for a coherent and authentic gender or sexual identity (see entry 3.17, p. 202) can create conflict, both within themselves and with their environment.

Erikson (1950) argues that without a stable independent identity, the young person will not be able to confidently enter adulthood and this lack may subsequently manifest in issues such as anorexia (see entry 3.12, p. 183), or depression (see entry 3.24, p. 229).

Identity formation can be hampered by a number of factors, such as early relational experiences and attachment (see entry 1.5, p. 16). From a humanistic point of view, conditions of worth (Rogers, 1959) affect identity development, where meeting the desires of another is prioritised above the organismic needs of the self. As the young person moves towards adolescence, they may be supported by a family which understands that development of an autonomous sense of self is vital to all children, or hampered by one where this development and its corresponding issues of separation and individuation is perceived as threatening in some way to the family structure or the wellbeing of individuals in the family. If growing up in the latter environment, the development of a separate identity can be loaded with feelings of guilt and ambivalence in the young person, and as they struggle to separate they may be compelled into a position of acting-out. This may manifest in presentations such as drug and alcohol use, anti-social behaviour, anger issues, eating disorders, etc.

Key Skills

1. Be aware that struggles with identity formation can underlie many clinical presentations in adolescent clients.
2. When developing a therapeutic relationship with a young person, be aware of the need to support their autonomy and development of a coherent sense of self. Where this is not something that has been previously provided, the therapeutic relationship can become an important space to support this.
3. Be aware of environmental factors that can potentially impact and influence identity development (see entry 1.10, p. 37), including cultural and family factors. When gathering information, be curious about how the client's family and community function. Listen for indications that this may be hampering development and for ways in which the therapeutic relationship and frame can be mobilised to facilitate this. For example, a young Black male client presenting with depression may be experiencing the effects of growing up in a social environment which projects identities of 'dangerous', 'criminal', 'gang member' onto him, making it difficult to develop a sense of worth as an individual (see entry 2.11, p. 93).
4. Be curious about identity development in the self as a therapist.

Exercise: Identity Formation

Consider your own identity formation during adolescence:

- What were the main factors influencing this?
- What factors 'told' you who you were and where you belonged?
- Where these different in adolescence than in childhood?
- How are they different now?

Summary

- Identity formation and individuation is a central process in the adolescent transition, as experienced in Western contemporary culture.
- Where identity formation has been hampered developmentally by early relational experiences or environmental factors, therapy can offer a facilitating space to work through this.
- Issues and confusion regarding identity may underly many clinical presentations among adolescent clients.

Additional Resources

- Erikson, E.H. (1950) 'Eight ages of man', *Childhood and Society*. New York: W.W. Norton & Co. (reprinted London: Vintage, 1995).
- Erikson, E.H. (1968) *Identity, Youth & Crisis*. New York: W.W. Norton & Co.

Associated Entries

1.7 Humanistic Theories of Development
1.9 Puberty & the Adolescent Transition
1.10 Environmental & Systemic Factors
3.17 Sexuality & Gender Identity
3.22 Self-Esteem
3.24 Depression
3.26 Neurodiversity: Autism Spectrum Disorder (ASD) & Attention-Deficit Hyperactivity Disorder (ADHD)

3.17 Sexuality & Gender Identity

Developing a coherent and authentic identity is a key task of the adolescent transition (see entry 3.16, p. 199). In this entry we consider issues related to sexuality and gender identity which may bring a child or young person into therapy, as well as the skills required to work appropriately in this important and complex area of development and functioning. As this is a developing area of understanding and practice, it is beyond the scope of this entry to offer an exhaustive understanding. Readers are directed to the additional resources at the end of the entry for suggestions of further reading and research.

Key Understandings

Contemporary Western culture is arguably founded on a 'heteronormative' series of understandings about gender and sexual identity and orientation (Barker, 2019). These include ideas about: gender identity as a 'binary' concept (i.e. people are either 'male' or 'female'), gender roles (i.e. what it means to be a man or a woman), sexuality (i.e. as either 'gay' or 'straight' and that everyone must have a 'sexuality' or a sexual orientation) and relationships (i.e. everyone needs a romantic attraction which leads to sexual and romantic attraction and that this leads to a normative 'ideal' of becoming a long-term monogamous couple) (Barker, 2019).

Barker (2019: 10) argues that this normative understanding relates to issues with mental health in a number of ways, particularly for those who 'fall into the less "normal" side of the various binaries'. They go on to argue that a client's understanding and experience in this respect will vary according to the time period in which they grew up as well as their cultural background. Young people growing up in an environment where they experience differing approaches to these areas in their family or among their peers may find this aspect of their development particularly troubling. For example, a young woman who comes from an orthodox Christian background where homosexuality is viewed as unacceptable may struggle with her own developing same-sex attraction, even though this is welcomed by her peer group at school.

Young people differing from this normative understanding experience a range of issues, including problems in identity development, discrimination, fear of or actual rejection by peers or community, bullying, depression, anxiety as well as suicidal ideation and self-harm. Intersectionality (Crenshaw, 1989) plays a vital role in understanding the experience of clients who not only experience themselves as outside the 'normative' view, but are also at the intersection of different identities, such as gender, race, religion, disability, etc. and are therefore affected in complex ways. For example, a white middle-class male who identifies as gay may find a supportive environment with peers, youth organisations or family within which to explore this, whereas this might be more problematic for a young Black male identifying in a similar way.

While gender may be medically assigned at birth depending on visible genitalia, a biopsychosocial view of gender acknowledges a range of factors which affect identity. Those children whose experience of gender is incongruent with their assigned gender identity may be experiencing gender dysphoria (GD) (Ristori & Steensma, 2016). Due to this incongruence, children may experience 'clinically significant distress and are consequently in need of clinical attention' (Ristori & Steensma, 2016: 13). GD as a diagnosis is included in the most recent edition of the *Diagnostic and Statistical Manual of Mental Disorders* (DSM) (American Psychiatric Association, 2013).

Practitioners need to be mindful of the past pathologising of non-normative identities within therapy, for example 'conversion therapies'. While young people may not be aware of this history, they may need reassurance that the aim of the therapeutic process is fundamentally affirmative of their identity, rather than seeking to change or 'normalise' this in any way. This is an area of rapid and sometimes controversial developments. It is vital that practitioners explore their own relationship with their gender, sexual and relational identities so they are prepared to support clients who need a supportive space for their own discoveries in this respect. This is an important aspect of cultural competence for therapists (see entry 2.11, p. 93).

Key Skills

1. While clients may present specifically with issues around gender and sexual identity, it's important to remember that every person has a complex relationship with their sexual/gender identity and this affects all aspects of their functioning in the world. Rather than see the issue as residing in the client, it can be helpful to view the difficulties they experience as being rooted in the attitudes of society and culture to those who fall outside the 'norm'. Beattie and Linehan (2018: 12) suggest affirmative counselling should be based on practitioner *reflexivity* and *education*. Reflexivity is identified as relating to the need for:

   > Developing an awareness for how we are all situated within a gendered world and how we all have an experience of gender identity and gender diversity – that the problems in living are 'in here' in relationship and not 'out there' in the bounded person of the client. (Beattie & Linehan, 2018: 13)

Education refers to the need for the counsellor to exercise their ethical duty to 'inform themselves about the field where our clients are experiencing distress and not leaving it to the client to educate their counsellor or therapist' (Beattie & Linehan, 2018: 13).

2. Counsellors need to develop skills and understanding with respect to gender and sexuality as it may be understood currently by children and adolescents. Young people presenting for counselling may feel comfortable expressing their identity using vocabulary unfamiliar to the practitioner. Counsellors may find it helpful to research current definitions and understandings used by young people to describe their identities and also to ensure they use the correct personal pronouns for their clients, for example she/her, he/him, they/them.
3. Clients may have experienced negative impact from the reactions of others to their identity. They may present with psychological and emotional issues related to experiences of bullying, discrimination or fear that their identity will place them at risk of rejection or even violence within their family or community. While counsellors need to practise in a way which is affirmative of all identities, it's important to understand that for some young people 'coming out' may be a complex and possibly dangerous process to even consider. There should not be an assumption that all young people need to be encouraged to accept their identity and express it to others. Each young person comes from a unique set of circumstances, and therapists should be mindful where their own views may interfere with fully understanding these circumstances and helping the client to manage themselves in the way which is best for them at this time.
4. Where a young client is exhibiting signs of gender dysphoria or other diagnosable conditions, counsellors should recognise the limits of their competency and seek advice or support from the wider community of professionals in this area, only referring on where there is consent to do so from the client or their family, as appropriate.

Exercise

Take some time to explore your own history of gender and sexual identity.

- How do you identify in terms of gender and sexual identity?
- Have you always felt comfortable with this identity? What were the main factors determining how comfortable you felt?
- What do you consider are the main factors which have determined your identity?
- Can you see any implications of this identity formation which might impede your capacity to hold an affirmative therapeutic space for children and young people, regardless of how they identify? If 'yes', how might you work on this to develop your skills as a practitioner?

Summary

- Gender identity and sexuality are central components of the identity and sense of self.
- Gender identity and sexuality development can be significantly affected by the environment and cultural background of the child or young person.
- Non-normative identities can lead to bullying, discrimination and rejection for young people. This can have significant implications for psychological and emotional wellbeing.
- Therapists need to hold an affirmative space for clients who are exploring their identity in therapy. It's vital to develop self-awareness of any prejudices or blocks we might have in facilitating this exploration.

Additional Resources

- Barker, M.-J. (2019) 'Good Practice across the Counselling Professions 001', in M.-J. Barker, *Gender, Sexual and Relationship Diversity (GSRD)*. Lutterworth: British Association for Counselling and Psychotherapy.
- Beattie, M., Linehan, P. & Dundas, R. (eds) (2018) *Counselling Skills for Working with Gender Diversity and Identity*. London: Jessica Kingsley.
- Krieger, I. (2017) *Counseling Transgender and Non-Binary Youth: The Essential Guide*. London: Jessica Kingsley.

Associated Entries

1.10 Environmental & Systemic Factors
2.11 Cultural Competence
3.18 Bullying

3.18 Bullying

Bullying is a form of abuse, commonly found among children and young people, but which can affect adult interpersonal relationships. The Anti-Bullying Alliance (ABA) defines bullying as: 'The repetitive, intentional hurting of one person or group by another person or group, where the relationship involves an imbalance of power' (Anti-Bullying Alliance, 2020).

Bullying can be direct, as in physical and verbal attacks and acts of social exclusion, or indirect, such as spreading rumours or damaging belongings or valued articles. More recently, cyberbullying has become a significant issue. Bullying causes young people considerable distress and can lead to self-harm and suicide. According to a 2020 report from the charity 'Ditch the Label', a fifth of those who responded to a survey of UK 12–20-year-olds had experienced bullying over the previous 12 months and 33% said that they had experienced suicidal thoughts as a result (Ditch the Label, 2020).

Key Understandings

When considering therapeutic interventions with both victims and perpetrators of bullying, it is useful to have an understanding of underlying dynamics and mechanisms as well as the external conditions which can reduce or exacerbate the effects of bullying. Child psychotherapist Margot Waddell (2007: 189) writes about the psychodynamics of bullying, suggesting that '[w]e are talking … of a dynamic relationship in which, aggravated or fuelled by external circumstances, negative aspects of the personality are played out – never without toll, and sometimes with tragic consequences'. Waddell (2007: 190) highlights relevant psychological aspects of adolescent development, suggesting:

> Anxiety about identity arouses an acute intolerance of difference either in the self or in the other – the seedbed of group identity if benign, or of gang or mob mentality when the shared purpose becomes that of cruelly bolstering the ego at the expense of others.

Of key importance in Waddell's (2007) analysis are early relational experiences, which offer some explanation for why some children have more resilience to bullying than others, and why some are compelled to act out against their peers in such a way. Waddell (2007) identifies Bion's (1962) concepts of 'reverie' and 'containment' (see entry 1.6, p. 20) as particularly relevant, arguing that in parent–infant relationships where containment of fragmented and overwhelming internal states does not occur, the infant is left alone to manage mental pain and unwanted aspects of the self:

> The individual can either disown and attribute elsewhere the vulnerable self and persecute it externally, or can disown a bully self and take up a hapless and helpless victim position in relation to denied aspects of the personality which then come to be represented by the persecutors. (Waddell, 2007: 195)

This perspective assists us in understanding why sometimes the most vulnerable young people are also the ones who themselves become bullies, as they try to manage intense internal feelings of vulnerability and distress.

While it is crucial to understand intrapsychic and interpersonal underpinnings of bullying, environmental and cultural factors also play a significant role. Whereas in the past bullying was accepted as a naturally occurring aspect of education, both between staff and pupils and between peers (Waddell, 2007), there is now an expressed intention to prevent bullying in schools and to address bullying and harassment of 'vulnerable' groups who are often singled out for harsh treatment. The UK government identifies schools as best placed to address bullying, stating that: 'By law, all state schools must have a behaviour policy in place that includes measures to prevent all forms of bullying among pupils' (gov.uk, n.d.). Schools must follow anti-discrimination law, taking active steps to prevent discrimination within school. While it is up to individual headteachers to implement policy and ensure all pupils, parents and staff adhere to it, bullying clearly remains an issue for many children and young people today. Since bullying can have a significant impact on young people's mental health, emotions and identity, as well as their capacity to attend and get the most out of educational opportunities, counselling is a vital resource for early intervention to support the wellbeing of all affected.

Key Skills

1. An integrative approach to working with clients who have experienced or perpetrated bullying is rooted in the need to understand the young person as an individual with a view to discovering their unique understanding of what the behaviour or experience means to them. This will require a therapeutic relationship based on the core relationship components, enabling an exploration of all aspects of their experience.
2. Young people who experience bullying may struggle with identity and with self-esteem (see entries 3.16, p. 199 and 3.22, p. 222). If bullying is understood as an attempt to project unwanted feelings of vulnerability onto the other, it is when these

projections are identified with and even internalised by the victim that they have their impact. It's as if the bully were trying to use the 'victim' as a dustbin for all the unwanted 'rubbish' pieces of their personality. If the victim implicitly agrees they deserve to be a receptacle for rubbish, they are more likely to receive these damaging projections. With this in mind, an effective method of supporting those affected by bullying therapeutically is to work on identity, exploring how negative aspects of their 'self-concept' leave them vulnerable to abuse. Developing self-esteem can act as a 'vaccination' against the impact of bullying. In this respect, school culture plays an important role. Where identities linked to race, gender, disability or LGBTQ are positively validated by staff and pupils and all harassment is responded to effectively, it will be easier to support the young person in dealing with feelings of shame or poor self-worth, and to develop a positive sense of their identity, rather than one dominated by the unchecked negative projections of others.

Both individual and group therapy can be effective in providing support with the effects of bullying. Individual interventions beyond integrative therapy might include CBT (see entry 3.6, p. 158) as well as play-based and creative-arts interventions (see entries 3.3, p. 147 and 3.4, p. 151) intended to support the client in developing a healthy self-concept and identity.

3. Where a young person is being placed at risk of harm through bullying, either from another or themselves, a collaborative risk assessment will be necessary (see entry 2.8, p. 79). Repeated bullying can lead to powerful feelings of hopelessness and helplessness potentially becoming unmanageable for the young person, who may have been compelled to withdraw from peer activities and self-isolate, adding to the risk factors to be considered at assessment.
4. Therapists working with young people who have experienced bullying may need to explore their own experiences of this in order to be able to hold a non-judgemental space for the client.

Summary

- Bullying is the intentional hurting of one person or group by another person or group, where the relationship involves an imbalance of power.
- Children and adolescents with low self-esteem may be vulnerable to bullying by peers.
- Bullying behaviour is often underpinned by difficult or abusive early relational experiences. It is important to explore these when children who bully others are referred for counselling.
- Certain groups and identities can be vulnerable to bullying and harassment. This can have a negative impact on self-concept, leading to issues with depression, self-harm and suicidality.

Additional Resources

- Anti-Bullying Alliance – www.antibullyingalliance.org.uk: the Anti-Bullying Alliance has worked with the Department for Education and the Anna Freud Centre to produce free online CPD training for professionals working with the effects of bullying. For more information, see: www.anti-bullyingalliance.org.uk/tools-information/free-cpd-online-training for more information (last accessed 14 June 2020).
- Other useful organisations include:
  - Bullying UK – www.bullying.co.uk
  - Kidscape – kidscape.org.uk
  - Internet Matters – internetmatters.org.uk

Associated Entries

3.10 Working with Risk
3.16 Identity
3.17 Sexuality & Gender Identity
3.19 Online Risk

3.19 Online Risk

For many children and young people, internet use occupies an ever-increasing amount of their time. According to a comprehensive report completed in 2017 by the UK Council for Child Internet Safety (UKCCIS), this increase, along with four in ten 3–4-year-olds now having internet access (UKCCIS, 2017), means that there is the potential for an increase in risk of harm for children and adolescents via the internet. This entry will consider some of the areas of risk and explore a range of skills for practitioners working in this area.

Key Understandings

In the UK we have now been living in the 'digital age' for over two decades. Those born post-1980, described as 'Digital Natives' (Prensky, 2001), are now in their 30s, and every subsequent generation has experienced even more of their lives in the dual locations of 'real life' and cyberspace. As therapists working with children and adolescents, it is important to develop an awareness of the impact digital technology has on children's development, the family and the overall environment as well as considering implications for therapy (Kirkbride, 2016a).

For many young people, the internet offers opportunities for interaction and creativity that they may not otherwise have had. Israeli et al. (2013: 282) ask: 'Does cyberspace open up new channels through which the adolescent may grow and deal with developmental burdens, or does it merely further complicate his life?' While theorists have suggested ways in which the internet provides a creative social space for young people, where they can 'play' with identity and self, free of the consequences of 'real-life' interactions (Turkle, 2011; Israeli et al., 2013), accessing the internet can be fraught with risk, particularly for those already vulnerable to harm (Katz & El Asam, 2019). Therapists require knowledge and skills to be able to engage with clients' online lives in a way that allows space for curiosity and exploration as well as the potential to identify and manage risk of harm.

Key Skills

1. Be curious about a client's engagement with online spaces. It's vital that counsellors demonstrate a non-judgemental attitude towards all aspects of their clients' lives, including online activities, such as social media, online video-games, video-sharing sites, etc. Practitioners should develop an awareness of any prejudices or biases they

might have regarding these, and set them aside in order to see material from the client's perspective, as in the following examples.

Counsellor: You've said you enjoy playing video-games. Which ones are you into? Can you tell me more about them?

Client (9 years): Well, you might not have heard of some of them, but I love Minecraft.

Counsellor: Oh yes, I've heard of that one. You build worlds, don't you? Can you tell me about something you've built?

Or:

Client: I started following her on insta [Instagram] and at first it was really nice. She kept liking my posts and making all these nice comments. She DM'd me and asked if I wanted to meet, but when I said yes, she laughed and said 'as if'. Now I'm worried she's gonna tell someone I'm gay. I don't know what I'll do if she does. This is a different account from my main one, so not many people I know are on there. But still... if she tells anyone, I don't know what I'll do. I can't stop worrying about it.

Counsellor: You're frightened that something is going to come out and you're not sure you're ready to deal with the consequences.

In these examples the counsellor is engaging with the client 'where they are'. They have created a therapeutic space where the client feels able to share their online experience. In the first example, this is used as a way of entering the client's world and learning more about them, and in the second, there is an opportunity for the counselling to address a significant area of concern for the client.

2. While exploring the client's online world, be alert to any indications that they may be at risk of harm. This could be due to engagements with:

   i. accessing violent or pornographic material
   ii. playing video-games with unsuitable age-related content
   iii. risky sexual behaviour, such as vulnerability to online grooming for sexual exploitation, exchanging images or content of a sexual nature (sexting)
   iv. grooming for exploitation by political, religious and/or criminal organisations
   v. cyber-bullying
   vi. social media sites where there is content related to self-harm, suicide, eating disorders, etc.

   Concerns regarding a client's online safety need to be managed in the same way as other safeguarding concerns, and protocols regarding confidentiality need to be observed (see entry 2.8, p. 79 and 3.10, p. 174). Counsellors should consider age and developmental capacity when reviewing safeguarding and online issues.

3. Counsellors need to be aware of their own online profile and activities. While all therapists have the right to a private life, the BACP's Ethical Framework (2018: 18) requires therapists to ensure that 'reasonable care is taken to separate and maintain

a distinction between our personal and professional presence on social media where this could result in harmful dual relationships with clients'. This may be of particular relevance in work with younger clients with active social networks that may cross-over with those of their counsellors.

Exercise

Consider your own online existence:

- What would your clients be able to discover about you were they to put your name into a search engine?
- What are the potential ethical and therapeutic implications of this?

The 'Online Therapy Institute' has produced some useful guidelines for practitioners around ethical use of social media (see additional resources at the end of this entry).

Summary

- Children and adolescents spend increasing amounts of time online, often unsupervised. This can place some at risk of harm.
- It's important to be aware of client online activity. Be curious about interactions and attuned to any indication that the client may be vulnerable to risk of exploitation or exposure to inappropriate and harmful material.
- Counsellors should be mindful of their own online activity and social media use in order to protect themselves and the clients from unwanted self-disclosure.

Additional Resources

- Katz, A. & El Asam, A. (2019) *Vulnerable Children in a Digital World.* Internet Matters/Youthworks [online]. Available at: internetmatters.org (last accessed 23 June 2020).
- Online Therapy Institute (n.d.) *Ethical Framework for the Use of Social Media by Mental Health Professionals.* www.onlinetherapyinstitute.com (last accessed 23 June 2020).
- Childnet International – childnet.com: provides a range of resources for teachers and professionals, including advice on 'professional reputation' online (childnet.com/teachers-and-professionals) (last accessed 23 June 2020).
- Internet Matters – Internetmatters.org
- NSPCC – nspcc.org.uk

Associated Entries

2.8 Risk Assessment & Safeguarding
2.11 Cultural Competence
3.10 Working with Risk
3.15 Risky Sexual Behaviour
3.18 Bullying

3.20 Family Breakdown & Instability

For most children, family provides the secure base within which they develop. As explored in previous entries, this begins with the development of the first bond between infant and primary caregiver and then extends gradually as the infant develops relationships with other family members and then the ecology of family system, culture and community (see entry 1.10, p. 37). Since this secure base is crucial to the healthy development of the child (Bowlby, 1988), it follows that instability, transition and breakdown occurring within the family system, for whatever reason, are likely to have a significant impact on development. For some, this will affect them in ways which require a referral for counselling. In this entry we explore some of the presentations linked to family instability and breakdown while considering the skills required by practitioners working in this area.

Key Understandings

Family instability takes many forms, including, but not limited to, parental separation and divorce. Instability can be caused by a range of issues, including, economic and employment instability, incarceration of parent figures or close family members, removal of children from the care of the parents (looked-after children), ill-health or bereavement, issues relating to immigration status or asylum applications, changes in parents' working arrangements, changes in family dynamics due to older children leaving home or due to the creation of new 'blended families' with step-parents and siblings introduced to the family system.

The impact of family instability and breakdown will depend on a number of complex factors. Perhaps the most significant factor is the developmental stage of the individual when the instability is experienced (Dissing et al., 2017), along with the relative longevity, repetition and severity of the instability and conflict. For example, the impact of parental separation will affect a 2-year-old differently from a 13-year-old and the conditions leading up to the separation will also contribute to impact. Research suggests under-5s and adolescents are the most vulnerable to the negative effects of divorce and separation (Wallerstein & Kelly, 1980). Younger children are more dependent on their parents and have fewer resources outside the parental couple for support, while adolescents are in the process of separating and can find parental separation at this point developmentally disturbing:

> In this situation of family fragmentation, common strategies employed by an adolescent are disengagement, distancing, and attempts to connect elsewhere. The adolescent might be seeking to escape from the toxic escalation of parental anger, depression and neediness or simply trying to find sustenance in the absence of parental support and supervision. (Isaacs et al., 1986: 184)

Clearly, these factors can bring young people into therapy, as they use whatever resources they can find to help them cope with their experience, perhaps leading to risk behaviour (see entry 3.10, p. 174), or emotional issues such as anxiety and depression (see entries 3.23, p. 225 and 3.24, p. 229). Adolescents experiencing divorce and separation are also likely to find new relationships formed by their parents challenging and potentially disturbing when they themselves are in the process of exploring their own sexuality and capacity for intimacy in relationships (Carr, 2006; Kirkbride, 2016a).

The developmental impact of separation is also relevant when children are removed from their family due to concerns that their needs are not being met by their parent/s. This process will have a range of impacts on the child, and these impacts are deeply affected by the degree of attachment and dependence present in the relationship at the time. Influencing factors will include the nature of the instability – whether temporary or permanent. Protective factors will include the quality of relationships within the family, support for the child within and external to the family, how quickly stability can be reinstated, how frequently or infrequently the child has been confronted by instability and change in their family system.

Such is the understanding of the impact of separation and instability on children that some separating parents will refer children for therapy even before an issue has appeared, perhaps due to their own fears about the potential negative impact. As in all therapy, it is crucial to allow an understanding to emerge of what the meaning is for the client, rather than the emphasis being on parental anxiety. The impact of family breakdown may need to be processed by the client at different stages of their development. For example, a young person whose parents separated when they were in primary school may find themselves dealing with the emotional and psychological consequences of this later in life, perhaps as they enter adolescence and begin to consider their own relational needs. Equally, a child or young person placed in foster care in their early years may need continued support to process this into adolescence and beyond. Practitioners need to be able to consider all aspects of the family history, recent or past, when helping clients to explore their feelings and relationships with others as they emerge in the therapeutic relationship.

Key Skills

1. Where a client has experienced family instability or breakdown, practitioners need to be open to exploring the meaning of this for the client. It's important to hold a balance between understanding that experiences of family instability are likely to have a significant impact and accepting that the nature of this impact will be unique for each person. It is especially important for therapists to look at their own history in this respect, whether in childhood or as an adult, and to be aware of prejudices and assumptions they may be transferring from this onto their client-work. Practitioners may have their own painful experiences of separation and instability, and while these might help in connecting empathically with the client, they also run the risk of interfering with being open to the uniqueness of the client's experience. Personal therapy and supervision can be useful for exploring experiences which have the potential to influence the therapeutic process in this way.
2. Clients experiencing family instability may need support in understanding their interpretation of what has happened. The way this is offered will depend on the age and developmental capacity of the client. For a young child this may be explored through play (see entry 3.3, p. 147). An attitude of open curiosity with regard to any symbolic meaning of the play will facilitate the emergence of clues as to how the client is internalising their experience, allowing the counsellor to help them in processing this in a way that gives it meaning that can be tolerated, as in the following example:

   Client: (Playing with toys in the sand – picking up a small elephant) This one can't play with these anymore. He's different now.
   Counsellor: That one's different so he can't play with the others.
   Client: They don't want him (the elephant is pushed by a giraffe). Oh no! They do want him. They want him back but it's too late. He's gone (elephant has been thrown in the toy box).
   Counsellor: (Aware that the client's dad has recently been sentenced to two years in prison) He's gone. They can't get him back.
   Client: No – it's just them now. I think they are quite sad but they need to be strong and not cry.
   Counsellor: They need to be strong and not cry, but I wonder if that might be hard sometimes, even for a rhino and a giraffe.
   Client: (Looking up at counsellor) It is very hard.

   In this example, the counsellor stays in the metaphor the child has created while beginning to make empathic conjectures intended to help the client understand and perhaps accept the complex and difficult feelings as they arise.
3. Children and young people experiencing instability may exhibit acting-out or risk-taking behaviour. They may not associate this directly with family issues, and therapy can be a way of facilitating their understanding of the impact of their environment on their emotional and psychological wellbeing. For example, a young person referred due to self-harming behaviour and suicidal ideation may be

indirectly responding to the effects of their parents' acrimonious relationship, which blights family interactions and is felt deeply by the client but never acknowledged directly by the parents. In some cases, the client will be relieved to understand that their feelings are arising from an issue in their environment, although working with this can be challenging where the parents are not ready to acknowledge this and/or work on their relationship (see entry 2.12, p. 97).

4. As with all aspects of family life, culture will have significance in how family instability is managed and spoken about by parents and other family members as well as on the impact it has on children and their understanding. Counsellors should be sensitive to cultural background when exploring their experience of family instability and breakdown, including the cultural meaning imposed on this. For example, in some communities, having divorced or separated parents may be experienced as shameful, while in others it may be seen as a cultural norm (see entries 1.10 p. 37 and 2.11, p. 93).

Summary

- The impact of family breakdown and/or instability will depend on the developmental stage and meaning for the individual client.
- The degree of dependence the client has on the family may be significant in respect of family instability and breakdown.
- A range of interventions can be offered to provide a space to explore feelings related to separation and loss of stability.

Additional Resources

- Carr, A. (2006) 'Separation and divorce', in A. Carr, *The Handbook of Child and Adolescent Clinical Psychology: A Contextual Approach* (2nd edition). New York: Brunner-Routledge.
- Isaacs, M.B., Montalvo, B. & Abelson, D. (1986) *The Difficult Divorce: Therapy for Children and Families*. New York: Basic Books.

Associated Entries

1.10 Environmental & Systemic Factors
3.21 Bereavement & Loss

3.21 Bereavement & Loss

Losing someone or something with significance is challenging whenever it occurs during the life-span. For children and young people, the repercussions can be substantial, with the impact often depending on the nature of the loss, when it occurs in their development, and the level of support they experience to help them to understand and process the loss. Adapting to a loss is described as 'bereavement', while 'mourning' is the process the individual goes through while making the adaptation. 'Grief' is generally understood to mean the feelings, thoughts and experiences that the individual associates with the loss. In this entry we consider some of the issues around bereavement and loss which bring children and adolescents into counselling, and how an integrative approach can be utilised to help this process.

Key Understandings

How a child understands death and the meaning they place on this understanding are significantly affected by their age, developmental stage and cognitive capacity (Bowlby, 1980). In the third part of his seminal series, *Loss*, Bowlby (1980: 271) outlines how a child comes to experience and understand death:

> In the ordinary course of life even very young children meet with examples of death – a dead beetle, a dead mouse, a dead bird. The phenomenon is puzzling. Contrary to all previous experience with the animal, the dead creature is immobile and fails to respond to anything done to it. ... What has happened? Is the creature asleep? Can we prod it into activity? In such circumstances no child is left for long without some explanation being given him by an adult or by another child; and it is from these explanations that he develops his own ideas.

Bowlby (1980) introduces several important ideas around how children understand death. Primarily children and adolescents are influenced in their understanding by the information given to them by others, including those conveyed by cultural and/or spiritual understandings of death and the afterlife. How a child is spoken to about death, whether this is in euphemistic terms, such as 'gone to sleep' or 'passed away', will affect the child's capacity to understand what has happened. Circumstances of death are also likely to be significant for the child. Experiencing a parent dying at the end of a long illness will be processed very differently from a sudden loss, for example, as a result of a fatal accident or the suicide of a parent or close family member. Bowlby (1980) is clear that in order to mourn, children need to understand the facts of death, even when these may be painful for the surviving parent to convey: 'Only, indeed, when he has been given true information, and the sympathy and support to bear it, can a child or adolescent be expected to respond to his loss with any degree of realism (1980: 271). While coping with death is a naturally occurring process in all people, children and adolescents may present for counselling when they have not received sufficient support with their mourning. This may be for many reasons, including the resources or capacity of the surviving family to support them adequately when they too are going through a process of mourning their own loss.

Key Skills

1. Worden (2002) describes four tasks of mourning for children and these are useful to have in mind when assessing and working with bereaved clients. Each person's experience of loss will take a different shape. The journey someone takes through the tasks will not necessarily be a linear process. It might be more helpful to consider that these are often returned to throughout life as the loss is experienced in different ways:

   Task 1: to accept the reality of the loss
   Task 2: to experience the pain or emotional aspects of the loss
   Task 3: to adjust to an environment in which the deceased is missing
   Task 4: to relocate the dead person within one's life and to find ways to memorialise the person.

   The role of the counsellor is to assess where the client might be 'stuck' within this process and use the therapeutic relationship and process to aid them in mourning appropriately. The interventions used will depend on the age and individual needs of the child. For example, a younger child may work through these tasks symbolically through play (see entry 3.3, p. 147), whereas an older adolescent may wish to make a 'memory box' and fill it with pictures and significant objects, while another may need to work with accessing emotions (see entry 3.7, p. 162).
2. Mourning may be complicated where there has been a difficult or ambivalent relationship with the dead person. For example, an 11-year-old girl is informed by her aunt that the father she has not seen since she was a baby has now died. Her family are surprised by the degree of distress this provokes: since she did not really know her father, they didn't imagine she would care. In counselling she might need to spend some time working on understanding the nature of her loss in all its complexity before being able to work through the tasks and process her grief.

There might also be complexities of this nature where the client had been experiencing difficult feelings towards the person they have lost. For example, a 13-year-old boy whose mother is killed in a car accident had been angry with her after she grounded him and took away his phone. After learning of her death, he became depressed and began to self-harm and express suicidal ideation. In therapy, he gradually became able to express the guilt he felt for having had hateful thoughts on the day she died. He felt he didn't deserve to feel sad or grieve for her and this then shifted into feeling he didn't deserve to continue to live. Through the process of exploring these feelings, over time he was able to see that they existed alongside others about his mum and he could see that they had loved one another deeply, in spite of their occasional difficulties. He moved on to being able to experience his sadness at her loss and chose to create a photo-montage of pictures of him and his mum sharing their lives in happy times.

3. Often a child's capacity to cope with loss will be influenced by how the important adults around them are coping. For this reason, it can sometimes be useful to suggest that a grieving parent or family member seeks therapeutic support for themselves as well as their child. By discovering their own capacity to cope with the pain of mourning and to move through this, they may find resources to similarly support their child/ren.
4. While bereavement through the death of a parent or significant other is profoundly significant in a child's life, there are other losses which occur and which they may need help to process in a similar way. These can include losing a pet or moving away from a home, community or previous school. Counselling is a space where the client can bring the loss as they have experienced it and make sense of its unique meaning for their life. In order for this to happen, the core components (see entry 2.2, p. 51) need to be offered, allowing the client to experience their loss in a relationship based on empathy and unconditional positive regard.
5. One aspect of this area for practitioners to be aware of is the loss of a peer during adolescence. Young people may find themselves bereaved at some point perhaps due to a friend's fatal accident, illness, drug and alcohol use, or suicide. Such close contact with mortality can be disturbing for young people moving towards adulthood with a sense of omnipotence and immortality. Many young people will find their own ways as a group to grieve and memorialise their friend, but counsellors should be aware of the vulnerability of some young people to this experience, particularly when they are already dealing with related experiences in their past. It's important to check with clients who are recently bereaved how they are coping with the loss and to support them in developing resources to help them manage.
6. As therapists, we are not immune from our own experiences of loss and bereavement, whether in the past or while we are in practice. Self-care is important here as well as recognising the limits of our competence to hold the therapeutic space for our client when we are experiencing loss or bereavement in our personal lives.

Summary

- Loss affects everyone at some point. The impact of loss depends on the meaning it has for the individual. This meaning can be affected by dependence and developmental stage.
- Children and adolescents may need counselling to help them cope with a loss when there are insufficient resources in their environment to support them in their grieving process.
- A therapeutic relationship based on the core relationship components provides a space for finding meaning and working through feelings associated with the loss in a developmentally appropriate way.

Additional Resources

- Worden, J.W. (2002) *Children and Grief: When a Parent Dies*. New York: Guilford Press.

Associated Entries

3.20 Family breakdown & Instability
3.23 Anxiety
3.24 Depression

3.22 Self-Esteem

Our self-concept (Rogers, 1959) is fundamental to how we function in the world and in relationships. In this entry we explore briefly what is meant by the term 'self-esteem' and consider how clients who are experiencing issues related to self-esteem might be helped by an integrative therapeutic approach.

Key Understandings

First coined by psychologist William James (1890), 'self-esteem' is a term used to describe our evaluation of our worth and value as a person. The term was popularised by social psychologist Morris Rosenberg (1973), who developed a scale to measure degrees of self-esteem in order to conduct research into how low or high self-esteem affects people in life. Rosenberg (1973: 554) defines self-esteem as 'the individual's global positive or negative attitude towards himself'. Zeigler-Hill (2013: 2) suggests a person's assessment of their self-worth is 'not necessarily accurate or inaccurate. ... This is important because self-esteem reflects perception rather than reality.' This last point is possibly the reason why cognitive-behavioural therapy (CBT) has become such a popular tool for working with low self-esteem, where the client's perceptions of self-worth, often in the form of negative core beliefs, can be tested against reality.

Levels of self-esteem are affected by a wide range of factors, including early relational experiences, abuse and neglect (see entry 3.14, p. 191). Rogers (1959) describes the conditions in early relationships that influence the development of the self-concept (see entry 1.7, p. 25), while Erikson (1950: 224) writes about the importance of 'basic trust' developed in infancy and resulting in 'a sense of identity which will later combine a sense of being "all right", of being oneself, and of becoming what other people trust one will become'. Young people without the facilitative experiences required to develop this sense of being 'all right' are likely to struggle in a number of areas. For example, children and adolescents with low self-esteem are more vulnerable to bullying and abuse (see entry 3.18, p. 206) as well as to risk, including risky sexual relationships as they seek validating experiences to shore up a vulnerable self-concept (see entry 3.15, p. 195).

Key Skills

1. Integrative approaches based on the core relationship components (see entry 2.2, p. 51) support the client in feeling valued 'as they are' without conditions of worth that may have been imposed on them in the past. Rogers (1959) asserted that with

these components in place, the client would feel valued, accepted and understood, and therefore able to reconnect with their organismic valuing principle as the central force for their ongoing existence (see entry 1.7, p. 25). With this in mind, the primary skills for working therapeutically with low self-esteem are the core relationship components. These may be offered as part of a non-directive play or creative intervention, or in talking therapy. As the client gradually experiences themselves as fully accepted in the therapeutic relationship, their sense of self-worth and value will increase, allowing them to feel more secure in their sense of self both in themselves and in their relationship with others, as shown in the following example:

Keisha, age 9 is referred for counselling having been bullied by other girls in her class. At the referral meeting, Keisha's mother presents as anxious and overly critical of her daughter, telling the counsellor that Keisha never helps at home and that she's afraid she'll do badly at school. In her play-therapy sessions, Keisha chooses to use paint. At first, she is cautious and frequently checks with her counsellor about what she is 'allowed' to do, worrying about 'making a mess'. The counsellor reflects that Keisha seems afraid of making a mess and reassures her that in here mess is not a problem, and that they will manage it together. Gradually, Keisha becomes more confident and paints large splodges of colour, which she enjoys watching run down the paper. As the sessions continue, Keisha's teacher remarks to the counsellor that Keisha is behaving differently in class: she has managed to find a couple of friends and it is lovely to see her laughing and playing with them. When the sessions end, Keisha tells her counsellor that she felt like a different person in their sessions when she was painting and that this was the person she feels like when she plays with her friends these days. Within the safety of a therapeutic relationship Keisha had been able to connect with a different sense of herself and through the counsellor's validation had begun to feel secure enough that she could risk forming friendships again.

2. Cognitive-behaviour therapy (see entry 3.6, p. 158) is used as a tool for working more directly with the thoughts and beliefs which can underpin low self-esteem. CBT techniques are used to identify negative core beliefs, such as 'I'm stupid', 'No one cares about me', 'I can't get anything right'. These can be worked with to help the client see how the beliefs have developed and how they are affecting their life, as in the following example:

   John is 15 and the youngest of three brothers. Both older brothers are serving jail sentences for burglary and violence. John is referred to a counsellor due to depression and self-harm. John and his counsellor discover a negative core belief for John that he is 'worthless' and will end up in prison like his brothers. The counsellor uses CBT to explore John's negative thoughts, demonstrating how these translate into his feelings of hopelessness and self-harming behaviours. Together they 'test' the beliefs, allowing John to see that the idea that because his brothers are in prison the same will happen to him is not 'fact', but an opinion or negative belief. The following week John tells his counsellor about his love of distance running. He stopped when his middle brother was incarcerated as they always trained together. John goes back to the club and starts running again, building a sense of hope and positivity about his future. Eventually, he writes to his brother to tell him that he's running again and reports to his counsellor that his brother had been pleased and proud of his achievement.

3. Self-esteem work can also be done in small groups where there are several young people with similar issues. Group-work (see entry 3.9, p. 171) can be useful for supporting participants in testing their opinions and beliefs about themselves against how others see them.

Summary

- Self-esteem is a term to describe the value we perceive ourselves to have as a person.
- Self-esteem can be affected by early relational experiences, trauma and abuse, and other environmental factors, including systemic racism and sexism.
- Low self-esteem can increase vulnerability to issues such as bullying, depression, self-harm and identity.
- Integrative therapy can be used as a means to explore clients' perceptions of self, to understand how it develops and how to work to improve self-esteem.

Additional Resources

- Stallard, P. (2019) *Think Good, Feel Good: A Cognitive Behavioural Therapy Workbook for Children and Young People.* London: John Wiley & Sons.

Associated Entries

1.5 Attachment Theory
1.7 Humanistic Theories of Development
1.10 Environmental & Systemic Factors
2.2 Core Relationship Components
3.6 Cognitive-Behavioural Therapy (CBT)
3.16 Identity
3.18 Bullying

3.23 Anxiety

Both anxiety and depression are commonly experienced by adults and children in the UK and worldwide. In this entry we will explore the meaning of anxiety and its application to children and adolescents. The entry will consider approaches to working with this common clinical presentation.

Key Understandings

Anxiety is broadly characterised by feelings of tension, worried thoughts and physical changes such as increased blood pressure. People with anxiety disorders often have recurring intrusive thoughts or concerns. They may avoid certain situations out of worry, for example, refusing to go to school or social activities. They may have physical symptoms, such as sweating, trembling, dizziness or a rapid heartbeat (www.apa.org/topics/anxiety). These symptoms are intricately connected to the autonomic and parasympathetic nervous system, which works with our brain to allow us to perceive threat and act accordingly. In this respect, symptoms of anxiety are adaptive and intended to keep us safe from harm by triggering our flight–fight response. However, anxiety can become maladaptive and cause distress in children and young people who experience an overwhelming sense of danger in seemingly benign circumstances, or who exaggerate the significance of certain situations, seeing them as 'life or death', eliciting an anxiety response. Beck et al. (1985) identify a central theme of anxiety as a preoccupation with the concept of danger and an underestimation of the personal ability to cope. This concept can be understood as an equation which assesses the degree of anxiety experienced by dividing perceived threat or danger by perceived capacity to cope. This is useful when we take into account that children and young people are likely to have a less developed sense of coping skills, increasing their vulnerability to anxiety states.

Childhood anxiety clinical presentations can take several forms, for example, selective mutism, general anxiety disorder (GAD), panic disorder, separation anxiety disorder, specific phobia or social anxiety disorder (American Psychiatric Association, 2013). Anxiety is experienced on a spectrum from mild and short-lived to chronic and debilitating. The causes of anxiety are considered to be a combination of biological factors, such as genetic make-up, neurochemistry, hormones, psychodynamic and social or environmental factors. The quality of early relational experiences, including containment (Bion, 1962) of difficult feelings (see entry 1.6, p. 20), have an impact on how a child or adolescent experiences their world and their capacity to cope with the challenges life brings.

Social and environmental factors play a part in anxiety in young people. For example, children growing up in poverty or as part of a discriminated-against minority may experience the world as a threatening place where they need to be constantly prepared for and ready to respond to danger. The 'Black Lives Matter' protests of June 2020 demonstrated a community's frustration regarding the fear of harm at the hands of the police they had been forced to endure for decades (Guardian, 2020). This has highlighted the reality for many Black, Indigenous and (young) People of Colour (BIPOC) in the UK and beyond who don't have confidence in society to protect them from harm. Rather, people of colour may be viewed perpetrators of crime and violence, contributing to anxiety and depression in this community. It is crucial for counsellors to understand the role discrimination, oppression and inequality play in the development of anxiety states. Children who grow up in households where there is financial insecurity and/or housing instability may also be prone to anxiety. This is also the case in households experiencing parental illness or addiction. Where parenting is inconsistent, aggressive or unpredictable, this can predict anxiety states in children. Overprotective parenting can also affect the development of anxiety as parents 'teach' their child that the world is a dangerous place and they have little control or capacity to manage it (Perini & Rapee, 2014).

Key Skills

1. For clients presenting with anxiety, a therapeutic frame based on the core relationship components (see entry 2.2, p. 51) which provides validation, consistent holding and containment of anxieties and experiences will provide the therapeutic support they require to work on their feelings and potentially reduce the negative impact of anxiety in their daily lives.
2. Play-based interventions can be used with anxiety in younger children or where cognition-based interventions are not appropriate. Play-based interventions (see entries 3.2, p. 144 and 3.3, p. 147) offer an accepting and non-threatening environment in which children can play out their fears and anxieties through the safety of symbolic play (Landreth et al., 2018).
3. There is evidence that CBT (see entry 3.6, p. 158) is effective in helping older children and adolescents who experience overwhelming anxiety states (Perini & Rapee, 2014; Stallard, 2019). Stallard (2019) suggests that a range of CBT interventions can be deployed for anxiety, such as encouraging clients to explore and engage with difficult thoughts and feelings, as well as in challenging anxiety-provoking situations rather than avoiding them, as is typical in anxiety presentations. An effective therapeutic intervention is to use CBT to demonstrate to the client how

they can become stuck in a cycle of negative cognitions that affect their emotions and behaviours and to offer them tools to address this, as in the following example:

Malik is a 12-year-old boy experiencing symptoms of separation anxiety. He is a talented football player and has been offered a place on a training camp over the summer. However, Malik is afraid of being away from home and experiences physical symptoms of panic when he thinks about spending time away from his family. Malik's mother is keen for him to go, but is herself anxious about him being away from home. She identifies her anxiety as being related to having a stillbirth prior to becoming pregnant with Malik.

Malik's counsellor uses CBT techniques to explore some of his negative cognitions. Together they identify that Malik has core assumptions such as 'If I go away from home, something terrible will happen to my mum' and 'If I leave my home, it will not be there for me to return to'. They work on testing these assumptions and developing some more functional understandings of the pros and cons of spending time away from his family. In addition, they work on breathing and grounding techniques that Malik can use if he experiences symptoms of panic or nausea. Gradually, Malik spends time away from his parents, beginning with a sleepover at a family member's house and then extending this to a weekend away with school. Malik's experiences on these times away from home are worked on in his counselling sessions as he begins to develop a sense of confidence that he can be away from his home and be OK. At the same time, Malik's parents begin their own couples' therapy to explore the loss of their child and the ongoing impact it has had on their family.

4. As in the previous example, breathing, mindfulness and grounding techniques can be used with clients to help them manage their symptoms of anxiety when they arise in the session and outside (see entry 3.8, p. 168).
5. Anxiety and depression can place clients at risk of harm from themselves. A risk assessment regarding the degree of anxiety and its impact needs to be made at an appropriate time in the work.
6. Anxiety in adolescence can be masked by substance and alcohol use. When working with clients who use substances, it is important to consider whether this may be due to social or other anxiety issues. In these cases, the counsellor needs to establish a therapeutic relationship where the client feels secure enough to reduce their substance use and engage therapeutically with feelings they may have been avoiding.

Summary

- Anxiety is a common issue for children and adolescents presenting for counselling.
- While anxiety has an important evolutionary function, anxiety responses can become maladaptive and create significant issues for children and adolescents.
- Counselling can be offered to provide a space to explore anxiety symptoms with a view to helping the client find more appropriate ways of responding, freeing them from the restrictions of chronic anxiety states.

Additional Resources

- Landreth, G., Ray, D.C., Sweeney, D.S., Homeyer, L.E. & Glover, G.J. (2018) *Play Therapy Interventions with Children's Problems: Case Studies with DSM-IV-TR Diagnoses*. New York: Jason Aronson.
- Stallard, P. (2019) *Think Good, Feel Good: A Cognitive Behavioural Therapy Workbook for Children and Young People*. London: John Wiley & Sons.

Associated Entries

1.5 Attachment Theory
1.6 Object Relations Theory
1.8 Neurobiological Development
3.6 Cognitive-Behavioural Therapy (CBT)
3.8 Mindfulness & Relaxation Techniques
3.11 Self-harm
3.13 Alcohol & Substance Misuse
3.24 Depression

3.24 Depression

Depression is a common emotional disorder experienced by increasing numbers of children and adolescents (NHS Digital, 2018). In this entry we develop our understanding of the clinical presentations of depression and how these can be worked with therapeutically.

Key Understandings

As with anxiety, depression can be understood as an adaptive aspect of human functioning which can become maladaptive and lead to powerfully debilitating symptoms, including:

- Persistent sadness or low mood and/or
- Loss of interest or pleasure
- Fatigue or low energy
- Disturbed sleep
- Poor concentration or indecisiveness
- Poor or increased appetite
- Suicidal thoughts or acts
- Agitation or slowing of movements
- Guilt or self-blame (ICD-10) (World Health Organisation, 1992).

Symptoms can be precipitated by the autonomic arousal system, which governs the limbic or fight–flight system. Gilbert (2007: 51) identifies the connection of depressive symptoms with perceived helplessness in the face of threat: 'The central requirement when confronted with a threat or stressor is that you will have to do something. But supposing you cannot?'. Rather than the 'flight' response becoming activated as with anxiety, in depression it is the 'freeze' response which is triggered, along with corresponding states of numbness, hopelessness, conservation of energy and preparation for death, all of which are characteristic symptoms of depression. Seligman (1975) coined the term 'learned helplessness' to describe the phenomenon observed in animals who become apathetic and passive when no escape from a stressor is available; the passivity remains even after the stressor is removed. As with anxiety, depression can be viewed as an adaptive response to the individual's perceived lack of resources to cope with a threat. This is a functional response in something like bereavement, where the individual withdraws from 'normal' life as their emotional and psychological resources are repurposed to help process the loss. However, when the person becomes 'stuck' in cycles of depression and unable to function, the response becomes pathological and will require intervention to facilitate a reconnection with an ability to engage with and enjoy life.

Depression can be caused by a range of biological, psychological and environmental factors. Genetics and neurochemistry play a part, but generally in relation to environmental factors (Gerhardt, 2015). Gerhardt (2015) writes extensively on the impact of early relationships on the development of the capacity to manage stress and on the neurochemical underpinnings of depression in later life:

> Babies who can't get the attention they need and who do not feel adequately protected from distress are forced to become aware of their own helplessness and powerlessness. But such awareness is premature because a young baby has virtually no capacity to regulate his own distress or act in his own interests. There is little he or she can do if no one responds to his protests and cries, except to try not to feel and to 'play dead'. This may be the safest course of action if his needs are an irritation to his caregivers. (Gerhardt, 2015: 142)

This understanding is crucial for counsellors looking to help a client make sense of seemingly irrational feelings of hopelessness and dread.

Trowell and Miles (2011: 19) consider the history of depression in children and young people in the introduction to their research as part of the Tavistock Clinic's 'Childhood Depression Project'. This project explores psychoanalytic understandings of depression and highlights the importance of understanding 'masked depression', where depression in children is hidden behind aggressive behaviour and somatic complaints.

Key Skills

1. Where clients are experiencing symptoms of depression and low mood, they may be disinclined to self-refer for counselling or to imagine there is any hope for them in engaging with the process. Often teachers or parents will spot signs and refer. It is then important to find a way of identifying and engaging with a 'hopeful' part of the client, even if they are not able to experience this themselves to begin with. With this in mind, seeing the client as a 'whole' person and not just as someone experiencing depression is a vital part of the therapeutic process. This might mean inviting a younger child to engage with play or other materials in whatever way they choose, or asking an adolescent who doesn't know what to talk about in their session what music they enjoy or what the last thing they saw on TV was (see entry 3.5, p. 154). This not only helps to build rapport (see entry 2.4, p. 63) but also allows the client to connect with aspects of themselves beyond their symptoms or behavioural issues.
2. Often clients experiencing depression find it difficult to articulate or understand their internal emotional landscape. Once a solid therapeutic relationship has

been established and trust has developed, techniques of working with emotions (see entry 3.7, p. 162) can be used to help the client to explore and express their feelings. Where in the past these feelings have been rejected or dismissed by caregivers, it can take some time for the client to trust they can bring them into awareness in therapy without meeting with a similar response, as in the following example:

Ceridwen is an 11-year-old girl seeing a counsellor due to depression and anger issues. Her mother was hospitalised with post-partum depression after both Ceridwen's birth and that of her younger sister just 15 months later. Ceridwen is reported to have been an easy child throughout primary school, but following the transition to secondary school she has not been coping.

In their initial sessions, Ceridwen cautiously uses art materials, always asking the counsellor which colours he would like her to use and what he would like her to draw. The counsellor is aware that perhaps she is making sure that he is not overwhelmed by her presence in the way she might perceive her mother to have been. After some weeks, Ceridwen's drawings change and become pictures of gardens where only dark things can grow. The counsellor explores these with her, demonstrating that he is not afraid of Ceridwen's difficult feelings and thoughts.

3. CBT has been used effectively with young clients with depression and low mood (Stallard, 2019). By using thought and mood diaries, underlying cognitive distortions can be explored and addressed using CBT techniques (see entry 3.6, p. 158).
4. Depression and low mood can provoke suicidal ideation and suicide attempts in children and young people. Counsellors need to ensure that they have adequately assessed for risk in their clients and have an established safeguarding plan in place where necessary (see entry 2.8, p. 79).

Summary

- Symptoms of depression can be common in children and adolescents presenting for counselling.
- Depressive symptoms can be experienced in differing degrees of intensity and with a range of presentations.
- Depression in children and adolescents may not manifest in ways we are familiar with in adults. For example, depression can be 'masked' by behaviours such as aggression or somatic illness.
- Counselling can be offered to provide a space to help the client to process their emotional experience and perhaps to connect to a more hopeful aspect of themselves.

Additional Resources

- National Institute for Health and Clinical Excellence (NICE) (2019) *Depression in Children and Young People*. Clinical Guideline NG134. London: NICE.
- Stallard, P. (2019) *Think Good, Feel Good: A Cognitive Behavioural Therapy Workbook for Children and Young People*. London: John Wiley & Sons.
- Trowell, J. & Miles, G. (eds) (2011) *Childhood Depression: A Place for Psychotherapy*. London: Karnac.

Associated Entries

3.7 Working with Emotions
3.10 Working with Risk
3.11 Self-Harm
3.21 Bereavement & Loss
3.22 Self-Esteem
3.25 Diagnosis, Medication & Psychiatric Presentations

3.25 Diagnosis, Medication & Psychiatric Presentations

While it is beyond the scope of most counsellors to diagnose or prescribe medications for their clients, knowledge of medications that are commonly prescribed for childhood diagnoses and their possible side effects can be useful. Counsellors must also be aware of the indications that a young person might require a psychiatric referral due to worsening mental health or risk of harm.

Key Understandings

Diagnosis

The term 'diagnosis' is generally associated with the medical model, with its focus on physical disorders perceived as clearly defined and measurable. Diagnosis is commonly defined as the identification of a disorder by the investigation of its symptoms. The integrative therapeutic approach takes the view that the client should be seen as a whole person, rather than a collection of symptoms leading to a diagnosis and targeted treatment. While supporting the general use of diagnostic manuals such as the *Diagnostic and Statistical Manual of Mental Disorders* (DSM; American Psychiatric Association, 2013), Gilbert and Orlans (2011: 102) stress the importance of viewing 'any diagnosis as a "tentative hypothesis" open to regular revision, and not a "label for life"'. This can be considered as particularly significant in diagnosing children and adolescents, who may be significantly impacted by receiving a diagnosis during this developmental period.

Psychopharmacology

The BACP's Competence Framework (2019) places 'Knowledge of psychopharmacology' as a core competence for practice with children and young people They suggest practitioners need to develop knowledge of the following areas:

1. An ability to draw on knowledge of the role of medication in the treatment of children and young people with mental health problems.

2. An ability to draw on knowledge of evidence for the benefits both of medication alone and medication offered in combination with psychological interventions.
3. An ability to draw on knowledge of medications commonly prescribed in child and adolescent psychopharmacology, and the conditions for which they are employed.
4. An ability to draw on knowledge that medications have both benefits and risks.
5. An ability to discuss with children, young people and their families the potential role of medication in their treatment.
6. An ability to discuss with appropriately qualified health professionals the risks, benefits and appropriateness of medication for particular clients. (BACP, 2019: 49)

Goodman and Scott (2012) acknowledge the 'uneasy feelings' of parents and professionals regarding the prescribing of medication to children and adolescents. However, they also make the point that 'suitable doses of the right medication used for an appropriate indication can be of great benefit' (2012: 319).

Commonly prescribed medications for children and adolescents include:

- For Attention-Deficit Hyperactive Disorder (ADHD):
  - Atomoxetine
  - Dexamphetamine
  - Methylphenidate
- Anti-psychotics:
  - Chlorpromazine
  - Clozapine
  - Olanzapine
  - Risperidone
- Antidepressants:
  - Citalopram (SSRI)
  - Duloxetine
  - Fluoxetine
  - Paroxetine
  - Sertraline
- For anxiety/insomnia:
  - Diazepam
  - Lorazepam
  - Melatonin
  - Zopiclone
- Mood stabilisers:
  - Lamotrigine
  - Lithium

This list is not exhaustive and readers are advised to see the additional resources section at the end of this entry for further information on psychopharmacology.

Psychiatric presentations

While most psychiatric presentations are beyond the limits of competence for counsellors to work with in practice, practitioners need to be aware of the signs that a client may require a psychiatric referral. For more detailed descriptions of psychiatric presentations see Goodman and Scott (2012).

Mania

Manic episodes can be experienced by young people, although this does not necessarily mean they will be diagnosed with bipolar disorder. Hypomanic episodes are a lesser version of mania and may have a reduced impact on functioning and are shorter in duration. Manic episodes can be caused by drug and alcohol use. Signs of a manic episode may include:

- Increased purposeful activity
- Being more talkative
- Flights of ideas or a subjective sense of accelerated thought
- Loss of normal social inhibitions
- Exaggerated self-esteem or grandiosity (Goodman & Scott, 2012).

Obsessive-Compulsive Disorder (OCD)

Approximately one-third of adults with OCD have their first symptoms before the age of 15 (Goodman & Scott, 2012). While counsellors may work with clients at the mild end of the OCD spectrum, it is important to be aware when symptoms and behaviours increase to a degree where psychiatric consultation is required. Characteristic features of OCD include:

- Obsessions – unwanted repetitive or intrusive thoughts. Common obsessions include:
  - Contamination
  - Disasters
  - Symmetry
  - Religion
- Compulsions – unnecessary repetitive behaviours (or mental activities such as counting). Common compulsions include:
  - Washing
  - Cleaning
  - Repeating

- ○ Checking
- ○ Touching

OCD is often hidden by the sufferer and may be comorbid with depression and anxiety symptoms. Other conditions, such as anorexia and schizophrenia, as well as autism may be accompanied by elements of OCD (Goodman & Scott, 2012).

Schizophrenia and psychosis

'Schizophrenia' is a term used to describe a major psychiatric disorder (or cluster of disorders) that alters a person's perception, thoughts, affect and behaviour. Characteristics of schizophrenia are divided into 'positive' and 'negative'. In this context, 'positive' characteristics refer to the symptoms that would not be present in 'normal' functioning for example:

- Hallucinations
- Delusions
- Thought disorder
- Motor abnormalities.

'Negative' characteristics refer to a reduction in symptoms which are part of 'normal' functioning, for example, less of the following:

- Speech
- Sociability
- Emotional involvement
- Motivation (Goodman & Scott, 2012).

National Institute for Health and Clinical Excellence (NICE) guidelines state:

> When a child or young person experiences transient or attenuated psychotic symptoms or other experiences suggestive of possible psychosis, refer for assessment without delay to a specialist mental health service such as CAMHS or an early intervention in psychosis service (14 years or over). (NICE, 2013: 11)

Key Skills

1. According to ethical principles (see entry 2.20, p. 124), counsellors need to always have the best interests of the client in mind. Where a client shows signs of needing psychiatric attention, a referral should be made to Child and Adolescent Mental Health Services (CAMHS) (see entry 4.4, p. 270). Where possible this should be done in collaboration with the client and their family, as appropriate, although

there may be circumstances where practitioners have to proceed without consent if this is in the best interest of the client.

2. Develop a 'bank' of appropriate resources to support work with clients who are taking medication and/or who are supported by psychiatric services alongside their counselling or who might require a referral. See the 'additional resources' section at the end of this entry for suggested sources of information. Counsellors will benefit from developing relationships with colleagues and professionals working in CAMHS who might be able to offer support and consultation when a client is suspected of needing psychiatric support. Connecting with a child and adolescent psychiatrist can provide useful insight into their role and ethos for work with young people experiencing major episodes of mental ill-health.
3. Clinical supervision is essential when working with clients who have been prescribed medication, or who are likely to require psychiatric intervention. Decisions in this complex and challenging area of practice should not be made by the counsellor alone. Rather, practitioners should seek as much appropriate support and guidance as needed in order to work effectively and ethically at all times.
4. Culture can play a part in the development, form and degree of psychiatric disorder. Counsellors should use cultural competence skills (see entry 2.11, p. 93) in understanding and supporting young people from a range of cultural backgrounds who experience difficulties in this area.

Summary

- While counselling is limited to non-psychiatric issues on the whole, counsellors need to be aware of the signs that a client might require psychiatric support for their difficulties.
- Counsellors should develop knowledge of common psychiatric diagnoses and medication prescribed for their symptoms.
- Where a client requires a psychiatric referral, this should always be approached collaboratively and with correct ethical protocols in place.

Additional Resources

Diagnosis

- MindEd – www.minded.org.uk: 414-030 *Diagnosis and Classification*.
- Goodman, R. & Scott, S. (2012) *Child and Adolescent Psychiatry* (3rd edition). London: Wiley-Blackwell.

Psychopharmacology

- Kutcher, S. (2002) *Practical Child and Adolescent Psychopharmacology*. This publication is available, with the author's permission, as a free pdf download from: www.youthinmind.info/GoodmanScott3rdEdition2012.pdf (last accessed 2 July 2020).
- British National Formulary (BNF) and British National Formulary for Children (BNFC) – www.BNF.org These are available to download as a free smartphone 'app'. They provide comprehensive and accessible information on current UK prescribing of medications.

Psychiatric Presentations

- MindEd – www.minded.org.uk: 428-020 *Bipolar Disorder and Psychosis in Young People (CT): Families and Professionals*.
- MindEd – www.minded.org.uk: 428-022 *Psychosis in Young People: Combining Therapies and Collaborative Treatment*.
- National Institute for Health and Clinical Excellence (NICE) – www.nice.org.uk/guidance: website provides guidance on evidence-based treatment for a range of mental health and psychological disorders.
- Royal College of Psychiatrists (RCPsych) – www.rcpsych.ac.uk: website contains useful resources for young people, parents and professionals looking for information related to psychiatric diagnoses. For more information, see: www.rcpsych.ac.uk/mental-health/parents-and-young-people (last accessed 3 July 2020).
- Thapar, A., Pine, D., Leckman, J.F., Scott, S., Snowling, M.J. & Taylor, E. (eds) (2015) *Rutter's Child and Adolescent Psychiatry* (6th edition). London: Wiley-Blackwell.

Associated Entries

2.8 Risk Assessment and Safeguarding
2.20 Ethical Issues
2.22 Working with Other Professionals
4.4 Child & Adolescent Mental Health Services (CAMHS)

3.26 Neurodiversity: Autistic Spectrum Disorder (ASD) & Attention-Deficit Hyperactivity Disorder (ADHD)

In this entry we explore the common neurodevelopmental issues that are likely to be encountered in practice. We consider the key understandings, along with skills and approaches, to therapeutic work with clients with Autistic Spectrum Disorder (ASD) and Attention-Deficit Hyperactivity Disorder (ADHD). Other neurodevelopmental disorders include Tourette's syndrome and tics as well as 'Developmental Coordination Disorder' (DCD or Dyspraxia) and Dyslexia, which will be covered in entry 3.27 (p. 244). This is a complex and developing area of clinical understanding, and interested readers are advised to explore the 'additional resources' section at the end of this entry for more sources of information and professional development in this area.

Key Understandings

There have been significant developments in recent years regarding how society views neurodiversity. Dyck and Russell (2020: 170) offer the view of the 'Neurodiversity Movement' (NDM) that '"Neurodiversity" is a concept that implies that neurological difference is best understood as an inherent and valuable part of the range of human variation, rather than a pathological form of difference'. The NDM takes as a central tenet a denial of pathologisation of neurodiversity and critiques 'labelling' as a potentially harmful action against diversity (Dyck & Russell, 2020: 173).

Neurodevelopmental issues such as ASD and ADHD usually become apparent in early childhood. They progress as the child's body and brain grow. Some children with neurodevelopmental issues will experience additional difficulties, such as anxiety or depression. They may have specific learning difficulties (SpLD), including Dyslexia and Dyspraxia, issues with motor control, and speech and language issues.

Neurodevelopmental disorders are generally assessed and diagnosed by Child and Adolescent Mental Health Services (CAMHS) and are often treated with a combination of medication prescribed by a medical practitioner and therapy.

Characteristics of ASD

The term 'Autistic Spectrum Disorders' refers to a spectrum of autistic traits ranging from 'classical' autism at one end to 'typically developed children' at the other (Goodman & Scott, 2012). For some, autistic traits can be severe and impact functioning, while for others their autistic features may be experienced as 'gifts' and offer advantages, depending on the context and how they are treated by others.

Approximately 1% of the population have some form of ASD with a male to female ratio of 4:1 (Goodman & Scott, 2012). Childhood autism is defined by the early onset of symptoms in three areas:

1. Social impairment, for example:

   i. Poor eye contact
   ii. Lack of interest in people as people
   iii. Issues in social responsiveness, reciprocity, capacity for empathy.

Children with autism tend to attach to parents, can be affectionate and can interact socially 'on their terms' (Goodman & Scott, 2012). They may struggle to receive social cues and be unable to respond in a 'socially acceptable' manner. Children with ASD tend to have a deficit in capacity for Theory of Mind (ToM) (see entry 1.3, p. 9) and spontaneous play (see entry 1.2, p. 5). These are important considerations for developing rapport and the therapeutic relationship (see entry 1.11, p. 43).

2. Communication impairment, for example issues with:

   i. Comprehension
   ii. Speech
   iii. Gesture
   iv. Expression.

These issues are understood as a spectrum, with variations in severity and type of impairment. Some children with autism will use repetitive 'stock' phrases or will talk about particular areas of interest or preoccupation. Speech may have a particular intonation or pitch.

3. Restricted and repetitive activities and interests, for example:

    i. Resistance to change
    ii. Insistence on routines and rituals
    iii. Hand-flapping/twirling
    iv. Ordering play items, i.e. lining-up toys
    v. Attachment to unusual objects
    vi. Preoccupations with certain subjects, i.e. train timetables, makes of car, etc.

'Asperger's Syndrome' shares some characteristics of 'classical' autism but without certain features, such as developmental delay in vocabulary. Restricted and repetitive behaviours are most evident in preoccupations or circumscribed interests.

Some children with ASD may experience other issues, such as seizures, intellectual disability (see entry 3.27, p. 244), and other psychiatric problems, such as ADHD (Goodman & Scott, 2012).

Characteristics of ADHD

Prevalence for ADHD (DSM-IV diagnosis) is 2–5% of the population, with a male to female ratio of 3:1. It is more common in younger children than in adolescents and is linked with deprivation and families of low socio-economic status (Goodman & Scott, 2012). ADHD can be recognised by the following indications:

- Marked restlessness, inattentiveness and impulsiveness, including:
    - Wriggling and squirming in seat
    - Fiddling with objects or clothing
    - Difficulty in staying 'on task'
    - Being easily distracted
    - Inability to suppress activity when circumstances require
    - Engaging in rash and possibly dangerous activities.
- Pervasiveness, such as:
    - Symptoms must occur across different settings, i.e. home and school.

Additional features include:

- Defiant, aggressive and anti-social behaviours
- Problems with social relationships
- Specific learning problems
- Coordination problems.

Key Skills

1. The core principles of the integrative therapeutic approach are to meet and engage with the client as a whole person rather than as a label or as someone reduced to a set of diagnostic criteria. While the criteria mentioned briefly above may be used to diagnose and treat neurodevelopmental disorders, they can be held lightly in the counselling relationship and met with curiosity as to their meaning for the client experiencing them. Prizant and Field-Meyer (2016: 18) caution against the 'behavioural-assessment' approach to ASD, suggesting that it:

   > ...means defining a child as the sum of his deficits ... and what denotes success? The more we can make a child look and act 'normal' the better. ... It treats the person as a problem to be solved rather than an individual to be understood.

   An underlying rationale for therapeutic work is therefore to try to understand the client's communications and make sense of them together. The more the counsellor is prepared to listen carefully for meaning, the more likely it is that they will be able to form an effective therapeutic relationship from which to proceed.
2. The therapeutic relationship and frame may need to be adapted for counselling with children and adolescents with ASD and ADHD. Counsellors need to be flexible with the frame and sensitive to how their words and actions impact the client in the room. Session length may need to be adjusted, according to the capacity of the client to remain comfortably engaged. When this flexibility is offered with consistency, it can provide secure holding for the client, facilitating their engagement with and capacity to benefit from the therapeutic process, as shown in this case study from Landreth et al. (2005):

   > Play therapy permitted Tim to experience play in which he could securely be in control. The therapist's responsiveness to Tim's need to control the relationship helped Tim feel less vulnerable and thereby more willing to risk greater investment in the therapist. (Landreth et al., 2005: 53)

3. Child-centred play therapy has been used successfully with children with ASD and ADHD (Landreth et al., 2005; Schottelkorb et al., 2020). Play therapy emphasises non-verbal skills and therefore can be accessed by children for whom verbal communication is challenging. Art therapy and creative-arts interventions can also be used with children with ASD and ADHD (Evans & Dubowski, 2001).
4. Older and adolescent clients with ASD and ADHD may want to explore issues of identity and 'labelling'. They may experience issues with peer relationships as well as discrimination and bullying as they get older. It is important for counsellors to set aside their own views of what is 'success' or 'normal' for a young person and to meet the client where they are without prejudice. This can sometimes be particularly difficult for practitioners who themselves have experience of diagnoses, either for themselves or family members. While individuals may have navigated their own journey in coming to terms with a diagnosis, they should not imagine the client will need to take a similar path. Counsellors will need to use personal therapy and

clinical supervision to work on their own relationship with neurodevelopmental issues in order to be able to provide a clear space within which to meet the client.

Summary

- Working with forms of neurodiversity is an important aspect of practice with children and adolescents.
- Clients with ASD, ADHD or other neurodivergent presentations may require flexibility in the therapeutic frame in order to benefit fully from the therapeutic process.
- Consideration should be given to the often-difficult experiences of neurodivergent children and adolescents who may be bullied or discriminated against by others.

Additional Resources

- Goodman, R. & Scott, S. (2012) *Child and Adolescent Psychiatry* (3rd edition). London: Wiley-Blackwell.
- Landreth, G.L., Ray, D.C., Sweeney, D.S., Homeyer, L.E. & Glover, G.J. (2018) *Play Therapy Interventions with Children's Problems: Case Studies with DSM-IV-TR Diagnoses*. New York: Jason Aronson.
- NICE (National Institute for Health and Clinical Excellence) (2011) *Autistic Spectrum Disorder in under 19s: Recognition, Referral and Diagnosis*. NICE Guideline CG128. London: NICE (last updated December 2017).
- NICE (National Institute for Health and Clinical Excellence) (2018) *Attention Deficit Hyperactivity Disorder*. NICE guideline NG87. London: NICE (last updated September 2019).
- Prizant, B. & Fields-Meyer, T. (2016) *Uniquely Human: A Different Way of Seeing Autism*. London: Souvenir Press.

Associated Entries

1.3 Theory of Mind
1.8 Neurobiological Development
1.11 Developmental Implications for Counselling
2.14 Developing & Sustaining the Therapeutic Relationship
3.18 Bullying
3.22 Self-Esteem

3.27 Special Educational Needs & Disabilities (SEND)

The term 'Special Educational Needs and Disabilities' (SEND) is used to describe those children or young people who

> ...have a learning difficulty or disability which calls for special educational provision. A child of compulsory school age, or a young person, has a learning difficulty if they:
>
> - Have a significantly greater difficulty in learning than the majority of others of the same age, or
> - Have a disability which prevents or hinders them from making use of facilities of a kind generally provided for others of the same age in mainstream schools or mainstream post-16 provision. (NHS England, 2018)

SEND includes children with a 'specific learning disability' (SpLD). These are children who are as able as any other child apart from in one or two areas of their learning. There are many different types of SpLD, the most common of which is Dyslexia.

In this entry we consider the role of counselling for children and young people who fall under the SEND umbrella.

Key Understandings

As seen in the above NHS England (2018) definition, SEND is an umbrella term covering a variety of children and young people with differing degrees of difficulties affecting capacity to engage with learning as provided by mainstream education. Approximately 14% of children are considered to have an identified special educational need (NHS England), although numbers are considerably larger when we consider those whose difficulties fall outside accepted criteria. Some of those under the SEND umbrella will be considered to have a disability, defined in the Equality Act 2010 as 'a physical or mental impairment which has a substantial and long-term adverse effect on a person's ability to carry out normal day-to-day activities'.

The impacts of being a child with SEND are varied and unique to the individual experiencing them. Each young person affected will have a different experience of their difficulty and of the response to them from others. There is a strong association between poor mental health and SEND (Lindsay, 1999; Department for Education, 2016), and correspondingly there has been increasing interest in the role of counselling as part of inclusive provision for SEND (Pattinson, 2005, 2006).

Key Skills

1. Children and young people with SEND may need counselling provision to be adapted for their needs (Pattinson, 2006; Department for Education, 2016). The integrative approach outlined in this book is designed to be flexible to the needs of the client, basing interventions on the developmental stage and needs of the client rather than on an assumption that all clients have the same need or capacity to engage with and benefit from the therapeutic process. Pattinson (2006: 127–128) identifies six indicators of inclusive practice among therapists from a range of theoretical orientations:

    1. A proactive approach to counselling.
    2. Relationship-building.
    3. Operationalisation of equal opportunities policies.
    4. Inclusive initial assessment.
    5. Flexible and creative approaches to counselling.
    6. Training and awareness raising.

    Ensuring that services are advertised and made available to children and young people with learning disabilities facilitates an increased awareness that SEND children can be offered counselling and that services are adapted to ensure equal access. Pattinson (2006: 128) argues that a duty to ensure that practice is anti-discriminatory makes it, 'imperative that counselling becomes more inclusive of this marginalised group of young people'. By adopting an inclusive attitude to practice in this respect, we are offering the possibility for less marginalisation and for more clients to benefit from counselling.
2. Counsellors need to understand the implications of SEND for children's experience of education. It is important to be curious about the messages clients may have 'heard' and internalised in terms of their educational 'worth' and how this might have affected their self-concept and self-esteem (see entry 3.22, p. 222), including in the area of academic attainment. In studies, children with a learning disability are generally found to have lower self-esteem than those without SEND, and are inclined to consider themselves failures (Lahane et al., 2012). Demonstrating an inclusive approach, as outlined above, particularly in terms of initial assessment and relationship-building, as well as in the provision of the core relationship components, provides a facilitating environment within which to address self-esteem issues as well as to explore identity and sense of self (see entry 3.16, p. 199).
3. Skills in cultural competence and an acknowledgement of the impact of environmental factors on development (see entry 1.10, p. 37) are essential in understanding the

SEND client and their experiences as they grow up, including the development of low self-esteem, anxiety and depression. How disability is viewed by society, families and wider communities is likely to impact the client's sense of self and self-worth (Blanchett et al., 2009; Ravindran & Myers, 2012). The social construction of labels and terminology can have an impact beyond the practical for individuals (Cluley, 2018). Disability labels are often associated with stigma and can result in children being vulnerable to discrimination, bullying and abuse, both in school and in their wider community.

4. Counsellors need to be aware of the discrimination and abuse received by young people with SEND as well as of issues related to the intersectionality of race, culture and disability. Young people at the intersection of multiple vectors related to oppression and discrimination are likely to experience a greater negative impact of a learning disability than those belonging to the majority group (Blanchett et al., 2009).

Summary

- Children and adolescents with SEND may also experience further issues impacting psychological and emotional wellbeing.
- Services and interventions need to be accessible for all clients, including those with SEND.
- For some, it is the response of others which creates difficulties, for example bullying, discrimination, negative educational experiences. These can leave children with SEND experiencing low self-esteem, anxiety and depression.

Additional Resources

- British Dyslexia Association – www.bdadyslexia.org.uk
- Dyspraxia Foundation – www.dyspraxiafoundation.org.uk

Associated Entries

2.2 Core Relationship Components
3.16 Identity
3.18 Bullying
3.22 Self-Esteem
3.23 Anxiety
3.24 Depression
3.26 Neurodiversity: Autism Spectrum Disorder (ASD) & Attention-Deficit Hyperactivity Disorder (ADHD)
3.31 Resilience
4.2 Educational Settings

3.28 Visual & Hearing Impairments

In this entry we consider the impact of sensory impairments on children and adolescents and explore the skills required to adapt counselling for those with hearing and/or visual impairments.

Key Understandings

Research over the last two decades has increased understanding regarding the emotional and psychological impact of hearing and visual impairments on children and adolescents. For example, estimates suggest that deaf children are 60% more likely to have experience mental health problems than other children (Department of Health, 2005).

It should be recognised that it is often not the impairment itself which increases the incidence of emotional difficulties, but rather the implications of impairment in a society oriented towards those who can hear and see without impairment. While children and adolescents may have issues to bring to therapy related to their impairment, they also have the same need for therapy as other young people, and in that respect much of this entry is focused on ensuring that counselling is as accessible and inclusive as possible for those with sensory impairments.

Key Skills

1. Ensure that services, especially those offered in school, are tailored for the specific needs of visually and hearing-impaired children and adolescents. In this way the service can be easily accessed by those who feel they would benefit from counselling or who are referred by others.

    - **Hearing impairment**: With hearing-impaired clients this might mean ensuring that the environment is suitable to enable lip-reading, and that it is quiet enough to ensure that those with hearing aids are not affected by outside noise. Seating needs to be positioned or adjusted to support effective communication.

      Use visual aids such as objects, art and play materials, whiteboards as appropriate. These help engage a hearing-impaired client who might find lengthy spoken conversations challenging. Information from the National Deaf

Children's Society (NDCS) suggests clients might find lip-reading and following sign language tiring, and that therefore agreements and information should be written down to allow the client to take them away and read in their own time (see additional resources at the end of this entry) (see entry 2.5, p. 68).

- **Visual impairment**: Adjustments may need to be made to counselling spaces which allow the client to negotiate the space safely. It may be useful to describe the space to the client the first time you meet them, and invite them to ask questions regarding any information they need. Together, you can make the space as accessible as possible. Remember to keep things as consistent as possible in the room after the first session to help the client build a sense of familiarity. Let them know if anything has moved or changed place.

  Remember that non-verbal communications, especially facial expressions and body language, will not be picked up on by visually-impaired clients. Particular consideration needs to be given to building a therapeutic relationship which enables the client to experience the core relationship components through verbal expression, tone of voice, etc.

  Seating may need to be rearranged to allow closer proximity for clients who can see if they are close to the person. Again, it will be important to assess needs during the initial collaborative assessment process with the client (see entry 2.7, p. 75).
- In counselling with younger children, where play might be an appropriate therapeutic medium, a range of toys can be provided which offer tactile experiences, encouraging the client to engage with and explore objects in the context of play therapy. The Royal National Institute for the Blind (RNIB) produces a range of resources for professionals working with visually-impaired children which offer ideas on appropriate play materials and 'Treasure Boxes' that can be adapted for the play therapy context (Royal National Institute for the Blind, 2020) (see additional resources at the end of this entry).

2. Therapeutic interventions should be provided that are appropriate for the developmental needs of the client and which take the impairment into consideration. As in other areas of practice, the counsellor needs to develop their knowledge and understanding in the field of sensory impairments rather than expecting the client to provide all the information. The degree, type and duration of impairments will vary considerably from client to client. Allow them to tell you the nature of their impairment if they want to and try not to make assumptions about what it means to have an impairment without understanding as fully as possible the client's own experience in this respect.
3. As with all interventions based on an integrative approach, the client needs to be met as a unique individual as they are in the moment, and all assumptions or prejudices around what it means to have a sensory impairment need to be set aside. Many clients coming for counselling will not be concerned with issues relating to their impairment. Adjustments to the frame are made so as to be able to facilitate a therapeutic relationship within which their concerns and difficulties can be explored in the same way as is offered to children without impairments of this nature.

Summary

- Accessible counselling means ensuring that services are available for as many children and adolescents as possible, including those with sensory impairments.
- Adjustments may need to be made in order to meet the needs of this group.
- While some may want to work on issues relating to their impairment, this should not be assumed by the counsellor. An integrative approach sees the whole client, not just the disability or impairment.

Additional Resources

- MindEd – www.minded.org.uk: 430-1005 *Deaf Communication Matters*.
- National Deaf Children's Society – www.ndcs.org.uk: for information on deafness and school counselling, see: www.ndcs.org.uk/media/1633/c11120_school-based_counselling_inserts_eng_web.pdf (accessed 5 July 2020).
- Royal National Institute for the Blind (RNIB) – rnib.org.uk: for information on teaching and learning guidance, see: www.rnib.org.uk/professionals/education-professionals/teaching-and-learning-guidance (accessed 5 July 2020).
- Royal Society for Blind Children (RSBC) – rsbc.org.uk

Associated Entries

2.2 Core Relationship Components
3.3 Play-Based Interventions

3.29 Physical Disability

According to UK government figures, there are 13.9 million disabled people in the UK with 8% of UK children defined as disabled (Department for Work and Pensions, 2018). In a 2018 report, the disability equality charity SCOPE asserts: 'Disabled children must get the same opportunities to thrive as every other child. As a society we need to do more to support disabled children and their families' (Samarasinghe, 2018: 3). In this entry we consider the understandings and skills required to ensure that counselling is accessible for children with physical disabilities who might benefit from this provision.

Key Understandings

Under the UK Equality Act 2010, a physical disability is understood to mean:

> ...a physical impairment that has 'substantial' and 'long-term' negative effect on the person's ability to do normal daily activities.
>
> - 'substantial' is more than minor or trivial, e.g. it takes much longer than it usually would to complete a daily task like getting dressed
> - 'long-term' means 12 months or more, e.g. a breathing condition that develops as a result of a lung infection (Definition of disability under the Equality Act 2010, www.gov.uk (accessed 12 July 2020)).

Physical disability affects a range of functions, including mobility, dexterity and stamina. It includes disabilities which effect physical functioning, such as epilepsy, blindness, respiratory and sleep disorders. Clients may present with a range of physical disabilities with varying degrees of impact on their lives. These disabilities may have existed since or prior to birth or may be acquired through trauma or have developed during the child's or adolescent's life-span.

Disability is viewed from a range of perspectives. The most common is the medical (or biomedical) model, which takes as central the assumption that pathology is present and that disabilities are objective conditions existing in and of themselves (Smart & Smart, 2012). In contrast, the social (or socio-political) model of disability locates the 'problem' of disability in a societal requirement for disabled people to 'fit' with 'normal' able-bodied society. Smart and Smart (2012: 62) argue that the concept of disability 'is changing to a paradigm in which disability is thought to be an interaction among the individual, the disability, and the environment (both social and physical)'. By considering the lens of the social model, disability can be defined as a social construction, and therefore 'society can deconstruct disability. Stigmatization, prejudice, discrimination, inferiority and handicapism are not inevitable, natural, or unavoidable consequences of disability' (Smart & Smart, 2012: 68). With this in mind, the aim of counselling for children and adolescents with physical disabilities must be to ensure services are accessible and that the client is met as a whole person, without prejudice or assumptions regarding the client's experience of their disability.

Key Skills

1. Before beginning work with a client with a physical disability, counsellors should consider their own experience and understanding of physical disability. It is vital for all practitioners to develop an awareness of any assumptions they hold regarding physical disabilities that might interfere with their capacity to offer a therapeutic space for the client. For example, if I hold the view that it is 'a personal tragedy' (Smart & Smart, 2012) for a child to be unable to walk, how can I get alongside the client and understand the world from their perspective? Segal (1997) argues that this process cannot be done in isolation, and therefore supervision or personal therapy are useful spaces to facilitate this process.
2. The BACP Ethical Framework (2018: 15) advises counsellors to 'make adjustments to overcome barriers to accessibility, so far as is reasonably possible, for clients of any ability wishing to engage with a service'. Counsellors wishing to work with clients with physical disabilities will need to ensure premises are accessible and fitted with appropriate facilities. This might mean adjusting furniture and equipment to ensure clients can access play materials easily. By providing a space which holds the client in mind, a message is conveyed that they are welcome and that this is a space for them as much as for a client without disability.
3. Some clients with a physical disability may need to explore their experience of this in counselling. They may want to work through loss or trauma associated with their disability. Adolescent clients may need to understand how their disability will affect them as they develop into young adults. They may experience emotional issues, such as anxiety and depression (see entries 3.23, p. 225 and 3.24, p. 229), as well as issues around identity and low self-esteem (see entries 3.16, p. 199 and 3.22, p. 222). The core relationship conditions (see entry 2.2, p. 51) provide a secure base of acceptance and empathy from which to work on these or any other issues which are pertinent for the client. Segal (1997: 403) suggests that the meaning of the disability is as important as the disability itself, emphasising the importance of exploring both practical aspects experienced by the client and existential meanings, such as 'will anyone want to go out with me when I have an artificial limb?' Therapeutic interventions can be provided for children and adolescents which empower them in developing a framework for understanding themselves beyond any physical limitations they may have experienced (Vance, 2016).

4. Children and adolescents with physical disabilities may attend frequent medical appointments and have experienced traumatic interventions, such as surgical operations, since birth or early childhood. The impact these have had on attachment and early relational experiences may need to be considered as part of an ongoing collaborative assessment and formulation.
5. Family and cultural views may impact the client's self-concept as well as their understanding of the meaning of disability. Counselling which is affirmative of all clients may be useful in addressing negative impacts related to this.
6. While some clients may want to explore issues related to their disability, this may not always be the case. Counselling that is 'as near to 'normal' as possible should be offered to all children and adolescents (Segal, 1997).

Summary

- A significant number of UK children and adolescents have a physical disability of some kind. Counselling provision should recognise the needs of this group and provide appropriate services which are accessible for all.
- Clients with a physical disability may need space to explore issues related to this, but may also need to access therapy for other, unrelated issues.
- Self-concept and self-esteem can be negatively impacted by the response of others to disability. The therapeutic relationship, based on core relational components, provides an opportunity for exploring and working through impacts on the individual.

Additional Resources

- e-learning for Healthcare – https://portal.e-lfh.org.uk/: for information on the child with additional needs, see 'Long-standing Illness or Disability' (accessed 12 July 2020).
- Segal, J. (1997) 'Counselling people with disabilities/chronic illnesses', in G. McMahon & S. Palmer (eds), *Handbook of Counselling* (2nd edition). London: Routledge.
- Smart, J.F. & Smart, D.W. (2012) 'Models of disability: Implications for the counseling profession', in M.A. Stebnicki & I. Marini (eds), *The Psychological and Social Impact of Illness and Disability* (6th edition). New York: Springer.
- Vance, J. (2016) 'Who am I now? How play therapy can empower children and adolescents in their "search for self" following severe acquired brain injury', in D. Le Vay & E. Cuschieri (eds), *Challenges in the Theory and Practice of Play Therapy* (pp. 86–103). London: Routledge.

Associated Entries

1.10 Environmental & Systemic Factors
2.2 Core Relationship Components
3.31 Resilience

3.30 Chronic Illness

Chronic illness can be defined as a condition for which there is no immediate cure but which can be controlled by medication or other treatments and therapies. About 16% of children aged 0–15 years in the UK are diagnosed with a long-term medical condition (NHS Digital, 2019). This entry builds on understanding developed in the preceding entry on physical disability (see entry 3.29, p. 000) to explore the skills and knowledge required to offer effective integrative counselling for children and adolescents living with chronic health conditions.

Key Understandings

Common chronic conditions experienced by children and adolescents include asthma, eczema, diabetes, cancer, epilepsy, sickle-cell anaemia and chronic fatigue syndrome (Edwards & Titman, 2010). Conditions are generally treated by local NHS services, but rarer chronic conditions may require specialist facilities. Children with chronic conditions are likely to have had a range of experiences relating to the condition and treatment. For example, children who have undergone treatment for cancer may have had repeated operations, chemotherapy, etc., possibly requiring lengthy periods in hospital, invasive treatments, and separations from family and school, along with frequent medical appointments which disrupt 'normal life'. Treatment can involve pain and severe discomfort, which may be experienced as trauma, particularly by young children. '*Invasive medical procedures* are potential sources of trauma that inevitably become stored as emotional memories for children' (Parson, 2014: 124).

Edwards and Titman (2010: 10) state:

> Children who are cared for in terms of both their medical and psychological well-being are more likely to adjust positively to any challenges arising from their condition, enabling them to participate more fully in ordinary childhood activities and lead as normal a life as possible.

Research has found that children with chronic illness are at risk of low self-esteem (see entry 3.22, p. 222) with the lowest levels found in children with chronic fatigue and chronic headaches (Pinquart, 2012). Children and adolescents with chronic illness may experience themselves as 'different' and experience rejection or exclusion by peers, further impacting self-concept and self-esteem (Pinquart, 2012). Chronic illness often has a negative impact on educational attainment and attendance, with one study estimating that children with chronic illness miss an average of 16 days of school per year, compared with three days for a healthy child (Shaw & McCabe, 2008), although this will vary depending on the nature and severity of the illness as well as intensity of treatments. Effects are likely to be varied and complex. For example, children will miss out not only on learning in class, but also on opportunities to develop and/or maintain friendships and gain important skills in social and emotional functioning (Layte & McCrory, 2012). Given the likely impact of these factors on healthy development, counselling has an important role to play in ensuring the psychological and emotional needs of young people with chronic conditions are met.

Key Skills

1. As with all the disabilities and conditions explored in Part III of this book, the primary skill is to provide a therapeutic relationship based on the core conditions and to meet the client as a whole person, rather than as a diagnosis or condition. Children and adolescents who have undergone frequent medical interventions may lack a sense of themselves beyond their illness. They may react to this negatively and become non-compliant with important aspects of treatment if their psychological and emotional needs are not recognised and responded to appropriately.
2. Counselling provides an opportunity to support the client in 'coming to terms' with their condition and what it means to and for them at whichever developmental stage they have reached. Counselling is also a space for the client to explore their understanding and relationship to their condition as well as treatment, past and current. The integrative approach emphasised so far is well placed to provide a space for this exploration and understanding of the client's fears or ambivalence regarding treatment. The counsellor needs to make it clear they are not able to advise the client on treatment, but can offer a space, where appropriate, for them to explore any fears, anxieties or difficult feelings, such as shame or embarrassment, they may experience.
3. Counselling for children and adolescents with chronic illness may need to be flexible to adapt to the needs of the client. Every effort should be made to provide a consistent frame to offer a secure base for the therapy to build on. However, where clients are unable to attend sessions due to health issues or medical appointments, allowance will need to made for this in the therapeutic frame. Parson (2014: 128) suggests using Bronfenbrenner's (1979) ecological systems model (see entry 1.10, p. 37) to identify elements in the client's environment which support reducing stress in the child and in exploring different places therapy could be offered within the client's world for the most positive impact on their wellbeing.
4. Working with clients with chronic illness is likely to require counsellors to engage with other professionals and the client's family in order to support the wellbeing of the child (see entries 2.12, p. 97 and 2.22, p. 131). The parents of children and adolescents with chronic illness may themselves experience secondary trauma when accompanying their children through difficult procedures, and require therapeutic and other support to help them manage this difficult experience.

5. Some children and adolescents will experience illness which becomes terminal at some stage. Children and young people's need of psychological and emotional support is increasingly recognised as an important aspect of palliative and end-of-life care (Edwards & Titman, 2010). Counsellors providing support in this complex area of practice will need to be prepared to work with the client in responding to their needs for emotional support in a developmentally appropriate way, in conjunction with family members and other professionals. Siblings of a dying child are also likely to benefit from therapeutic intervention, along with parents and other family members. Counsellors working in this area will need to find appropriate support networks, including clinical supervision, in order to be mindful of their own needs for support and self-care.

Summary

- Like physical disability, chronic illness effects many children and adolescents. Their capacity to cope with its effects is likely to be improved by effective therapeutic intervention.
- The core relationship components provide a frame for the exploration of experiences related to illness and treatment.
- The therapeutic frame and contract may require adaptation to meet the needs of clients with chronic illness.

Additional Resources

- Edwards, M. & Titman, P. (2010) 'Palliative care and bereavement', in M. Edwards & P. Titman, *Promoting Psychological Well-Being in Children with Acute and Chronic Illness*. London: Jessica Kingsley.
- Parson, J.A. (2014) 'Holistic mental health care and play therapy for hospitalized, chronically ill children', in E.J. Green & A.C. Myrick (eds), *Play Therapy with Vulnerable Populations: No Child Forgotten*. Boulder, CO: Rowman & Littlefield.

Associated Entries

2.12 Working with Parents/Carers
2.22 Working with Other Professionals
3.18 Bullying
3.22 Self-Esteem
3.23 Anxiety
3.24 Depression

3.31 Resilience

In recent decades, resilience is an area which has sparked interest among those working with children and adolescents (Masten, 2018). Throughout this book we have considered issues that impact children's development, quality of life and sense of self. In this entry we consider what part resilience might play in development and how counselling can be used to identify and develop resilience in children and adolescents.

Key Understandings

The scientific study of resilience began in the 1970s and has continued to develop ever since. Masten (2001) describes resilience as '[p]ositive adaptation to adversity despite serious threats to adaptation or development', going on to suggest:

> Resilience does not come from rare and special qualities, but from the everyday magic of ordinary, normative human resources in the minds, brains and bodies of children, in their families and in their communities. ... The task before us now is to delineate how adaptive systems develop, how they operate under diverse conditions, how they work for or against success for a given child in his or her environmental and developmental context, and how they can be protected, restored, facilitated, and nurtured in the lives of children. (Masten, 2001: 235)

Key Skills

1. The integrative approach to counselling outlined in this book is based on the centrality of a therapeutic relationship that is intended to facilitate the development of a stable and positive self-concept in clients. In this way the approach is intended to identify resilience factors and aid their development. Understanding how adverse experiences affect development and which aspects of a client's environment may increase the likelihood of further adverse experiences is an important starting point in understanding resilience in the context of an individual child or family.
2. Hart et al. (2012) have developed a *Resilience Framework* as part of their *Resilient Therapy* (Hart et al., 2007) approach to working therapeutically and supporting the development of resilience in disadvantaged children and families. Their model is based on 'Four Noble Truths' of resilience:

> Working with these Noble Truths involves developing the skills of *Accepting* the precise starting point of children/families, *Conserving* any good that has occurred hitherto,

Commitment to working with them over a sensible time period and thoughtfully *Enlisting* appropriate others to help. (Hart et al., 2007: 2, original emphasis)

The framework (Hart et al., 2012) focuses on aspects of functioning, including building relationships, coping, and the core self, as areas where clients can be supported in developing resilience through therapeutic interventions.

3. Some clients may not experience themselves as resilient. In this respect, the therapeutic process can offer opportunities for children and young people to develop a sense of their resilience in terms of challenges they have coped with and the skills they may have developed along the way.
4. Resilience is also an important quality for counsellors to identify and develop in themselves. Use the following exercise to identify your own experience of resilience and to consider ways of developing this further.

Exercise

Think of a challenging experience in your life that you consider you coped well with.

- What were the circumstances? What happened? Who was with you?
- What helped you to cope? Write down as many factors as you can think of. These could be historical factors from your past or things in the here and now that helped you.
- Which of these factors would you associate with resilience? Are they factors that can be cultivated and strengthened?

Consider what you can take from your discoveries into your therapeutic practice.

Repeat this exercise as many times as you like for different experiences as you develop your own resilience map.

Summary

- Resilience is an important concept for those working with vulnerable children and adolescents.
- Counselling can assist children to identify resilience factors that may help them to cope with future difficulties.
- Counsellors and therapists also need resilience to cope with the demands of this challenging profession. Understanding our own resilience factors and how to develop them can support ongoing practice.

Additional Resources

- Boingboing – www.boingboing.org.uk: organisation researching and promoting resilience for disadvantaged children and families. The website offers lots of downloadable resources for therapists working in this area: www.boingboing.org.uk/resilience/resilient-therapy-resilience-framework/ (accessed 19 July 2020).

Associated Entries

2.23 Self-Care for Counsellors
3.14 Trauma & Abuse
3.22 Self-Esteem
4.7 Refugee Communities
4.8 Looked-After Children (LAC)

Part IV

Key Considerations: Contexts & Client Groups

4.1 Introduction: Considerations & Contexts

In Part IV we begin to explore the application of the integrative approach to a range of groups and contexts. Returning to the analogy described in the Introduction of the tree-pose in yoga, we might see these entries as the environments in which our tree will grow. How does this dynamic 'tree' grow in an educational or CAMHS setting? What are the considerations for the approach in work with looked-after or refugee community children? How does the shape of the tree change when applied to working online with children and young people?

These are some of the contexts and groups considered in this part of the book. In each entry we consider the key understandings required to develop appropriate services and interventions, as well as the skills needed to deliver them. This is by no means an exhaustive list of all contexts and groups to which this approach can be applied, although hopefully the aspects considered in these entries can be adapted and applied to work elsewhere.

These entries all connect to those in previous parts of the book, but primarily to those which explore aspects of the therapeutic relationship as well as those related to the understanding of child and adolescent development and the ecological systems within which this occurs.

4.2 Educational Settings

Since the 1970s, educational settings in the UK have provided a natural 'home' for the provision of counselling to young people (Pearce et al., 2018b). School is universally accessible up to the age of 18 years and therefore counselling services, where there is provision in school, should be accessible by all who attend. Many counsellors working with children and adolescents practise in educational settings at some point in their career and perhaps for its entirety. In this entry we explore some of the important understandings and skills required for this area of practice.

Key Understandings

While providing counselling in educational settings makes sense from the point of view of broad accessibility, this does not mean the relationship between counselling and education is a straightforward one, or that practice in this context is easy. Across the UK there are considerable variations in how counselling is provided in schools, including whether counselling provision is government policy or something individual schools 'buy' into (Pearce et al., 2018b). The UK government's *Taskforce on Mental Health in Society* has recommended:

> All children should be able to access professional, qualified counselling and therapy services in their school or college in an age-appropriate form. The government should set out a strategy to achieve this, with schools, local authorities and the NHS working together to deliver it. (Department of Health, 2015: 10)

While school counselling has for some time been provided by the Welsh and Northern Ireland governments as part of statutory provision and is now funded by the Scottish government, Parliament has yet to support the provision of counselling in schools in England, despite strong evidence for its effectiveness (McArthur et al., 2013; Pearce et al., 2018b; Stafford et al., 2018).

When working therapeutically in an educational setting, it's important to understand the role of therapeutic interventions in a context which is primarily organised around education and academic attainment. While universal access is a compelling reason to offer counselling in school or college, counselling places emotional and psychological needs of the individual over the need for academic achievement, and this can be counter to contemporary educational priorities. Complex dynamics between learning and emotional wellbeing play out in various aspects of the provision of counselling: for example, in the referral process, when a teacher identifies that a child's anxiety is interfering with his capacity to focus in class, or when an A-level student's exam-phobia threatens to derail them in the lead up to public exams. These pupils might be referred because an explicit threat to their educational achievement is viewed as having a psychological or emotional cause. If a therapeutic relationship can be developed, then they may be able to use the counselling process to understand these difficulties and work through them, enabling them to access educational opportunities more effectively. Some referrals, however, may be made on the basis of wanting a child to be 'fixed' by counselling so they behave better in class or achieve the high grades expected by parents or teachers. School counsellors may at times feel under considerable pressure to prioritise the goals of teachers or parents rather than those of most benefit to the client. However, since counselling is rooted in ethical principles (see entry 2.20, p. 124) as well as the core relationship components (see entry 2.2, p. 51), these must be the primary concerns for the counsellor working with any client in school. This demonstrates the importance of developing an approach that is firmly grounded in the ethical and theoretical principles of practice and is strengthened by returning to these regularly through reading, supervision, peer support and CPD activities.

Key Skills

1. Get a sense of the school 'culture'. Find out how counselling is viewed by the Head and other staff. Many teachers value the contribution of a counsellor to the school, but some may be less open, and even envious or suspicious of a school counsellor. Depending on how well a counselling service is integrated into the functioning of the whole school, it may be useful to offer workshops to staff on how counselling works, providing information on how they might benefit from having the support of a counsellor in school.
2. Ensure practicalities are in place before beginning to work with students. This might mean ensuring that a suitable location has been identified. The therapy space should be a sound-proof room where sessions will not be disturbed. There should be space for art and play materials to be used and stored safely, and where confidential materials will not be accessed by other staff or students.
3. Make sure you have established a frame for provision of counselling which is well integrated in the school system as a whole. These require identifying protocols for getting clients to their sessions in a way which is as respectful of their need for as much confidentiality as possible.
4. Ensure services are accessible to as many students as possible. Consider ways of promoting services within school that communicate to all students that this is a service for them. It might mean providing information about the service in languages other than English which are spoken in the school community, and using images on promotional materials which promote diversity and accessibility. Counselling spaces

in schools need to be accessible for clients with disabilities (see entries 3.28, p. 247 and 3.29, p. 250).

5. Working as a school counsellor can be isolating. It can be difficult to form relationships with a range of school staff when counsellors work in school perhaps as little as half-a-day a week. Even where relationships in school are formed, it's also important to connect with other school counsellors. Where counselling provision comes under the umbrella of larger counselling providers, it may be easier to develop connections with others. Where this is not the case, building a network of peers can provide much needed support for the challenges of counselling in school as well as opportunities for sharing good practice and other resources.

Additional Resources

- Kirkbride, R. (2018a) 'Educational settings', in R. Kirkbride, *Counselling Young People: A Practitioner Manual*. London: Sage.
- Stafford, M.R., Cooper, M., Barkham, M., Beecham, J., Bower, P., Cromarty, K., Fugard, A.J.B., Jackson, C., Pearce, P., Ryder, R. & Street, C. (2018) 'Effectiveness and cost-effectiveness of humanistic counselling in schools for young people with emotional distress (ETHOS): Study protocol for a randomised control trial', *Trials*, 19: 175.

Associated Entries

1.11 Developmental Implications for Counselling
2.2 Core Relationship Components
2.11 Cultural Competence
2.20 Ethical Issues
2.22 Working with Other Professionals
3.9 Groups
3.18 Bullying
3.27 Special Educational Needs & Disability (SEND)

4.3 Private Practice

Given the challenges of providing counselling through educational and NHS services for all who need it, inevitably some families will want to access private counselling services for their children. In this entry we consider the key understandings and skills required to offer effective, ethical counselling for children and adolescents in private practice.

Key Understandings

Counselling young clients in private practice is more complex than work with adults in the same context. Primarily this is because the child or young person themselves does not have the same degree of independence as an adult and there is likely to be a need for a relationship to be established with a parent or carer as well as the relationship with the client themselves (see entry 2.12, p. 97). Managing these relationships in order that confidentiality and the primacy of the client's needs are maintained at all times takes a great degree of skill and preparation on the part of the counsellor. Children are not able to refer themselves for counselling in private practice without the knowledge or consent of their parents, unlike in an educational setting where this may be possible for some. It can be tricky to establish what a client's goals are for therapy if they have been referred by a concerned parent who has strong desires for the outcome of their child's counselling sessions and is paying a fee for this provision. As in school counselling (see entry 4.2, p. 264), it is vital to maintain a sense of the ethical basis for counselling as well as the core relationship components when establishing the therapeutic relationship at the outset of the work.

Key Skills

1. Develop a clear process for referral and assessment. This should be flexible enough to respond to the developmental level of any client. For example, the process for under-10s may need to consist of interviews with parent/s to gather information on the referral as well as joint assessment sessions with parent/s in addition to any with the child on their own. With older clients this process can be adapted according to the needs and capabilities of individual clients. It's important to establish a sense of what information is needed prior to work beginning, and then what is the best way of gaining this information (Kirkbride, 2016a). With adolescent clients it may

be sufficient to gather information from parents over the phone. Older adolescents, who have a reasonably clear sense of why they are coming for therapy and what they hope to achieve, may not need to come with a parent, unless this is helpful for the initial consultation. With these clients, the work can continue as it would with an adult client, although a relationship with the parent will need to be maintained to facilitate the payment of fees and practicalities such as getting the client to sessions, communicating as needed regarding breaks, etc.

2. Develop appropriate contracts for work with children and adolescents as well as parents. The clearer these contracts are, the easier it is for everyone to understand their role in the counselling process. For example, contracting with the client may consist of an information sheet, written in developmentally appropriate language, outlining important aspects of the relationship, such as confidentiality and when this might be broken (see entry 2.5, p. 68). For parents/carers, contracting is an opportunity to discuss the confidentiality of their child's counselling and how important it is to respect this. Parents are naturally curious about their child's activities and may need reminding that it is not appropriate to ask your child how their session was as soon as they get in the car afterwards. Most parents respect this boundary if it is explained in an appropriate way that also offers information on the safeguarding process and how they will be informed of any concerns around risk.
3. Make boundaries clear at the start of counselling so the client understands you are there to support them and they can trust you. If you break boundaries by discussing things with parents without the client's knowledge, this will damage trust and is a breach of the ethical principles underlying counselling for all clients (see entries 2.5, p. 68 and 2.9, p. 84).
4. Make sure the space where you see clients is appropriate for the kind of work you will be doing. For example, if you are planning to work with younger children, you will need a consulting room which is appropriate for use of play and art materials (Kirkbride, 2016b).
5. Private practice involves managing relationships with both client and parent/s. It's important for counsellors to find a clinical supervisor who understands these complex dynamics and is able to offer support working in this area. Peer support can also be helpful and counsellors may want to work alongside others in developing their private practice in order to reduce isolation and share ideas and resources for good practice.

Additional Resources

- Kirkbride, R. (2016a) *Counselling Children and Young People in Private Practice: A Practical Guide*. London: Routledge.

Associated Entries

2.9 Confidentiality & Consent
2.11 Cultural Competence
2.12 Working with Parents/Carers
2.24 Clinical Supervision
3.29 Physical Disability

4.4 Child & Adolescent Mental Health Services (CAMHS)

In the UK, the Child and Adolescent Mental Health Service (CAMHS) (aka Children and Young People's Mental Health Service [CYPMHS]) is part of NHS provision, supporting the mental health needs of children and young people (CYP). CAMHS is provided by a range of professionals, including nurses, doctors, psychologists, psychiatrists, therapists, etc. In this entry we consider briefly some of the key understandings for counsellors working with or in CAMHS as well as some of the skills required to do this successfully.

Key Understandings

'Comprehensive' CAMHS refers to all services for CYP which have a role in mental health and wellbeing. This includes school nurses, GPs, etc., who support children's general wellbeing.

'Specialist' CAMHS refers to services which are for clients with more severe, long-lasting or complex mental health issues. This might include eating disorder services, early intervention for psychosis teams, etc.

Each NHS authority has their own CAMHS provision and the form it takes varies between authorities. All CAMHS operate a 'tier' system (Department for Education, 2004) which allows service users to be directed to the right service for them. The tiers are:

Tier 1: Services in 'comprehensive' CAMHS, provided by practitioners who are not necessarily mental health specialists but who support and promote emotional and psychological wellbeing and resilience in CYP. It is a primary level of care.

Tier 2: A service provided by specialist individual professionals relating to workers in primary care. Counselling is often viewed as a tier 2 intervention.

Tier 3: A specialised multidisciplinary service for more severe, complex or persistent disorders. Services may be provided by psychiatrists, social workers, psychotherapists, community psychiatric nurses, etc.

Tier 4: Essential tertiary level services, such as day units, highly specialised outpatient teams and inpatient units (Department for Education, 2004).

As well as the tier structure for provision, CAMHS are also categorised according to those they work with, that is, Universal (for all CYP), Targeted (community-based early interventions for vulnerable CYP), Specialist (for those CYP with more complex and long-term needs), and Highly Specialist (for those CYP with severe or complex difficulties requiring specialist support).

In terms of equality of provision, the National Service Framework states:

> Services for children and young people should be provided irrespective of their gender, race, religion, ability, culture or sexuality. This standard emphasises the importance of improving access to CAMHS to ensure greater equity is achieved. (Department for Education, 2004: 8)

Key Skills

1. Working with or within CAMHS means working closely with other professionals (see entry 2.22, p. 131). Research looking into the relationship between CAMHS and counselling suggests this is aided by mutual knowledge and understanding of the services each party provides, mutual respect for differences in working practices, and good communication and contact between services (Spong et al., 2013).
2. Working as a counsellor within CAMHS may mean working within particular parameters. For example, there is often a focus on assessment and evidence-based provision and the use of approaches supported by National Institute for Health and Care Excellence (NICE) guidelines, such as cognitive-behavioural therapy (CBT) (see entry 3.6, p. 158), family therapy and medication. Counselling may involve the use of goals and measures and be offered in a strictly time-limited form. This can require the development of a different skill-set from less directive therapeutic work with CYP.
3. Making a referral to CAMHS should be done on the basis of a clear understanding of referral criteria. The more knowledge practitioners have about services provided by CAMHS and how these differ from and are related to those provided by counselling, the more straightforward this referral process will be. Most specialist CAMHS services operate a service for phone consultations regarding potential referrals.
4. Get a sense of CAMHS provision in your area or authority and how referral systems work. You might like to complete the exercise below to help with this. As services and systems change and develop, it is important to keep your knowledge up to date. This will help when supporting a client who has been referred to CAMHS.

Exercise: Mapping Local CAMHS Provision

- Do some research to map out CAMHS provision in your locality, or that of your client group if these are different.
- What universal services are there?
- What tier 2 services operate and how can these be accessed?
- Is counselling part of CAMHS provision?
- How are school- and community-based counselling services integrated with CAMHS?
- Does CAMHS in your area provide a consultation service for professionals looking for advice about potential referrals and information on who can refer to CAMHS?

Additional Resources

- MindEd – www.minded.org.uk: 412-011 *Counselling and Specialist CAMHS.*
- Department for Education (2004) *National Service Framework for Children, Young People and Maternity Services: The Mental Health and Psychological Well-Being of Children and Young People.* London: HMSO.
- Spong, S., Waters, R., Dowd, C. & Jackson, C. (2013) *Scoping Report: The Relationship between Specialist Child and Adolescent Mental Health Services (CAMHS) and School- and Community-based Counselling for Children and Young People.* Lutterworth: British Association for Counselling and Psychotherapy.

Associated Entries

2.7 Assessment & Integrative Formulations
2.10 Outcome & Process Measures
2.12 Working with Parents/Carers
2.22 Working with Other Professionals
3.6 Cognitive-Behavioural Therapy (CBT)
3.10 Working with Risk
3.25 Diagnosis, Medication and Psychiatric Presentations
3.26 Neurodiversity: Autism Spectrum Disorder (ASD) & Attention-Deficit Hyperactivity Disorder (ADHD)

4.5 Voluntary & Community Sector (VCS) Counselling Services

Voluntary and community counselling services for children and adolescents have a long and vibrant history in the UK. The voluntary and community sector (VCS) exists within the 'third sector' of services, outside statutory and private sector services. In spite of struggles to maintain funding, the VCS offers a huge variety of provision to clients who find it easier to access services provided in this way, rather than through educational settings or CAMHS. In this entry we consider some of the knowledge and skills required to work as a counsellor within the VCS.

Key Understandings

Counselling has been provided by VCS agencies over several decades (Kirkbride, 2016a). Estimates suggest that approximately 400 community-based, VCS-provided counselling services for children, young people and young adults currently operate across England (Street, 2013a). These services vary in size and in terms of how they are staffed. Many benefit from providing voluntary placements for trainee counsellors or those looking to gain experience in this area. A typical service might consist of a paid counselling coordinator, two paid counsellors providing assessments and supervision, and six to eight volunteer counsellors. VCS counsellors provide interventions from a range of modalities, including humanistic, psychodynamic, CBT and integrative. Some organisations may focus on one modality, while others may offer a range of approaches.

Services are provided to a range of client groups and may focus on a particular age range, such as 5–12 years or 14–25 years, or group of clients, such as those from the LGBTQ community. Youth Information, Advice and Counselling Services (YIACS) offer provision spanning adolescence and young adulthood, thus avoiding the 'cut-off' point experienced by clients using school counselling and CAMHS. YIACS offer services alongside counselling for young people, such as sexual health advice, housing and employment support. Individual services are tailored to meet the needs of a particular community so as to be accessible and welcoming for all in the community. For example, a service in a community where many languages are spoken in addition to English might offer leaflets and information in different languages.

VCS organisations work alongside CAMHS, the NHS and other agencies providing support for children and young people.

Key Skills

1. Counsellors working in VCS need to be proficient using outcome and process measures (see entry 2.10, p. 89). An important part of VCS provision is proving to stakeholders that services offered are appropriate and effective for the young people they are serving. Collecting data regarding the kinds of issues young people bring to counselling and the outcome of interventions allows agencies to demonstrate their efficacy in order to continue to receive the necessary funding. It is also vital that VCS services gather feedback from young people and their families regarding the services offered in order to ensure that these are effectively meeting their needs.
2. Young people accessing VCS counselling may be initially uncertain that they can trust counsellors or that counselling will be helpful for them. With this in mind, counsellors need to develop their rapport-building skills (see entry 2.4, p. 63) in order to be able to engage with clients from a variety of backgrounds and with differing presenting issues and needs.
3. Due to funding, VCS counselling may be time-limited so that services are available to as many young people as possible. Counsellors will therefore need to be able to offer brief therapeutic interventions as well as refer clients on to other services as necessary.
4. Skills in communicating with other professionals are important for practitioners working within VCS. This may include colleagues within YIACS services where clients might benefit from services in addition to counselling, such as housing and employment advice. It might also involve working with other agencies, such as youth offending teams or addiction services. Counsellors need to be able to refer on as needed while ensuring that information is shared appropriately and that the client's voice is respected throughout (see entry 2.22, p. 131).

Additional Resources

- MindEd – www.minded.org.uk: 412-008 *Counselling in the Community.*
- Youth Access – www.youthaccess.org.uk: Youth Access is the advice and counselling network supporting the provision of counselling services in the community to all young people.
- Street, C. (2013a) *Voluntary and Community sector (VCS) Counselling Provision for Children, Young People and Young Adults in England.* Lutterworth: British Association for Counselling and Psychotherapy/MindEd. Available at: www.bacp.co.uk/media/2051/counselling-minded-online-counselling-provision-children-young-people-street.pdf (last accessed 29 July 2020).

Associated Entries

2.4 Building Rapport
2.8 Risk Assessment & Safeguarding
2.10 Outcome & Process Measures
2.11 Cultural Competence
2.22 Working with Other Professionals

4.6 Online Counselling

Over the past 15 years, provision of online counselling services for children and adolescents has become a growing sector, often driven by the voluntary and community sector (VCS) (Street, 2013a). This growth has occurred alongside rapid developments in online, mobile phone and broadband technology, leading to an interesting phenomenon wherein methods of delivering counselling online may become obsolete as the technology they are based on itself goes through various transformations. The COVID-19 pandemic, when physical face-to-face counselling was not possible, led to a rapid acceleration in the provision of online therapy (Brown, 2020). This has the potential to profoundly change future delivery of counselling services for children and adolescents. In this entry we consider some of the key understandings for online counselling as well as the skills required to deliver it successfully.

Key Understandings

Prior to the COVID-19 pandemic when growth in the area increased rapidly, online counselling services for children and young people (CYP) represented a small but growing sector of provision (Street, 2013b).

Before offering online counselling services, practitioners need to have considered the various ethical, therapeutic and legal implications, and be confident they can provide services which will be of benefit to their clients. The BACP's recommendation is that child and adolescent counsellors refer to BACP adult competences for online and telephone work (see additional resources section) and, in addition, 'undertake appropriate training, linking this with the additional neurodevelopmental, psychological and legal knowledge required for working with this age group' (BACP, 2021).

There are currently two main forms of online counselling for young people, although there is potential for these to be extended in the future by other technologies, such as artificial intelligence (AI):

1. Face-to-face therapy carried out via video conferencing software such as Skype, Zoom or mobile phone-based services such as FaceTime. Some services also offer platforms which are designed specifically for therapy.
2. Text-based services/email counselling/synchronous chat-room counselling.

There are clear strengths and advantages of online counselling provision as well as disadvantages. Strengths include:

- Flexible provision that can be made widely available, including at times outside 'normal' school or working hours.
- Clients are able to access services from home, which may be useful for those with illnesses, disabilities or caring responsibilities which prevent them from accessing services in the community. This might also be beneficial for CYP in rural communities who don't find it easy to attend regular face-to-face sessions.
- Some young people find it easier to open up when working online (Hanley, 2012). There is an identified disinhibitory factor to online communications (Suler, 2005) which can profoundly affect how young people communicate online in their counselling sessions and this must be actively understood and managed as part of the therapeutic process (Hanley, 2012).

Disadvantages include:

- CYP may find it difficult to have privacy for their session when at home. They may find it more difficult to discuss their issues when parents and siblings are around.
- It may be more difficult for counsellors to pick up on body language or other non-verbal aspects of presentation.
- Play and creative-arts interventions are not easy to provide or facilitate online, which may make online work with younger children more of a challenge than with older clients.
- Online counselling is dependent on clients having access to appropriate technology and connectivity, such as 'high-speed' broadband. While online counselling does extend accessibility for some, it can also highlight existing societal inequalities between those with access to technology and those without.

Another consideration for online counselling is that of the therapeutic relationship. As discussed throughout this book, this is viewed as the main engine of the therapeutic change process. Hanley (2012: 36), in identifying the potential for young people to access support via the internet, suggests that '[a] major question revolves around the ability of counsellors to establish relationships of a sufficient quality to create psychological change online'. Online counsellors working in either text format or face to face need to consider how they will develop rapport with clients and work with ruptures or miscommunications in the relationship.

Further considerations include consent, confidentiality and the legal aspects of working therapeutically online. The Information Commissioner's Office (ICO) has produced guidelines regarding children and data protection (see additional resources below). Counsellors need to consider whether they need parental consent to work with a young person online, and how they will ensure their practice meets requirements for encryption, the confidentiality of data and safeguarding.

Key Skills

1. Before beginning online counselling, counsellors should work with their clinical supervisor, line manager or service manager and/or trainers to ensure they have a frame and contract for online work which is safe, ethical and based in sound therapeutic practice (see additional resources for this entry). This will need to be adapted for work with clients of different ages and developmental capacity. The BACP's Ethical Framework (2018) states that practitioners must not work beyond the limits of their capabilities, and this includes beginning online work without adequate training, preparation and supervisory support.
2. At the outset of the work, 'etiquette' for sessions will need to be established. This should include a discussion of what is and isn't acceptable in the counselling process. For example, it may be important to establish guidelines regarding where the client is when they have their session. Are you happy for them to have a video session on their phone while they shop for clothes? With older children and adolescents, this discussion can be developed collaboratively and offers an opportunity to think through together how to get the most benefit from online sessions.
3. Before working online, develop confidence and patience with technology. Counsellors need to be confident using the software and applications for online counselling and aware of considerations such as encryption and record-keeping. Counsellors using video platforms and other services will need to be able to advise their clients regarding the system and broadband requirements for accessing their sessions. Patience is required to contain and manage the inevitable problems connecting and interruptions to the session due to technological issues.
4. Counsellors need to work with supervisors and service managers to develop rigorous protocols regarding safeguarding when working online. With young children, information should be discussed with parents and carers and shared in a developmentally appropriate way with the client. With older clients there should be a clear agreement regarding the limits of safeguarding in an online setting and how safeguarding concerns will be managed. When working online as part of school or agency counselling, there should be a designated safeguarding lead to discuss concerns with before taking appropriate action.
5. Counsellors need to develop their understanding of how the therapeutic relationship works online, including transference and countertransference implications and how to build rapport and manage rupture and repair.

Additional Resources

- MindEd – www.minded.org.uk: 412-009 *Counselling and its Contexts: Counselling Online.*
- BACP resources for working with children and young people online: *Competences for Telephone and e-Counselling*. Available at: www.bacp.co.uk/media/8113/bacp-competences-for-telephone-ecounselling-apr20.pdf (last accessed 30 July 2020).
- *Working Online with Children and Young People: Guidance for Members*. Available at: www.bacp.co.uk/news/news-from-bacp/coronavirus/working-online-with-cyp-faqs/ (accessed 30 July 2020).
- Information Commissioner's Office (ICO) guidelines on children and data protection: https://ico.org.uk/for-organisations/guide-to-data-protection/key-data-protection-themes/children/ (last accessed 30 July 2020).
- NSPCC – nspcc.org.uk: the website provides guidelines for teachers on safeguarding when working online. See https://learning.nspcc.org.uk/news/2020/march/undertaking-remote-teaching-safely (accessed 30 July 2020).
- Online Therapy Institute – www.onlinetherapyinstitute.com: regularly updated guidance and training for working therapeutically online, including their *Ethical Framework for the Use of Technology in Mental Health*: www.onlinetherapyinstitute.com/ethical-training/ (accessed 30 July 2020).
- Street, C. (2013b) *Online Counselling for Children, Young People and Young Adults*. Lutterworth: British Association for Counselling and Psychotherapy/ MindEd.
- BACP resources for children, young people and families in the COVID-19 pandemic (June 2020): *Counselling CYP in the Time of Coronavirus*. Available at: www.bacp.co.uk/bacp-journals/bacp-children-young-people-and-families-journal/june-2020/counselling-cyp-in-the-time-of-coronavirus/ (accessed 30 July 2020).

Associated Entries

2.2 Core Relationship Components
2.4 Building Rapport
2.5 Contracting
2.8 Risk Assessment & Safeguarding
2.13 Record-Keeping and Data Protection
2.15 Managing Ruptures in the Therapeutic Alliance
2.16 Transference & Countertransference
2.21 Self-Disclosure

4.7 Refugee Communities

The UK is currently home to over 120,000 refugees and recent UK government statistics suggest that in the 12 months up to March 2020 there were 3,463 applications from unaccompanied children, 69% of whom were granted asylum (Office for National Statistics, 2020). Over recent years there has been increasing concern regarding the mental health of children from refugee and asylum-seeking communities. Many of them have experienced not only the loss of their home and sense of secure belonging to a community, they may also have suffered profound loss and trauma both at home and on their migratory journey (Warr, 2010). In this entry we consider the key understandings for counselling children and adolescents from refugee communities as well as the skills required to work in this context.

Key Understandings

According to The Children's Society:

> A refugee is a person who is fleeing armed conflict or persecution in their homeland or country of residence. In order for someone to be considered a refugee due to persecution, they must have been persecuted because of their religion, race, nationality, social group or political opinion.
>
> An asylum seeker is someone who has applied for refugee status, but their case hasn't been evaluated. (www.childrenssociety.org.uk/what-we-do/our-work/refugee-and-migrant-children/facts-about-child-refugees, accessed 30 July 2020)

The impact of the refugee journey and resettlement on both families and individuals is complex, and exploring this in comprehensive detail is beyond the scope of this book. However, research suggests that psychological distress is prevalent among refugee children, with diagnoses of post-traumatic stress disorder (PTSD), anxiety disorders and depression commonly found among this population (Henley & Robinson, 2011). This research also found an 'elevated need for psychological services among child refugees' as well as evidence for the effectiveness of therapy with this group when therapy was 'adapted sensitively' (Henley & Robinson, 2011: 51).

Key Skills

1. Children and adolescents who have sought asylum in the UK are likely to be living in conditions of uncertainty and insecurity, whether they have come to the UK alone or accompanied by family members. Given our understanding of the fundamental need for security experienced by all human beings, attending to this lack of security is likely to be a primary task for any kind of psychological and emotional support provided for this group. This might mean addressing issues such as food, safety and housing prior to beginning therapeutic interventions.
2. Given their experiences prior to coming for counselling, clients from refugee communities may struggle to form trusting therapeutic relationships. It is important to be aware of this and to allow trust to develop over time. Van der Veer and Van Waning (2004) describe the process of creating a 'safe therapeutic sanctuary' for asylum seekers and refugees.
3. Cultural competence (see entry 2.11, p. 93) is a vital skill for counsellors working with refugee children. Interventions should be provided using methods which are respectful of the culture of the client and without imposing 'Eurocentric' values or ideals on the therapeutic work (Warr, 2010).
4. Play-based, creative arts and interventions which work with symbol and metaphor may be useful in work with traumatised refugee children (Warr, 2010) (see entries 3.2, p. 144, 3.3, p. 147 and 3.4, p. 151). These allow engagement with difficult material with objective distance at a pace determined and controlled by the client, enabling exploration of potentially traumatic material without it becoming overwhelming.
5. It may be necessary with some children and families to use an interpreter in order to communicate effectively with the client or with their parents. The BACP's (2019) Competence Framework provides guidance to counsellors on considerations for working with an interpreter. It is important also to consider the effect of an interpreter on the therapeutic alliance in work with refugee children and families (Miller et al., 2005).
6. Counsellors working with children from this community need to practise self-care in order to ensure they can continue to hear and engage with the client in challenging material without themselves experiencing secondary trauma (see entry 2.23, p. 134).

Additional Resources

- MindEd – www.minded.org.uk: 410-043 *Vulnerable Groups – An Overview*.
- Rutter, J. (2006) *Refugee Children in the UK*. London: McGraw-Hill Education.
- The Children's Society – www.childrenssociety.org.uk: for resources supporting young refugees and migrants, see: www.childrenssociety.org.uk/what-we-do/our-work/refugee-and-migrant-children/services-supporting-young-refugees-and-migrants (accessed 30 July 2020).
- The Refugee Council – www.refugeecouncil.org.uk: for resources supporting young refugees and migrants, see: www.refugeecouncil.org.uk/our-work/mental-health-support-for-refugees-and-asylum-seekers/ (accessed 30 July 2020).

Associated Entries

2.2 Core Relationship Components
2.4 Building Rapport
2.11 Cultural Competence
2.22 Working with Other Professionals
2.23 Self-Care for Counsellors
3.2 Symbol & Metaphor
3.14 Trauma & Abuse
3.16 Identity
3.21 Bereavement & Loss
3.31 Resilience

4.8 Looked-After Children (LAC)

UK government statistics suggest there are approximately 80,000 'looked-after' children (LAC) in the UK, a number which has increased every year since 2010 (Department for Education, 2020. 'Looked-after' means children who are the responsibility of the local authority. Around 60% of children in care are looked-after due to abuse and neglect, and are four times more likely to suffer mental health issues than those not in care (Smith et al., 2018). In this entry we consider some of the key understandings and skills necessary for effective therapy with this often-vulnerable group of children and young people.

Key Understandings

The experiences of looked-after children are complex and unique to each individual. Prior to being removed from the care of their family, children may have experienced varying degrees of abuse, trauma and neglect as well as experienced parenting which has not met fundamental developmental needs. As a result, LAC may manifest emotional, psychological and behavioural issues related to traumatic or inadequate early relational experiences. LAC may have significant difficulties with attachment and affect-regulation. They may have witnessed domestic violence or have had parents who were emotionally and physically unavailable due to issues such as addiction or severe mental health difficulties.

Once removed from their family, a child or adolescent in the care system may experience frequent changes of placement and carers. They may be placed separately from siblings, adding to their experiences of separation, loss and instability. Our understanding of the importance of attunement and secure attachment in development informs an awareness of the likely cumulative negative impact on the child's wellbeing and growth (see entry 1.5, p. 16). In addition, LAC may go on to experience further trauma and abuse within the care system itself, leaving them mistrusting of adults in authority and at increased risk of harm as they move into adolescence and beyond (La Valle et al., 2016).

Having an understanding of common experiences of LAC is vital to the process of supporting a client in recovering from trauma and moving into a more positive place in terms of development and the capacity to form appropriate, beneficial relationships built on trust.

Key Skills

1. Meet the child and young person where they are. Looked-after children may be referred for counselling due to a long list of painful and difficult experiences of trauma, separation and loss (see entry 3.14, p. 191). They may demonstrate behavioural issues that lead to further experiences of rejection and abandonment by adults and peers. The integrative approach of this book allows practitioners to hold referral information in our minds in a way that informs our approach, but also allows us to meet the child as they are in the room and assist them in developing a sense of themselves as an individual, not just a collection of experiences or legal processes (see entry 2.2, p. 51).
2. Looked-after children and adolescents will have experienced a range of complex trauma and difficulties in their relationships with adults. They may therefore take time to develop trust in the therapeutic relationship. Depending on the age and developmental capacity of the client, counsellors may need to be flexible in terms of the frame, while setting clear limits and boundaries for clients who struggle to regulate their emotions and behaviour (see entry 3.7, p. 162). In some cases, the opposite may be true and the client may form a bond rapidly, but without an appropriate sense of boundaries.
3. As well as trust taking time to develop, LAC may be more sensitive than other clients to aspects of the therapeutic relationship such as breaks and endings. Counsellors need to have this in mind throughout the work and make sure they prepare the client as well as possible for any breaks, or to transition carefully when work is coming to an end. When working in a school context, this might mean counting together how many more sessions there are before the end of term, but also allowing plenty of space for exploring the client's feelings around endings, however hard this may be for them and the counsellor. Working in this way allows the potential for a different kind of ending than those they may have experienced previously, enabling them to consider their needs in this respect and how ending can be managed in a way that allows the inevitability of separation in life to be tolerated and understood as part of a developmental process.
4. Therapeutic work with LAC may be undertaken alongside other professionals and carers. Williams and Richardson (2016: 52) suggest a model for multidisciplinary work in partnership with other professionals which recognises 'that professionals from different disciplines can also work together in ways that welcome birth and substitute families into the partnership, and that have direct therapeutic benefits for the child'. Often LAC have several different professionals involved with their 'case' at any time. Counsellors need to work alongside other professionals while maintaining the confidentiality of the therapeutic work with the child (see entry 2.22, p. 131). This includes careful consideration of what they will or will not undertake in a child protection conference or other meetings, ensuring that this is discussed in advance with their supervisor.
5. Older LAC and adolescents may be at increased risk of acting out and engaging in harmful behaviours. Due to early relational experiences impacting their capacity for

regulation and increased impulsivity, along with low self-esteem and unmet attachment needs, they are at increased risk of engaging in risky or dangerous behaviour as well as sexual acting out and inappropriate relationships (see entry 3.10, p. 174). Adolescents in the care system are vulnerable to grooming for sexual exploitation (La Valle et al., 2016) as well as exploitation by gangs looking for children to work in 'county lines' drug supply chains (National Crime Agency, 2016). Counsellors working with this group need to be aware of indications that the client is at risk in these ways and be prepared to act appropriately to safeguard the child or young person.

6. Working with LAC therapeutically is challenging and in order to be able to work consistently with these vulnerable clients and avoid the potential for re-traumatising children or exposing them to further experiences of rejection or abandonment, counsellors need to develop robust supervision and self-care practices (see entry 2.23, p. 134 and entry 2.24, p. 137). Working closely with colleagues and supervisors who have experience and expertise in this field of work is vital to support counsellors. Personal therapy is important in providing a space for exploration of the counsellor's personal material brought up by contact with clients who have experienced significant trauma and loss.

Additional Resources

- MindEd – minded.org.uk: 410-047 *Children Adopted or in Care 06* and 410-043 *Vulnerable Groups – An Overview.*
- NSPCC learning: https://learning.nspcc.org.uk/children-and-families-at-risk/looked-after-children (accessed 31 July 2020).

Associated Entries

1.5 Attachment Theory
1.10 Environmental & Systemic Factors
1.11 Developmental Implications for Counselling
2.2 Core Relationship Components
2.4 Building Rapport
2.8 Risk Assessment & Safeguarding
2.19 Endings
2.22 Working with Other Professionals
2.23 Self-care for Counsellors
3.10 Working with Risk
3.14 Trauma & Abuse
3.20 Family Breakdown & Instability
3.22 Self-Esteem
3.31 Resilience

References

Abbass, A., Rabung, S., Leichsenring, F., Refseth, J.S. & Midgely, N. (2013) 'Psychodynamic psychotherapy for children and adolescents: A meta-analysis of short-term psychodynamic models', *Journal of the American Academy of Child and Adolescent Psychiatry*, 52(8): 863–875.

Ainsworth, M.D.S. (1985) 'Patterns of infant–mother attachments: Antecedents and effects on development', *Bulletin of the New York Academy of Medicine*, 61(9): 771–791.

Ainsworth, M.D.S., Blehar, M., Aters, E. & Wall, S. (1978) *Patterns of Attachment: A Psychological Study of the Strange Situation*. Hillsdale, NJ: Lawrence Erlbaum.

Akilapa, R. & Simkiss, D. (2012) 'Cultural Influences and safeguarding children', *Paediatrics and Child Health*, 22(11): 490–495.

Aldgate, J. (2006) 'Children, development and ecology', in J. Aldgate, W. Rose & C. Jeffery (eds), *The Developing World of the Child*. London: Jessica Kingsley.

American Psychiatric Association (2013) *Diagnostic and Statistical Manual of Mental Disorders*, (5th edition) (DSM-5). Washington, DC: APA.

American Psychological Association (APA) (2020) 'Cognition', in *APA Dictionary of Psychology* (online). https://dictionary.apa.org/cognition

Anderson, R. (ed.) (1991) *Clinical Lectures on Klein and Bion*. London: Routledge.

Anti-Bullying Alliance (ABA) (2020) *'The ABA definition of bullying'*. Available at: https://www.anti-bullyingalliance.org.uk/tools-information/all-about-bullying/what-bullying/aba-definition-bullying (accessed 9 January 2021).

Archibald, A.B., Graber, J.A. & Brooks-Gunn, J. (2006) 'Pubertal process and physiological growth in adolescence', in G.R. Adams & M.D. Berzonsky (eds), *The Blackwell Handbook of Adolescence*. Oxford: Blackwell Publishing.

Astington, J. & Gopnik, A. (1991) 'Theoretical explanations of children's understanding of the mind', *British Journal of Developmental Psychology*, 9(1): 7–31.

Axline, V. (1947) *Play Therapy*. New York: Ballantine.

Baer, R. (2014) 'Introduction to the core practices and exercises', in R.A. Baer (ed.), *Mindfulness-Based Treatment Approaches* (2nd edition). London: Academic Press.

Barker, M.-J. (2019) 'Good practice across the counselling professions 001', in *Gender, Sexual and Relationship Diversity (GSRD)*. Lutterworth: British Association for Counselling and Psychotherapy.

Bateman, A. & Fonagy, P. (2013) 'Mentalization-based treatment', *Psychoanalytic Inquiry*, 33(6): 595–613.

Bateman, A. & Holmes, J. (1995) *Introduction to Psychoanalysis: Contemporary Theory and Practice*. London: Routledge.

Bava, S. & Tapert, S. (2010) 'Adolescent brain development and the risk for alcohol and other drug problems', *Neuropsychology Review*, 20: 398–413.

Beattie, M. & Linehan, P. (2018) 'Introduction', in M. Beattie, P. Linehan & R. Dundas (eds), *Counselling Skills for Working with Gender Diversity and Identity*. London: Jessica Kingsley.

Beattie, M., Linehan, P. & Dundas, R. (eds) (2018) *Counselling Skills for Working with Gender Diversity and Identity*. London: Jessica Kingsley.

Beck, A. et al. (1985) *Anxiety Disorders and Phobias: A Cognitive Perspective*. New York: Basic Books.

Biegel, G.M., Chang, K., Garrett, A. & Edwards, M. (2014) 'Mindfulness-based stress reduction for teens', in R.A. Baer (ed.), *Mindfulness-Based Treatment Approaches* (2nd edition). London: Academic Press.

Bion, W.R. (1962) *Learning from Experience*. London: Heinemann.

Bion, W.R. (1967) 'Notes on memory and desire', *The Psychoanalytic Forum*, 2: 272–273.

Blake, P. (2008) *Child and Adolescent Psychotherapy*. London: Routledge.

Blanchett, W.J., Klingner, J.K. & Harry, B. (2009) 'The intersection of race, culture, language, and disability: Implications for urban education. *Urban Education*, 44(4): 389–409.

Bond, T. (2015) *Standards and Ethics for Counselling in Action* (4th edition). London: Sage/British Association for Counselling and Psychotherapy.

Bond, T. & Mitchels, B. (2015) *Good Practice in Action 014: Breaches in Confidentiality*. Lutterworth: British Association for Counselling and Psychotherapy.

Bordin, E.S. (1979) 'The generalizability of the psychoanalytic concept of the working alliance', *Psychotherapy: Theory, Research, and Practice*, 16(3): 252–260.

Bott-Spillius, E. (1992) 'Clinical experiences of projective identification', in R. Anderson (ed.), *Clinical Lectures on Klein and Bion* (pp. 59–73). London: Routledge.

Bowlby, J.M. (1951) *Maternal Care and Mental Health*. Geneva: World Health Organisation.

Bowlby, J.M. (1973) *Attachment and Loss*. Vol. 2: *Separation*. London: The Hogarth Press and the Institute of Psycho-Analysis (reprinted London: Pimlico, 1988).

Bowlby, J.M. (1980) *Loss: Sadness and Depression*. London: The Hogarth Press (reprinted London: Vintage, 2008).

Bowlby, J.M. (1988) *A Secure Base: Clinical Applications of Attachment Theory*. London: Routledge.

Brady, M.T. (2016) *The Body in Adolescence: Psychic Isolation and Physical Symptoms*. London: Routledge.

Bratton, S. (2010) 'Meeting the early mental health needs of children through school-based play therapy: A review of outcome research', in A.A. Drewes & C.E. Schaefer (eds), *School-Based Play Therapy* (2nd edition, pp. 17–58). Hoboken, NJ: Wiley.

Briggs, S., Maxwell, M. & Keenan, A. (2015) 'Working with the complexities of adolescent mental health problems: Applying time-limited adolescent psychodynamic psychotherapy (TAPP)', *Psychoanalytic Psychotherapy*, 29(4): 313–329.

British Association for Counselling and Psychotherapy (BACP) (2018) *Ethical Framework for the Counselling Professions*. Lutterworth: BACP.

British Association for Counselling and Psychotherapy (BACP) (2019) *Competence Framework for Therapeutic Work with Children and Young People 4–18 Years*. Lutterworth: BACP.

British Association for Counselling and Psychotherapy (BACP) (2019) *Working with Children and Young People: Guidance for Members*. Available at: https://www.bacp.co.uk/news/news-from-bacp/coronavirus/working-with-cyp/ (accessed 10 January 2021).

Bronfenbrenner, U. (1979) *The Ecology of Human Development: Experiments by Nature and Design*. Cambridge, MA: Harvard University Press.

Brown, S. (2020) 'How are counsellors coping with COVID 19?', *Therapy Today*, 31(4).

Bruch, H. (1973) *Eating Disorders: Obesity, Anorexia Nervosa, and the Person Within*. New York: Basic Books.

Bryant-Waugh, R. & Lask, B. (1995) 'Eating disorders – An overview', *Journal of Family Therapy*, 17: 13–30.

Bryant-Waugh, R. & Lask, B. (2013) 'Overview of eating disorders in childhood and adolescence', in R. Bryant-Waugh & B. Lask (eds), *Eating Disorders in Childhood and Adolescence* (4th edition, pp. 33–49). Hove: Routledge.

Campbell, A.F. & Simmonds, J.G. (2011) 'Therapist perspectives on the therapeutic alliance with children and adolescents', *Counselling Psychology Quarterly*, 24(3): 195–209.

Campos, J.J., Campos, R.G. & Barrett, K.C. (1989) 'Emergent themes in the study of emotional development and emotion regulation', *Developmental Psychology*, 25(3): 394–402.

Carr, A. (2006) *The Handbook of Child and Adolescent Clinical Psychology: A Contextual Approach* (2nd edition). New York: Brunner-Routledge.

Casey, B.J., Jones, R.M. & Hare, T.A. (2008) 'The adolescent brain', *Annals of the New York Academy of Science*, 1124: 111–126.

Cashmore, J. & Shackel, R. (2013) 'The long-term effects of child sexual abuse', *Child Family Community Australia Information Exchange (CFCA)*. Paper 11. Available at: www.aifs.gov. au/cfca/pubs/papers/a143161/cfca11.pdf.

Cattanach, A. (1997) *Children's Stories in Play Therapy*. London: Jessica Kingsley.

Cattanach, A. (2008) *Play Therapy with Abused Children* (2nd edition). London: Jessica Kingsley.

Children Act (1989) London: HMSO.

Clarkson, P. (1995) *The Therapeutic Relationship*. London: Whurr.

Cluley, V. (2018) 'From "learning disability to intellectual disability" – Perceptions of the increasing use of the term "intellectual disability" in learning disability policy, research and practice', *British Journal of Learning Disabilities*, 46(1): 24–32.

Cohen, D. (2017) *How the Child's Mind Develops*. London: Routledge.

Constantino, M.J., Castonguay, L.G., Zack, S.E. & DeGeorge, J. (2010) 'Engagement in psychotherapy: Factors contributing to the facilitation, demise, and restoration of the therapeutic alliance', in D. Castro-Blanco & M.S. Karver (eds), *Elusive Alliance: Treatment Engagement Strategies with High-Risk Adolescents*. Washington, DC: American Psychological Association.

Cooper, M. (2013) 'Developmental and personality theory', in M. Cooper, M. O'Hara, P.F. Schmid & A. Bohart (eds), *The Handbook of Person-Centred Psychotherapy and Counselling* (2nd edition). London: Palgrave Macmillan.

Cooper, M., O'Hara, M., Schmid, P.F. & Bohart, A.C. (eds) (2013) *The Handbook of Person-Centred Psychotherapy and Counselling* (2nd edition). London: Palgrave Macmillan.

Coren, A. (1996) 'Brief therapy – base metal or pure gold?', *Psychodynamic Practice*, 2(1): 22–38.

Courtland, C.L. & Na, G. (2011) 'Identity development and its impact on the therapy relationship', in C. Lago (ed.), *The Handbook of Transcultural Counselling and Psychotherapy*. Maidenhead: McGraw-Hill/Open University Press.

Crenshaw, K. (1989) 'Demarginalizing the intersection of race and sex: A Black feminist critique of antidiscrimination doctrine and antiracist politics', *University of Chicago Legal Forum*, Issue 1, Article 8.

Creswell, C. & Waite, P. (2009) 'The use of CBT with children and adolescents', in P. Waite & T. Williams (eds), *Obsessive Compulsive Disorder: Cognitive Behaviour Therapy with Children and Young People*. Hove: Routledge.

Crisp, A. (1983) 'Anorexia Nervosa', *British Medical Journal*, 287: 855–858.

Crittenden, P. (2015) *Raising Parents: Attachment, Representation and Treatment*. London: Routledge.

Daniels, D. & Jenkins, P. (2010) *Therapy with Children: Children's Rights, Confidentiality and the Law* (2nd edition). London: Sage.

Dashorst, P., Mooren, T.M., Kleber, R.J., de Jong, P.J. & Huntjens, R.J.C. (2019) 'Intergenerational consequences of the Holocaust on offspring mental health: A systematic review of associated factors and mechanisms', *European Journal of Psychotraumatology*, 10(1).

Davids, J., Green, V., Joyce, A. & McLean, D. (2016) 'Revised diagnostic profile: 2016', *Journal of Infant, Child and Adolescent Psychotherapy*, 16(2): 149–157.

Department for Education (DfE) (2004) *National Service Framework for Children, Young People and Maternity Services: The Mental Health and Psychological Well-Being of Children and Young People*. London: HMSO.

Department for Education (DfE) (2015a) *Information Sharing: Advice for Practitioners Providing Safeguarding Services to Children, Young People, Parents and Carers*. London: HMSO.

Department for Education (DfE) (2015b) *Working Together to Safeguard Children: A Guide to Inter-agency Working to Safeguard and Promote the Welfare of Children*. London: HMSO.

Department for Education (DfE) (2016) *Counselling in School: A Blueprint for the Future*. London: HMSO.

Department for Education (DfE) (2018) *Working Together to Safeguard Children: A Guide to Inter-Agency Working to Safeguard and Promote the Welfare of Children*. London: HMSO.

Department for Education and Skills (DfES) (2006) *What to Do if You're Worried a Child is Being Abused: Departmental Advice Providing Best Practice Information for Those who Work with Children in Order to Safeguard their Welfare*. London: HMSO.

Department for Education and Skills (DfES) (2015) *What to Do if You're Worried a Child is Being Abused: Departmental Advice Providing Best Practice Information for Those who Work with Children in Order to Safeguard their Welfare*. London: HMSO.

Department for Education and Skills (DfES) (2020) *Children Looked After in England Including Adoptions*. London: HMSO. Available at: https://explore-education-statistics.service.gov.uk/find-statistics/children-looked-after-in-england-including-adoptions/2020 (accessed 10 January 2021).

Department for Work and Pensions (DWP) (2018) *Family Resources Survey: Financial Year 2016/17*. London: HMSO.

Department of Health (2005) *Mental Health and Deafness: Towards Equity and Access: Best Practice Guidance*. London: HMSO.

Department of Health (2015) *Taskforce on Mental Health in Society*. London: HMSO.

Dissing, A.S., Dich, N., Andersen, A.N., Lund, R. & Naja, H. (2017) 'Parental break-ups and stress: Role of age and family structure in 44,509 pre-adolescent children', *European Journal of Public Health*, 27(5): 829–834.

DitchtheLabel (2020) *The Annual Bullying Survey 2020*. Available at: https://www.ditchthelabel.org/research-papers/ (accessed 9 January 2021).

Duncan, B.L., Sparks, J.A., Miller, S.D., Bohanske, R.T. & Claud, D.A. (2006) 'Giving youth a voice: A preliminary study of the reliability and validity of a brief outcome measure for children, adolescents and caretakers', *Journal of Brief Therapy*, 5(2): 71–87.

Dunn, J., Brown, J., Slomkowski, C., Tesla, C. & Youngblade, L. (1991) 'Young children's understanding of other people's feelings and beliefs: Individual differences and their antecedents', *Child Development*, 62(6): 1352–1366.

Dyck, E. & Russell, G. (2020) 'Challenging psychiatric classification: Healthy autistic diversity and the neurodiversity movement', in S.J. Taylor & Y.A. Brumby (eds), *Healthy Minds in the Twentieth Century: Mental Health in Historical Perspective*. London: Palgrave Macmillan.

Eddo-Lodge, R. (2018) *Why I'm No Longer Talking to White People about Race*. London: Bloomsbury.

Edwards, M. & Titman, P. (2010) *Promoting Psychological Well-Being in Children with Acute and Chronic Illness*. London: Jessica Kingsley.

Elliot, R., Watson, J.C., Goldman, R.N. & Greenberg, L. (2003) *Learning Emotion-Focused Therapy: The Process-Experiential Approach to Change*. Washington, DC: American Psychological Association.

Equality Act (2010) London: HMSO. Available at: www.legislation.gov.uk/ukpga/2010/15/contents (accessed 5 July 2020).

Erikson, E.H. (1950) 'Eight ages of man', *Childhood and Society*. New York: W.W. Norton & Co. (reprinted London: Vintage, 1995).

Erikson, E.H. (1968) *Identity, Youth & Crisis*. New York: W.W. Norton & Co.

Eubanks, C.F., Muran, C.J. & Safran, J.D. (2018) 'Alliance rupture repair: A meta-analysis', *Psychotherapy*, 55(4): 508–519.

Evans, K. & Dubowski, J. (2001) *Art Therapy with Children on the Autistic Spectrum: Beyond Words*. London: Jessica Kingsley.

Ferguson, K.T. & Evans, G.W. (2019) 'Social ecological theory: Family systems and family psychology in bioecological and biocultural perspective', in B.H. Fiese, M. Celano, K. Deater-Deckard, E.N. Jouriles & M.A. Whisman (eds), *APA Handbook of Contemporary Family Psychology: Foundations, Methods, and Contemporary Issues across Lifespan*. Washington, DC: American Psychological Association.

Fiese, B.H., Tomcho, T.J., Douglas, M., Josephs, K., Poltrock, S. & Baker, T. (2002) 'A review of 50 years of research on naturally occurring family routines and rituals: Cause for celebration?', *Journal of Family Psychology*, 16(4): 381–390.

Figley, C.R. (2002) 'Compassion fatigue: Psychotherapists' chronic lack of self care', *Journal of Clinical Psychology*, 58(11): 1433–1441.

Fonagy, P., Gergely, G., Jurist, E.L. & Target, M. (2004) *Affect Regulation, Mentalization and the Development of the Self*. London: Karnac.

Freud, A. (1946) *The Ego and the Mechanisms of Defence*. New York: International Universities Press.

Freud, A. (1965) *The Writings of Anna Freud*. Vol. VI: *Normality and Pathology in Childhood: Assessments of Development*. New York: International Universities Press.

Freud, A. (1974) *Introduction to Psychoanalysis: Lectures for Child Analysts and Teachers 1922–1935*. London: The Hogarth Press and the Institute of Psycho-Analysis.

Freud, S. (1905/1953) 'Three essays on the theory of sexuality', in J. Strachey (ed.), *The Standard Edition of the Complete Psychological Works of Sigmund Freud* (Vol. 7, pp. 123–246). London: The Hogarth Press.

Freud, S. (1912/1958) 'The dynamics of transference', in J. Strachey (ed.), *The Standard Edition of the Complete Psychological Works of Sigmund Freud* (Vol. 12, pp. 97–108). London: The Hogarth Press.

Freud, S. (1914/1958). 'Remembering, repeating and working-through (further recommendations on the technique of psycho-analysis II), in J. Strachey (ed.), *The Standard Edition of the Complete Psychological Works of Sigmund Freud* (Vol. 12, pp. 145–156). London: The Hogarth Press.

Freud, S. (1923/1961) 'The ego and the id', in J. Strachey (ed.), *The Standard Edition of the Complete Psychological Works of Sigmund Freud* (Vol. 19, pp. 3–309). London: The Hogarth Press.

Freud, S. (1926/1959) 'Inhibitions, symptoms and anxiety', in J. Strachey (ed.), *The Standard Edition of the Complete Psychological Works of Sigmund Freud* (Vol. 20: An Autobiographical Study, Inhibitions, Symptoms and Anxiety, The Question of Lay Analysis and Other Works, pp. 75–176. London: The Hogarth Press.

Fuggle, P., Dunsmuir, S. & Curry, V. (2013) *CBT with Children, Young People & Families*. London: Sage.

Garza, Y., Falls, L. & Bruhn, R. (2009) 'Measuring deeper meaning responses: A discrimination scale for play therapists in training', *International Journal of Play Therapy*, 18(3): 147–161.

Gerhardt, S. (2015) *Why Love Matters: How Affection Shapes a Baby's Brain* (2nd edition). Hove: Routledge.

Gilbert, M. & Orlans, V. (2011) *Integrative Therapy: 100 Key Points and Techniques*. Hove: Routledge.

Gilbert, P. (2007) *Psychotherapy and Counselling for Depression* (3rd edition). London: Sage.

Goodman, R. & Scott, S. (2012) *Child and Adolescent Psychiatry*. London: John Wiley & Sons.

gov.uk (n.d.) 'Bullying at school'. Available at https://www.gov.uk/bullying-at-school (accessed 14 January 2021).

Gray, A. (2013) *An Introduction to the Therapeutic Frame*. London: Routledge.

Greenberg, L. (2008) 'Emotion and cognition in psychotherapy: The transforming power of affect', *Canadian Psychology/Psychologie Canadienne*, 49(1): 49–59.

Greenberg, L.S. (2011) *Emotion-Focused Therapy*. London: EDS Publications.

Guardian (2020) 'As a Black police officer, I know the Met is still institutionally racist', *The Guardian*, 15 June. Available at: www.theguardian.com/commentisfree/2020/jun/15/black-police-officer-met-institutionally-racist-bame-officers.

Hall, D. (2011) 'The effects of an African Caribbean heritage: Living as a problem', in C. Lago (ed.), *The Handbook of Transcultural Counselling and Psychotherapy*. Maidenhead: McGraw-Hill/Open University Press.

Hall, G.S. (1904) *Adolescence: Its Psychology and its Relations to Physiology, Anthropology, Sociology, Sex, Crime, Religion and Education*, Vol. 1. New York: D. Appleton & Company.

Hanley, T. (2012) 'Understanding the online therapeutic alliance through the eyes of adolescent service users', *Counselling and Psychotherapy Research* 12(1): 35–43.

Hart, A., Blincow, D. & Thomas, H. (2007) *Resilient Therapy: Working with Children and Families*. London: Routledge.

Hart, A., Blincow, D. & Thomas, H. (2012) *Resilience Framework (Children & Young People)*. London: Routledge. (Adapted from Hart, Blincow & Thomas, 2007. Available at: www.boingboing.org.uk).

Hawkins, P. & Shohet, R. (2012) *Supervision in the Helping Professions* (4th edition). Maidenhead: Open University Press.

Hawton, K., Rodham, K. & Evans, E. (2006) *By Their Own Young Hand: Deliberate Self-harm and Suicidal Ideas in Adolescents*. London: Jessica Kingsley.

Hawton, K., Saunders, K.E.A. & O'Connor, R.C. (2012) Self-harm and suicide in adolescents. *The Lancet*, 379: 2373–2382.

Heimann, P. (1950) 'On countertransference,' *International Journal of Psychoanalysis*, 31: 81–84.

Henley, J. & Robinson, J. (2011) 'Mental health issues among refugee children and adoelscents', *Clinical Psychologist*, 15: 51–62.

Hobson, R. (1985) *Forms of Feeing: The Heart of Psychotherapy*. Hove: Routledge.

Howe, D. (2005) *Child Abuse and Neglect: Attachment, Development and Intervention*. London: Macmillan.

Human Rights Act (1988) London: HMSO.

Iqbal, N. (2020) 'Black Lives Matter isn't about statues or TV shows: It's about real lives being ruined', *The Guardian*, 10 July.

Isaacs, M.B., Montalvo, B. & Abelsohn, D. (1986) *The Difficult Divorce: Therapy for Children and Families*. New York: Basic Books.

Israeli, E., Asulin-Simhon, Z. & Sharabany, R. (2013) The interface between cyberspace and psychotherapeutic space: Relationship avoidance and intimacy in adolescent psychotherapy. *The Psychoanalytic Study of the Child*, 67: 279–297.

James, W. (1890) *The Principles of Psychology*. New York: Henry Holt and Co.

Jennings, S. (1993) *Playtherapy with Children: A Practitioner's Guide*. Oxford: Blackwell Scientific.

Katz, A. & El Asam, A. (2019) *Vulnerable Children in a Digital World*. Internet Matters/Youthworks [online]. Available at: internetmatters.org (accessed 23 June 2020).

Kegerreis, S. (2006) 'Working with children and adolescents – Is specialist training necessary?', *Psychodynamic Practice*, 12(4): 403–418.

Kirkbride, R. (2016a) *Counselling Children and Young People in Private Practice: A Practical Guide*. London: Karnac.

Kirkbride, R. (2016b) 'Preparing your practice for children', in British Association for Counselling and Psychotherapy, *Children and Young People*, June: 28–31.

Kirkbride, R. (2018a) *Counselling Young People: A Practitioner Manual*. London: Sage.

Kirkbride, R. (2018b) 'Eating disorders', in S. Pattison & M. Robson (eds), *The Handbook of Counselling Children and Young People* (2nd edition). London: Sage.

Klein, M. (1926/1975) 'The psychological principles of early analysis', in M. Klein, *The Writings of Melanie Klein* (Vol. 1). London: The Hogarth Press.

Klein, M. (1946) 'Notes on some schizoid mechanisms', *The International Journal of Psychoanalysis*, 27: 99–110.

Knox, R. & Cooper, M. (2015) *The Therapeutic Relationship in Counselling and Psychotherapy*. London: Sage.

Krieger, I. (2017) *Counseling Transgender and Non-Binary Youth: The Essential Guide*. London: Jessica Kingsley.

Kutcher, S. (2002) *Practical Child and Adolescent Psychopharmacology*. This publication is available, with the author's permission, as a free pdf download from: www.youthinmind.info/GoodmanScott3rdEdition2012.pdf (last accessed 2 July 2020).

Ladany, N., Mori, Y. & Mehr, K.E. (2013) 'Effective and ineffective supervision', *The Counselling Psychologist*, 41(1): 28–47.

Lago, C. (ed.) (2011) *The Handbook of Transcultural Counselling and Psychotherapy*. Maidenhead: McGraw-Hill/Open University Press.

Lago, C. & Hirai, T. (2013) 'Counselling across difference and diversity'. in M. Cooper, M. O'Hara, P.F. Schmid & A. Bohart (eds), *The Handbook of Person-Centred Psychotherapy and Counselling* (2nd edition). London: Palgrave Macmillan.

Lahane, S., Shah, H., Nagarale, V. & Kamath, R. (2012) 'Comparison of self-esteem and maternal attitude between children with learning disability and unaffected siblings', *The Indian Journal of Pediatrics*, 80: 745–749.

Landreth, G.L. (2012) *Play Therapy: The Art of the Relationship*. London: Routledge.

Landreth, G.L., Ray, D.C., Sweeney, D.S., Homeyer, L.E. & Glover, G.J. (2005) *Play Therapy Interventions with Children's Problems: Case Studies with DSM-IV-TR Diagnoses*. New York: Jason Aronson.

Lane, R. & Garfield, D. (2005) 'Becoming aware of feelings: Integration of cognitive-developmental, neuroscientific, and psychoanalytic perspectives', *Neuropsychoanalysis*, 7: 30–35.

La Valle, I., Graham, B. & Hart, D. (2016) *Child Sexual Exploitation: Support in Children's Residential Homes: Research Report* London: Department for Education.

Law, D. & Wolpert, M. (eds) (2014) *Guide to Using Outcomes and Feedback Tools with Children, Young People and Families*. London: CAMHS Press.

Layte, R. & McCrory, C. (2012) 'Paediatric chronic illness and educational failure: The role of emotional and behavioural problems', *Social Psychiatry and Psychiatric Epidemiology: The International Journal for Research in Social and Genetic Epidemiology and Mental Health*, 48(8): 1307–1316.

Leblanc, M. & Ritchie, M. (2001) 'A meta-analysis of play therapy outcomes', *Counselling Psychology Quarterly*, 14(2): 149–163.

Lerner, R.M. & L. Steinberg, L.D. (eds) (2004) *Handbook of Adolescent Psychology* (2nd edition). London: Wiley.

Levingston, B. & Melrose, J. (2009) 'Alcohol and young people', in K. Geldard (ed.), *Practical Interventions for Young People at Risk*. London: Sage.

Lindsay, W. R. (1999) Cognitive therapy. *The Psychologist*, 12(5): 238–241.

Ling, J., Hunter, S.V. & Maple, M. (2014) 'Navigating the challenges of trauma counselling: How counsellors thrive and sustain their engagement', *Australian Social Work*, 67(2): 297–310.

Main, M. & Solomon, J. (1986) 'Discovery of an insecure-disorganized/disoriented attachment pattern', in T. Brazelton & M. Yogman (eds), *Affective Development in Infancy*. Norwood, NJ: Ablex.

Malan, D. (1979) *Individual Psychotherapy and the Science of Psychodynamics*. London: Butterworth.

Malchiodi, C.A. (ed.) (2005) *Expressive Therapies*. New York: Guilford Press.

Mander, G. (2000) *A Psychodynamic Approach to Brief Therapy*. London: Sage.

Marks Mishne, J. (1986) *Clinical Work with Adolescents*. New York: The Free Press.

Martellozzo, E., Monaghan, A., Adler, J.R., Davidson, J., Leyva, R. & Horvath, M.A.H. (2016) *'I Wasn't Sure It Was Normal to Watch It': A Quantitative and Qualitative Examination of the Impact of Online Pornography on the Values, Attitudes, Beliefs and Behaviours of Children and Young People*. London: NSPCC.

Masten, A.S. (2001) 'Ordinary magic: Resilience processes in development', *American Psychologist*, 56(3): 227–238.

Masten, A.S. (2018) 'Resilience theory and research on children and families: Past, present and promise', *Journal of Family Theory & Review*, 10: 12–31.

McArthur, K. & Cooper, M. (2018) 'Evaluating counselling', in S. Pattison & M. Robson (eds), *The Handbook of Counselling Children and Young People* (2nd edition). London: Sage.

McArthur, K., Cooper, M. & Berdondini, L. (2013) 'School-based humanistic counselling for psychological distress in young people: Pilot randomized controlled trial', *Psychotherapy Research*, 23: 355–365.

McCall, B. (2016) 'Child poverty continues to rise in the UK', *The Lancet*, 38: 747.

Maslow, A.H. (1943) 'A theory of human motivation', *Psychological Review*, 50(4): 430–437.

Mearns, D. & Thorne, B. (2013) *Person-Centred Counselling in Action* (4th edition). London: Sage.

Meins, E. et al. (2003) 'Pathways to understanding mind: Construct validity and predictive validity of maternal mind-mindedness', *Child Development*, 74(4): 1194–1211.

Meins, E. et al. (2013) 'Mind-mindedness and Theory of Mind: Mediating roles of language and perspective of symbolic play', *Child Development*, 84(5): 1777–1790.

Melandri, F. (2017) 'Milk and tears: A very difficult beginning: The assessment and treatment of a young boy with atypical presentation', *Journal of Infant, Child and Adolescent Psychotherapy*, 16(2): 158–174.

Mendle, J. & Ferrero, J. (2012) 'Detrimental psychological outcomes associated with pubertal timing in adolescent boys', *Developmental Review*, 32: 49–66.

Mendle, J., Turkheimer, E. & Emery, R. (2007) 'Detrimental psychological outcomes associated with early pubertal timing in adolescent girls', *Developmental Review*, 27: 151–171.

Midgely, N., Hayes, J. & Cooper, M. (eds) (2017) *Essential Research Findings in Child and Adolescent Counselling and Psychotherapy*. London: British Association for Counselling and Psychotherapy/Sage.

Miller, K., Martell, Z., Pazdirek, L., Caruth, M. & Lopez, D. (2005) 'The role of interpreters in psychotherapy with refugees: An exploratory study', *American Journal of Orthopsychology*, 75(1): 27–39.

Miller, W.R. & Rollnick, S. (2012) *Motivational Interviewing: Helping People Change* (3rd edition). New York: Guilford Press.

Mirza, K.A.H. & Mirza, S. (2008) 'Adolescent substance misuse', *Psychiatry*, 7: 357–362.

Mitchels, B. (2015) *Good Practice in Action 031: Safeguarding Children and Young People in England and Wales*. Lutterworth: British Association for Counselling and Psychotherapy.

Mitchels, B. & Bond, T. (2010) *Essential Law for Counsellors and Psychotherapists*. London: Sage.

Mitchels, B. & Bond, T. (2011) *Legal Issues across Counselling & Psychotherapy Settings: A Guide for Practice*. London: Sage.

Mitchels, B. & Membrey, D. (2018) 'General data protection regulation (GDPR) and CYP', *BACP Children, Young People and Families Journal*, December.

Mueller, B. (2019) 'What is austerity and how has it affected British society', *The New York Times*, 24 February. Available at: www.nytimes.com/2019/02/24/world/europe/britain-austerity-may-budget.html (accessed 9 April 2020).

Music, G. (2017) *Nurturing Natures: Attachment and Children's Emotional, Sociocultural and Brain Development*. London: Routledge.

Music, G. (2019) *Nurturing Children: From Trauma to Growth Using Attachment Theory, Psychoanalysis and Neurobiology*. London: Routledge.

National Crime Agency (NCA) (2016) *County Lines Gang Violence, Exploitation & Drug Supply: 0346-CAD National Briefing Report*. London: National Crime Agency.

NHS Digital (2018) *Mental Health of Children and Young People in England, 2017: Summary of Key Findings*. Government Statistical Service: NHS Digital. London: HMSO.

NHS Digital (2019) *Health Survey for England 2018*. Government Statistical Service: NHS Digital. London: HMSO.

NHS England (2018) *Guidance for Health Services for Children and Young People with Special Educational Needs and Disability (SEND)*. London: The Children with Complex Needs/Special Educational Needs and Disability (CCN SEND) Board.

NICE (National Institute for Health and Clinical Excellence) (2011) *Autistic Spectrum Disorder in under 19s: Recognition, Referral and Diagnosis*. NICE Guideline CG128. London: NICE (last updated December 2017).

NICE (National Institute for Health and Clinical Excellence) (2013) *Psychosis and Schizophrenia in Children and Young People: Recognition and Management*. Clinical Guideline. London: NICE.

NICE (National Institute for Health and Clinical Excellence) (2018) *Attention Deficit Hyperactivity Disorder*. NICE guideline NG87. London: NICE (last updated September 2019).

Nof, A., Dolev, T., Leibovich, L., Harel, J. & Zilcha-Mano, S. (2019) 'If you believe that breaking is possible, believe also that fixing is possible: A framework for ruptures and repairs in child psychotherapy', *Research in Psychotherapy: Psychopathology, Process and Outcome*, 22: 45–57.

NSPCC (2020) *What is Child Abuse?* London: National Society for the Prevention of Cruelty to Children. Available at: NSPCC.org.uk/what-is-child-abuse (accessed 1 July 2020).

Office for National Statistics (2020) *Migrations Statistics Quarterly Report: August 2020*. Available at: https://www.ons.gov.uk/peoplepopulationandcommunity/

populationandmigration/internationalmigration/bulletins/migrationstatisticsquarterlyreport/august2020 (accessed 10 January 2021).
Palfrey, J. & Gasser, U. (2008) *Born Digital: Understanding the First Generation of Digital Natives*. New York: Basic Books.
Parson, J.A. (2014) 'Holistic mental health care and play therapy for hospitalized, chronically ill children', in E.J. Green & A.C. Myrick (eds), *Play Therapy with Vulnerable Populations: No Child Forgotten*. Boulder, CO: Rowman & Littlefield.
Pattinson, S. (2005) 'Making a difference for young people with learning disabilities: A model for inclusive counselling practice', *Counselling and Psychotherapy Research*, 5(2): 120–130.
Pattinson, S. (2006) 'Beyond the classroom: The inclusion of young people with learning disabilities in UK mainstream counselling services', *International Journal of Inclusive Education*, 10(6): 547–564.
Pearce, P. & Sewell, R. (2014) 'Tenuous contact', *Therapy Today*, 25(6): 28–30.
Pearce, P., Proud, G. & Sewell, R. (2018a) 'Group work', in M. Robson & S. Pattison (eds), *The Handbook of Counselling Children and Young People* (2nd edition). London: Sage.
Pearce, P., Sewell, R. & Cromarty, K. (2018b) 'School and education settings', in S. Pattison & M. Robson (eds), *The Handbook of Counselling Children and Young People* (2nd edition). London: Sage.
Perini, S.J. & Rapee, R.M. (2014) 'Theoretical foundations of CBT for anxious and depressed youth', in E.S. Sburlati, H.J. Lyneham, C.A. Schniering & R.M. Rapee (eds), *Evidence-Based CBT for Anxiety and Depression in Children and Adolescents: A Competencies Based Approach*. Chichester: Wiley Blackwell.
Piaget, J. (1962) *Play, Dreams, and Imitation in Childhood* (G. Gattegno & F. M. Hodgson, Trans.). New York: Norton.
Piaget, J. (1964) 'Development and learning', *Journal of Research in Science Teaching*, 2: 176–186.
Pinquart, M. (2012) 'Self-esteem of children and adolescents with chronic illness: A meta-analysis', *Child: Care, Health and Development*, 39(2): 153–161.
Prensky, M. (2001) 'Digital natives, digital immigrants', *On the Horizon*, 9: 1–6.
Prizant, B.M. & Field-Meyer, T. (2016) *Uniquely Human: A Different Way of Seeing Autism*. London: Souvenir Press.
Prochaska, J.O., DiClemente, C.C. & Norcross, J.C. (1992) 'In search of how people change: applications to addictive behavior', *American Psychologist*, 47: 1102–1104.
Ravindran, N. & Myers, B.J. (2012) 'Cultural influences on perceptions of health, illness, and disability: A review and focus on autism', *Journal of Child and Family Studies*, 21: 311–319.
Ray, D.C. (2018) 'Endings' in S. Pattison & M. Robson (eds), *The Handbook of Counselling Children and Young People* (2nd edition). London: Sage.
Reiss, D. (1981) *The Family's Construction of Reality*. Cambridge, MA: Harvard University Press.
Ristori, J. & Steensma, T.D. (2016) 'Gender dysphoria in childhood', *International Review of Psychiatry*, 28(1): 13–20.
Rogers, C.R. (1951) *Client-Centred Therapy: Its Current Practice, Implications and Theory*. London: Constable.
Rogers, C.R. (1959) 'A Theory of Therapy, personality, and interpersonal relationships, as developed in the client-centred framework', in S. Koch (ed.), *Psychology: A Study of Science*, Study 1, Vol. 3: *Formulations of the Person and the Social Context*. New York: McGraw-Hill.

Rogers, C.R. (1961) *On Becoming a Person: A Therapist's View of Psychotherapy*. London: Constable.
Rogers, C.R. (1980) *A Way of Being*. Boston, MA: Houghton Mifflin.
Rosenberg, M. (1973) 'Disturbance in the self-image at adolescence', *American Sociological Review*, 38(5): 553–568.
Roth, B. (2014) 'Mutual attention and joint gaze as developmental forerunners of the therapeutic alliance', *The Psychoanalytic Review*, 101(6): 847–869.
Royal National Institute for the Blind (RNIB) (2020) *Effective Practice Guide: Learning through Play in the Early Years*. London: RNIB. Available at: www.rnib.org.uk/professionals/education-professionals/teaching-and-learning-guidance (accessed 5 July 2020).
Rycroft, C. (1968) *A Critical Dictionary of Psychoanalysis*. New York: Basic Books.
Safran, J.D. & Muran, C.J. (2000) 'Resolving therapeutic alliance ruptures: Diversity and integration', *Journal of Clinical Psychology/In Session*, 56: 233–243.
Samarasinghe, S. (2018) *Now is the Time: Supporting Disabled Children and their Families*. London: SCOPE. Available at: www.scope.org.uk/campaigns/research-policy/ (accessed 12 July 2020).
Saunders, K.E.A., Hawton, K., Fortune, S. & Farrell, S. (2012) 'Attitudes and knowledge of clinical staff regarding people who self-harm: A systematic review', *Journal of Affective Disorders*, 139(3): 205–216.
Schore, A.N. (2003) *Affect Regulation and Repair of the Self*. New York: W.W. Norton.
Schottelkorb, A., Swan, K. & Ogawa, Y. (2020) 'Intensive child-centred play therapy for children on the autism spectrum: A pilot study', *Journal of Counseling & Development*, 98(1): 63–73.
Scott, M.E. (1998) 'Play and therapeutic action', *The Psychoanalytic Study of the Child*, 53(1): 94–101.
Segal, J. (1997) 'Counselling people with disabilities/chronic illnesses', in G. McMahon & S. Palmer (eds), *Handbook of Counselling* (2nd edition). London: Routledge.
Seligman, M.E.P. (1975) *Helplessness: On Depression, Development and Death*. San Francisco, CA: Freeman.
Semple, R. & Lee, J. (2014) 'Mindfulness-based cognitive therapy for children', in R.A. Baer (ed.), *Mindfulness-Based Treatment Approaches* (2nd edition). London: Academic Press.
Sexual Offences Act (2003). London: HMSO.
Shaw, S. & McCabe, P. (2008) 'Hospital-to-school transition for children with chronic illness: Meeting the new challenges of an evolving health care system', *Psychology in the Schools*, 45(1): 74–87.
Smart, J.F. & Smart, D.W. (2012) 'Models of disability: Implications for the counseling profession', in M.A. Stebnicki & I. Marini (eds), *The Psychological and Social Impact of Illness and Disability* (6th edition). New York: Springer.
Smith, B., Pattinson, P. & Bell, C. (2018) 'Health and social care services', in S. Pattison & M. Robson (eds), *The Handbook of Counselling Children and Young People* (2nd edition, pp. 415–430). London: Sage.
Sommers-Flanagan, J. & Bequette, T. (2013) 'The initial psychotherapy interview with adolescent clients', *Journal of Contemporary Psychotherapy*, 43: 13–22.
Spong, S., Waters, R., Dowd, C. & Jackson, C. (2013) *Scoping Report: The Relationship between Specialist Child and Adolescent Mental Health Services (CAMHS) and School- and Community-based Counselling for Children and

Young People. Lutterworth: British Association for Counselling and Psychotherapy.
Stafford, M.R., Cooper, M., Barkham, M., Beecham, J., Bower, P., Cromarty, K. Fugard, A.J.B., Jackson, C., Pearce, P., Ryder, R. & Street, C. (2018) 'Effectiveness and cost-effectiveness of humanistic counselling in schools for young people with emotional distress (ETHOS): Study protocol for a randomised control trial', *Trials*, 19: 175.
Stallard, P. (2005) *A Clinician's Guide to Think-Good-Feel-Good: Using CBT with Children and Young People*. London: Wiley.
Stallard, P. (2018) 'Cognitive behavioural therapy', in S. Pattison & M. Robson (eds), *The Handbook of Counselling Children and Young People* (2nd edition). London: Sage.
Stallard, P. (2019) *Think Good, Feel Good: A Cognitive Behavioural Therapy Workbook for Children and Young People*. London: John Wiley & Sons.
Steinberg, L.D. (2017) *Adolescence*. New York: McGraw-Hill.
Steinberg, L. & Morris, A. (2001) 'Adolescent development', *Annual Review of Psychology*, 52: 83–109.
Steinglass, P., Bennett, L.A., Wolin, S.J. & Reiss, D. (1987) *The Alcoholic Family*. New York: Basic Books.
Street, C. (2013a) *Voluntary and Community sector (VCS) Counselling Provision for Children, Young People and Young Adults in England*. Lutterworth: British Association for Counselling and Psychotherapy/MindEd.
Street, C. (2013b) *Online Counselling for Children, Young People and Young Adults*. Lutterworth: British Association for Counselling and Psychotherapy/MindEd.
Stroud, P., Pickett, K., Lupton, R., Capie, R. & Margo, J. (2010) *Deprivation and Risk: The Case for Early Intervention*. London: Action for Children.
Suler, J. (2005) 'The Online Disinhibition Effect', *International Journal of Applied Psychoanalytic Studies*, 2(2): 184–188.
Sunderland, M. (2016) *The Science of Parenting* (2nd edition). London: Dorling-Kindersley.
Susman, E.J. & Rogol, A. (2004) 'Puberty and psychological development,' in R.M. Lerner & L. Steinberg (eds), *Handbook of Adolescent Psychology* (2nd edition). London: Wiley.
Tanner, J.M. (1989) *Foetus into Man: Physical Growth from Conception to Maturity* (2nd edition). Ware, UK: Castlemead Publications.
Tartt, D. (1992) *The Secret History*. London: Penguin Books.
Thapar, A., Pine, D., Leckman, J.F., Scott, S., Snowling, M.J. & Taylor, E. (eds) (2015) *Rutter's Child and Adolescent Psychiatry* (6th edition). London: Wiley-Blackwell.
Troupp, C. (2013) 'Individual psychotherapy' in B. Lask & R. Bryant-Waugh (eds), *Eating Disorders in Childhood and Adolescence* (4th edition). London: Routledge.
Trowell, J. & Miles, G. (eds) (2011) *Childhood Depression: A Place for Psychotherapy*. London: Karnac.
Turkle, S. (2011) *Alone Together: Why we Expect More from Technology and Less from Each Other*. New York: Basic Books.
Turner-Daly, B. (2018) 'Sexual, physical and emotional abuse', in M. Robson & S. Pattinson (eds), *The Handbook of Counselling Children and Young People* (2nd edition). London: Sage.

UKCCIS (United Kingdom Council for Child Internet Safety) (2017) *Children's Online Activities, Risks and Safety: A Literature Review by the UKCCIS Evidence Group*. London: Crown Publishing.

United Nations (1989) *UN Convention on the Rights of the Child*. New York: United Nations.

Van der Veer, G. & Van Waning, A. (2004) 'Creating a safe therapeutic sanctuary', in: J.P. Wilson & B. Drozdek (eds), *Broken Spirits: The Treatment of Traumatized Asylum Seekers, Refugees, War and Torture Victims* (pp. 187–200). New York: Brunner-Routledge.

Vance, J. (2016) 'Who am I now? How play therapy can empower children and adolescents in their 'search for self' following severe acquired brain injury', in D. Le Vay & E. Cuschieri (eds), *Challenges in the Theory and Practice of Play Therapy* (pp. 86–103). London: Routledge.

Velez, G. & Spencer, M.B. (2018) 'Phenomenology and intersectionality: Using PVEST as a frame for adolescent identity formation amid intersecting ecological systems of inequality', *New Directions for Child and Adolescent Development*, 161: 75–90.

Vesoulis, A. (2020) 'Coronavirus may disproportionately hurt the poor – and that's bad for everyone', *Time*, 11 March. New York: Time Magazine. Available at: https://time.com/5800930/how-coronavirus-will-hurt-the-poor/ (accessed 9 April 2020).

Vygotsky, L.S. (1962) *Thought and Language*. Cambridge, MA: MIT Press.

Waddell, M. (2007) 'Grouping or ganging: The psychodynamics of bullying', *British Journal of Psychotherapy*, 23(2): 189–204.

Walker, S. (2005) 'Towards culturally competent practice in child and adolescent mental health', *International Social Work*, 48(1): 49–62.

Wallerstein, J.S. & Kelly, J.B. (1980) *Surviving the Breakup: How Children and Parents Cope with Divorce*. New York: Basic Books.

Wampold, B.E. & Imel, Z.E. (2015) *The Great Psychotherapy Debate: The Evidence for What Makes Psychotherapy Work* (2nd edition). London: Routledge.

Warr, S. (2010) 'Counselling refugee young people: an exploration of therapeutic approaches. *Pastoral Care in Education* 28 (4) 269–282.

Wheeler, S. & Elliot, R. (2008) 'What do counsellors and psychotherapists need to know about research?', *Counselling and Psychotherapy Research*, 8(2): 133–135.

Wilkinson, M. (2006) *Coming into Mind: The Mind–Brain Relationship: A Jungian Clinical Perspective*. Hove: Routledge.

Williams, J. & Richardson, M. (2016) 'Therapeutic multi-disciplinary collaboration', in M. Richardson & F. Peacock (eds), *Fostering Good Relationships: Partnership Work in Therapy with Looked after and Adopted Children* (Chapter 4). London: Taylor & Francis.

Winnicott, D.W. (1960) 'The theory of the parent–infant relationship', in D.W. Winnicott, *The Maturational Processes and the Facilitating Environment*. London: The Hogarth Press.

Winnicott, D.W. (1969) 'The use of an object', *International Journal of Psycho-Analysis*, 50: 711–716.

Winnicott, D.W. (1971) *Playing and Reality*. London: Tavistock Publications.

Winnicott, D.W. (1990) 'The capacity to be alone', in D.W. Winnicott, *The Maturational Processes and the Facilitating Environment: Studies in the Theory of Emotional Development*. London: Karnac.

Wood, D. (1998) *How Children Think and Learn* (2nd edition). Oxford: Blackwell.

Wood, E. & Attfield, J. (2005) *Play, Learning and the Early Childhood Curriculum*. London: Sage.

Worden, J.W. (2002) *Children and Grief: When a Parent Dies*. New York: Guilford Press.

World Health Organisation (WHO) (1992) *The ICD-10 Classification of Mental and Behavioural Disorders: Clinical Descriptions and Diagnostic Guidelines*. Geneva: World Health Organization.

Yalom, I.D. & Leszcz, M. (2005) *The Theory and Practice of Group Therapy* (5th edition). New York: Basic Books.

Yon, K., Malik, R., Mandin, P. & Midgley, N. (2018) 'Challenging core cultural beliefs and maintaining the therapeutic alliance: A qualitative study', *Journal of Family Therapy*, 40: 180–200.

Youell, B. (2008) 'The importance of play and playfulness', *The European Journal of Psychotherapy and Counselling*, 10(2): 121–129.

Zeigler-Hill, V. (2013) *Self-Esteem*. London: Taylor & Francis.

Index

abreaction, 162
abuse, 8, 11, 17, 38, 75, 80, 81, 82, 85, 104, 145, 152, 174, 177, 191–4, 206, 222, 246, 283
accessibility *see* reasonable adjustments
acting out, 164, 192, 200, 206, 216, 284, 285
actualisation *see* self-actualisation
addiction, 16, 31, 185, 188, 226, 274, 283
ADHD *see* attention-deficit hyperactive disorder (ADHD)
adolescence
  alcohol use *see* alcohol misuse
  brain development, 29, 30–1, 33–4, 174, 179
  eating disorders *see* eating disorders
  family routines and rituals, 39
  identity, 34–5, 51
  overview, 32–5
  parental separation *see* separation, parental
  play-based interventions *see* play-based interventions
  risky behaviours *see* risk, behaviours
  self-harm *see* self-harm
  substance use *see* substance misuse
advanced empathy, 114–16
aesthetic distance, 145, 154
affect, 13, 162, 163
  see also emotional regulation; emotions
Ainsworth, Mary, 17
alcohol misuse, 82, 188–90, 195, 200, 220, 235
amygdala, 30
amygdala-prefrontal connectivity, 30
anchoring, 169
anorexia, 183, 199, 236
Anti-Bullying Alliance, 206
antidepressants, 234
anti-psychotics, 234
anti-social behaviour, 200, 241
anxiety, 30, 82, 169, 171, 203, 215, 225–8, 229, 234, 236, 239, 246, 251, 265, 280
art, 58, 59, 69, 81, 86, 121, 145, 152, 163, 171, 196, 247, 265, 268
  see also creative-arts interventions
art therapy, 56, 242
artificial intelligence (AI), 276
Asperger's Syndrome, 241
assessment
  Child and Adolescent Mental Health Services (CAMHS), 271
  overview, 75–8
  physical disability, 252
  private practice, 267–8
  risk, 79–83, 124, 156, 175, 180, 184, 189, 190, 196, 208, 231
  role of parents in, 97
  sexual behaviour, 196
  special educational needs and disabilities (SEND), 245
  voluntary and community counselling services, 273
asylum-seekers, 280, 281
  see also refugees
attachment, 10–11, 16–19, 29, 32, 43, 76, 183, 195, 199, 215, 240, 252, 283, 285
attention-deficit hyperactive disorder (ADHD), 234, 239–40, 241, 242, 243
austerity, 40
authenticity, 52–3, 55, 104, 138, 151
  see also congruence
autistic spectrum disorder, 8, 65, 145, 236, 239–41, 242, 243
autonomic nervous system, 225, 229
Axline, V., 72–3, 145, 148

BACP *see* British Association for Counselling and Psychotherapy
Barker, M.-J., 202
Bateman, A., 3–4
Bava, S., 31
Beattie, M., 203–4
Beck, A., 225
behavioural experiments, 161
Bequette, T., 64
bereavement, 82, 132, 171, 214, 218–21, 229
bio-ecological model, 37–42
biomedical model, 250
Bion, Wilfred, 10, 22, 176–7, 206–7
bipolar disorder, 235
Black, Indigenous and (young) People of Colour (BIPOC), 226
Black Lives Matter, 95, 226
Black people, 200, 203
Blake, P., 8, 111–12, 113, 145, 154
blindness *see* visual impairment
body
  dysmorphia, 183
  image, 183–7
  language, 54, 56, 81, 114, 115, 117, 165, 248, 277
  scan, 169
Bond, T., 86–7
bonds, 63, 64, 108–9
Bordin, Edward, 63, 106
boundaries, 7, 52, 61, 65, 68, 69, 73, 124, 156, 172, 175, 268, 284
Bowlby, John, 16–18, 22, 26, 218–19
Brady, M.T., 179, 181
brain, 29–31, 32, 33–4, 174, 179
breaks, 59, 69, 175, 268, 284
breathing, 169, 227
brief therapy, 120–1, 274

Briggs, S., 121
British Association for Counselling and Psychotherapy
Competence Framework, xviii, 26, 89, 124–5, 127–8, 233–4, 276, 281
Ethical Framework, 80, 94, 124, 134, 137, 211–12, 251, 278
ethics hub and consultant, 127
supervision, 137
Bronfenbrenner, Urie, 37–9, 40, 255
bullying, 22, 82, 171, 195, 199, 202–3, 204, 206–9, 222, 242, 246
burnout, 104, 134

Campos, J.J., 162
cancer, 254
cannabis, 189
capacity to consent, 44, 76, 84–5, 196
care system, 283, 285
carers, 26, 63, 68, 75, 76, 82, 86, 97–100, 184, 267, 277
Carr, A., 185
catharsis, 162
Cattanach, A., 191, 193
CBT *see* cognitive-behavioural therapy (CBT)
Child and Adolescent Mental Health Services (CAMHS), 76, 132, 171, 175, 190, 236–7, 240, 270–2, 273, 274
child protection, 80, 82–3, 134
Child Session Rating Scale (CSRS), 90
Childhood Depression Project, 230
Children Act (1989), 80, 191
Children and Young People's Mental Health Service [CYPMHS], 270
The Children's Society, 280
chronic fatigue syndrome, 254
chronic illness, 254–6, 277
client-centred therapy, 72, 130, 148, 154
clinical supervision *see* supervision
cognition, 13–15, 158, 227
cognitive-behavioural therapy (CBT), 77, 158–61, 168, 171, 208, 222, 223–4, 226–7, 231, 271, 273
Cohen, D., 29
communication impairments, 240
compassion fatigue, 104, 134, 174, 177, 192
Competence Framework (BACP), xviii, 26, 89, 124–5, 127–8, 233–4, 276, 281
compulsive gaming, 156
conation, 13
conditions of worth, 26, 27, 108, 200
confidentiality, 33, 44, 58–9, 60–1, 68, 69, 81, 84, 85–7, 98, 99, 101, 108, 109, 125, 126, 138, 174, 175, 180, 184, 189, 193, 196, 211, 265, 267, 268, 277, 284
confrontation, 106, 107
congruence, 51–3, 56, 64, 94, 95, 109, 118, 129, 156
consent, 33, 44, 68, 76, 84–5, 87, 91, 125, 237, 277–8
containment, 10, 22, 72, 145, 163, 164, 176–7, 180, 181, 206–7, 225–6
continuous professional development (CPD), 16, 135, 137, 177, 191, 265
contracting, 44, 58–9, 68–71, 86, 98, 124, 175, 180, 184, 189, 196, 268, 278
Convention on the Rights of the Child (United Nations), 191
conversion therapies, 203
Cooper, M., 129
core beliefs, 160, 222, 223, 227
core conditions *see* core relationship components
core relationship components, 35, 44, 51–7, 72, 73, 93, 94, 95, 103, 104, 109, 114, 118, 129, 138, 143, 149, 151, 172, 176, 180, 184–5, 193, 196, 207, 222–3, 226, 245, 248, 251, 255, 265, 267
Coren, A., 120
countertransference, 111, 112, 180–1, 278
county lines, 189, 285
COVID-19 pandemic, 40, 276
creative-arts interventions, 144, 151–3, 171, 196, 208, 223, 231, 242, 265, 268, 277, 281
criminal justice system, 189
Crisp, A., 186
cultural competence, 41, 93–6, 203, 237, 245–6, 281
culture, 7, 33, 37, 38, 39, 40–1, 52, 63, 65, 66, 75, 81, 99, 183, 200, 202, 217, 237, 246, 252
cyberbullying, 206, 211

Daniels, D., 124
data protection, 68, 102, 277–8, 279
deafness *see* hearing impairment
death *see* bereavement
defence mechanisms, 20, 21–2, 156
deliberate self-harm *see* self-harm
depression, 30, 82, 158, 199, 202–3, 215, 220, 223, 226, 227, 229–32, 236, 239, 246, 251, 280
depressive position, 23
developmental coordination disorder, 239
diagnosis, 233, 237, 242, 255
Diagnostic and Statistical Manual of Mental Disorders (DSM), 203, 233
digital natives, 210
disability, 40, 123, 145, 171, 203, 208, 246, 250–3, 266, 277
see also special educational needs and disabilities (SEND)
discrimination, 38, 202–3, 204, 207, 226, 242, 246
disillusionment, 23
Ditch the Label, 206
divorce, 39, 99, 214, 217
see also parents, separation
domestic violence, 132, 283
dorsolateral prefrontal cortex, 30
drug abuse *see* substance misuse
Duncan, B.L., 89
Dyck, E., 239
dyslexia, 239, 240, 244
dyspraxia, 239, 240

eating disorders, 174, 183–7, 199, 200, 211, 236, 270
ecological systems theory, 37–42, 255

educational settings, 264–6, 273
Edwards, M., 254
ego-centredness, 10
The Eight Ages of Man, 199
Elliot, R., 89–90
Embodiment-Projection-Role (EPR), 7
emotional regulation, 11, 23, 31, 108, 162, 163–4, 166, 230, 283, 284
emotion-focused therapy, 162, 231
emotions, 162–7, 181, 207
empathy, 10, 18, 41, 44, 51, 55–6, 66, 93, 94, 104, 109, 114–16, 117, 118, 121, 138, 165, 175, 185, 220, 240, 251
endings, 120–3, 172, 175, 284
end-of-life care, 256
environmental factors, 37–42
Equality Act (2010), 94, 244, 250
Erikson, E., 23, 34–5, 199, 222
Ethical Framework (BACP), 80, 94, 124, 134, 137, 211–12, 251, 278
ethical issues, 80, 81, 85, 86, 94, 101, 124–8, 137, 138, 143, 174, 204, 236, 265, 267, 268, 276
ethnic minorities, 39, 63, 226
ethnicity, 93, 94, 200, 203
    see also Black, Indigenous and (young) People of Colour (BIPOC); Black Lives Matter; Black people
Evans, G.W., 39–40
evenly-suspended attention, 155
eye contact, 65, 66, 81, 240

facial expressions, 248
family
    adolescence, 39
    breakdown and instability, 214–17
    family sessions, 97, 98–9
    identity, 200
    impact of poverty, 39–40
    physical disability, 252
    routines and rituals, 38–9, 40
family therapy, 99, 271
family-systems theory, 181
female genital mutilation (FGM), 81
Ferguson, K.T., 39–40
Fields-Meyer, T., 242
Fiese, B.H., 39, 40–1
fight-flight response, 225, 229
Figley, C.R., 134, 177, 192
fitness to practise, 137
Fonagy, Peter, 9, 34
food issues *see* eating disorders
forced marriage, 81
formal operational stage, 13tab, 14, 33
formulation, 76–8, 95, 158, 159–60, 184, 252
foster care, 215
Four Noble Truths (resilience), 257–8
frame of reference, 55, 56
free association, 6, 147
free-floating attention, 22
freeze response, 229
Freud, Anna, 4, 21, 23–4, 37, 44, 63–4, 77, 97, 111, 147, 199
Freud, Sigmund, 6, 20, 111, 112, 129, 147, 155, 162

gay, 202, 203
gender, 33, 52, 63, 65, 82, 93, 94, 174, 199, 202, 203, 208, 271
gender dysphoria, 203, 204
gender identity, 199, 202–5
genetic factors, 183, 225, 230
genuineness, 51, 52
    see also congruence
Gerhardt, S., 30, 230
Gestalt, 162
Gilbert, M., 233
Gilbert, P., 229
Gillick competency, 76, 84
Goal-Based Outcome Measures (GBO), 90
good enough mother, 23
Goodman, R., 234
Gray, A., 59
Greenberg, L., 162
grief, 43–4, 152, 218, 219, 220, 221
grounding techniques, 164, 227
group-work, 171–3, 224

Hanley, T., 277
harm, 79–80, 82, 86, 87, 124, 125, 126, 128, 156, 174, 184, 188, 189, 191, 193, 208, 210, 225, 227, 283
Hart, A., 257–8
Hawkins, P., 137
hearing impairment, 247–8
Heimann, Paula, 112
heteronormativism, 202
hierarchy of needs, 25
Hirai, T., 94
holding, 7tab, 35, 83, 188, 189, 226
Holmes, J., 3–4
homosexuality, 202, 203
Hug-Hellmuth, Hermine, 147
Human Rights Act (1988), 84
humanistic psychotherapy, 25–8, 51, 53, 72, 129, 162, 200, 273
hypervigilance, 192

identity, 34–5, 51, 94–5, 185, 195, 199–201, 207, 208, 210, 242, 251
impulsivity, 241, 285
inclusive practice, 245
Information Commissioner's Office, 277
information sharing, 131, 274
insecure anxious attachment, 17, 18
insomnia, 234
intellectual disability, 241
intergenerational trauma, 38
internal working model, 16, 18
internet, 210–13, 277, 278
interpersonal neurobiology, 29, 30
interpreters, 281
intersectionality, 203, 246

introjection, 21, 22
Israeli, E., 210

James, William, 222
Jenkins, P., 124
Jennings, S., 6, 7
joint gaze, 65

Klein, Melanie, 6, 21–2, 23, 111, 112, 147
Knox, R., 129

labels, 179, 193, 233, 239, 242, 246
Lago, C., 94
Landreth, G., 73, 85, 117, 242
languages, 32, 265, 274, 281
learned helplessness, 229
learning difficulty, 244
legislation, 127
Leszcz, M., 171
Levingston, B., 189
LGBTQ, 208, 273
limit-setting, 17, 59, 68, 69, 72–4, 190, 284
Linehan, P., 203–4
Ling, J., 138
lip-reading, 247, 248
looked-after children, 214, 283–5
loss, 218–21, 251, 280, 283, 284, 285

magnetic-resonance imaging (MRI), 29, 31
Malan, David, 77, 121
Malchiodi, C., 151
mania, 235
Marks Mishne, J., 98
Maslow, Abraham, 25
Masten, A.S., 257
Maternal Care and Mental Health, 16
maternal reverie, 10, 22, 206–7
Mearns, D., 51
medical model, 233, 250
medication, 233–5, 237, 238, 240, 254, 271
Meins, E., 9, 10
Melrose, J., 189
memory box, 219
menstruation, 34
mental health problems, 11, 16, 40, 75, 80, 98, 131, 189, 207, 234, 245, 247, 280, 283
mentalisation, 9, 10–11, 22–3, 163, 164
metaphor, 103, 144–6, 149, 151, 154, 156, 163, 165, 180, 185, 216, 281
middle childhood, 32
Miles, G., 230
MindEd, xviii
mindfulness, 168–70, 175, 227
mind-mindedness, 10
mini-formulations, 159
mirror neurons, 30
Mirza, K.A.H., 189
Mirza, S., 189
Mitchels, B., 86–7
mood stabilisers, 234
motivational interviewing, 185, 190
mourning, 218, 219, 220
multidisciplinary work, 270, 284
Muran, C.J., 106–7
Music, G., 3, 11

National Deaf Children's Society, 248
National Institute for Health and Care Excellence (NICE), 158, 236, 271
National Service Framework, 271
negative symptoms, 236
neglect, 11, 18, 81, 174, 181, 191, 193, 222, 283
neurobiological development, 29–31, 179, 189
neurodevelopment disorders, 239–43
neurodiversity, 239
Nof, A., 108
non-directive play-based therapy (NDPB), 148, 149, 223
non-verbal communication, 56, 81, 152, 248, 277
note-taking *see* record-keeping
NSPCC, 191

object relations theory, 20–4, 76, 77, 130
obsessive-compulsive disorder (OCD), 235–6
Oedipal crisis, 111
online counselling, 210–13, 276–9
Online Therapy Institute, 212
orbitofrontal cortex, 30
organismic valuing principle, 26, 27, 53, 223
Orlans, V., 233
outcome measures, 89–90, 91, 274

pacing, 164
palliative care, 256
panic, 166, 168, 169, 225, 227
paranoid-schizoid defence, 21
parents
    confidentiality, 86
    contracting, 68, 70
    divorce, 39, 99, 214, 217
    eating and body issues, 184
    measuring effectiveness of counselling, 91
    parenting and anxiety, 226
    private practice counselling, 267–8
    role in assessment, 97
    role in therapy, 44, 50
    separation, 39, 99, 163, 175–6, 214–15, 217
    working with, 63, 97–100
Parson, J.A., 255
Pattinson, S., 245
peer supervision, 135, 139, 177
peer support, 177, 192, 265, 266, 268
personal therapy, 52, 56, 94–5, 104, 112, 135, 177, 180, 192–3, 197, 216, 242–3, 251, 285
personality disorders, 11
phenomenological perspective, 25–6, 49
phobias, 225, 265
physical disability, 250–3
    see also disability; special educational needs and disabilities (SEND)
Piaget, Jean, 6–7, 9, 13–14, 33

play, 5–8, 43, 59, 72–3, 77, 81, 138, 144–5, 147, 151, 240
Play Therapy, 72, 148
play-based interventions, 144, 145, 147–50, 151–2, 171, 193, 196, 208, 216, 219, 226, 230, 242, 248, 265, 268, 277, 281
pornography, 196, 211
positive symptoms, 236
post-traumatic stress disorder (PTSD), 280
  see also secondary post-traumatic stress disorder
poverty, 38, 39–40, 226, 241
practitioner competence, 124
pre-frontal cortex, 30
pregnancy, 195, 196
preparatory period, 63–4
private practice, 68, 98, 101, 138, 139, 175, 267–9
Prizant, B., 242
process measures, 89–91, 274
professional bodies, 135
professional networks, 135
projection, 21–2, 23, 111, 145, 183, 207–8
projective identification, 21–2
protective factors
  family breakdown, 215
  risk, 176–7
psychoanalytic theory, 20–4, 25, 26, 34–5, 37, 63–4, 77, 111–13, 147–8, 162, 206–7, 230
psychodynamic theory, 20, 77, 120–1, 129, 162, 184, 206–7, 273
psychopharmacology, 233–5, 238
psychosis, 189, 236, 270
puberty, 29, 30, 32, 33–4, 179, 183–4, 186, 195

race, 94, 203, 208, 246, 271, 280
racial inequality, 38
racism, 95
rapport, 18, 51, 63–7, 82, 103, 111, 192, 230, 240, 274, 277, 278
reasonable adjustments, 247, 248, 251, 265, 266
record-keeping, 68, 101–2, 278
referral, 58–9, 131–2, 137, 236–7, 265, 267–8, 271, 274, 284
reflexivity, 52, 137, 203
refugees, 280–2
regression, 20
relaxation techniques, 168, 169, 175
religion, 93, 94, 203
resilience, 257–9
Resilient Therapy, 257–8
reverie *see* maternal reverie
Richardson, M., 284
risk
  adolescence, 31, 79
  assessment, 79–83, 124, 156, 175, 180, 184, 189, 190, 196, 208, 231
  behaviours, 31, 79, 174, 179, 215, 216, 284–5
  looked-after children, 284–5
  management, 175, 179, 181, 184
  online counselling, 210–13
  private practice, 268
  protective factors, 176–7
  risk factors, 75, 82, 208
  sexual behaviour, 174, 189, 195–8, 199, 211, 222
  working with, 174–8
Rogers, Carl, 22, 25–8, 51, 53, 55, 72, 114, 148, 222–3
Rogol, A., 33–4
role confusion, 199
Rosenberg, Morris, 222
Roth, B., 65
Royal National Institute for the Blind (RNIB), 248
ruptures, in therapeutic alliance, 106–10, 122, 130, 277, 278
rural settings, 277
Russell, G., 239

safeguarding, 68, 80–1, 82–3, 98, 108, 124, 126, 127, 131, 134, 138, 174, 175, 184, 189, 193, 195, 196, 197, 211, 231, 268, 278, 285
Safran, J.D., 106–7
Sally-Anne test, 9–10
scaffolding, 14, 117, 199
schizophrenia, 236
schools, 171, 175, 207, 208, 246, 264–6, 273, 278
Schore, A.N., 30–1
SCOPE, 250
Scott, S., 234
screening, 76
secondary post-traumatic stress disorder, 134, 174, 192
  see also post-traumatic stress disorder (PTSD)
secondary schooling, 32
secure attachment, 17
Segal, J., 251
self-actualisation, 25, 27, 51
self-care, 82, 104, 134–6, 177, 197, 220, 256, 281, 285
self-concept, 26, 27, 41, 208, 222, 245, 252, 254
self-disclosure, 52, 66, 129–30
self-esteem, 11, 53, 82, 126, 171, 177, 195, 207, 208, 222–4, 245, 246, 251, 254, 285
self-harm, 16, 31, 75, 79–80, 81–2, 86, 174, 175–6, 179–82, 196, 197, 203, 206, 211, 216–17, 220, 223
self-talk, 14
Seligman, M., 229
sense of self, 26, 34, 35, 51, 52, 53, 54, 77, 95, 185, 199, 200, 223, 245, 246, 257
sensory impairments, 247–9
separation, parental, 39, 99, 163, 175–6, 214–15, 217
separation anxiety, 225, 227
sexting, 211
sexual abuse, 80, 82, 85, 169, 174, 191, 195, 196, 197
sexual assault, 163, 195, 196, 197
sexual behaviour, 174, 189, 195–8, 199, 211, 222, 285
sexual exploitation, 196, 211, 285
sexual health, 132

sexual identity, 199
Sexual Offences Act (2003), 196
sexual orientation, 65, 82, 93, 94, 95, 202
see also homosexuality; LGBTQ
sexuality, 52, 94, 95, 184, 195, 202–5, 215
sexually-transmitted diseases, 195, 196
Shohet, R., 137
significant harm, 80, 191, 193
sign-language, 248
Smart, D.W., 250–1
Smart, J.F., 250–1
social anxiety, 171, 225
social brain, 30
social impairments, 240
social media, 93, 210, 211, 212
social model, 250–1
Socratic questioning, 160
Sommers-Flanagan, J., 64
special educational needs and disabilities (SEND), 244–6
specific learning disability, 240
see also special educational needs and disabilities (SEND)
speech and language issues, 240
splitting, 21, 99, 132
Stages of Change model, 159
Stallard, P., 159
stigma, 246, 251
Strange Situation test, 17
Strengths and Difficulties Questionnaire (SDQ), 90
substance misuse, 75, 82, 132, 174, 188–90, 195, 196–7, 200, 220, 227, 235, 285
suicide, 75, 82, 179, 203, 206, 211, 216–17, 219, 220, 229, 231
supervision, 83, 95, 99, 104, 108, 122, 125, 126, 134, 137–40, 174, 177, 180, 192, 197, 216, 237, 242–3, 251, 256, 265, 268, 273, 278, 285
Susman, E.J., 33–4
symbol, 103, 144–6, 151, 163, 165, 180, 181, 185, 216, 219, 281

Tapert, S., 31
Tartt, Donna, 5
Taskforce on Mental Health in Society, 264
Tavistock Clinic, 230
telephone-based counselling, 276
terminal illness, 256
text-based counselling, 276, 277
theory of mind, 9–12, 240
therapeutic alliance, 3, 43, 49, 63, 65, 93, 95, 103, 104, 106–10, 138, 147, 151, 152, 154, 158, 159, 164, 169, 184, 189, 196, 277, 281
therapeutic 'chat', 144, 154–7
therapeutic contract *see* contracting
therapeutic frame, 58–62, 65, 68, 69, 72, 103, 121, 180, 193, 200, 226, 242, 248, 255, 265, 278, 284
third-party involvement, 124
Thorne, B., 51
thoughts and mood diaries, 160, 231
tics, 239
Tier system (CAMHS), 270–1
time-limited counselling, 120–1
Titman, P., 254
Tourette's syndrome, 239
tracking, 117–19, 156
trafficking, 189
transference, 111–13, 115, 129, 181, 216, 278
transitional objects, 23
trauma, 5, 8, 11, 17, 18, 23, 43, 44, 65, 80, 104, 134, 138, 144, 145, 174, 177, 181, 191–4, 251, 252, 254, 255, 280, 281, 283, 284, 285
Triangles of Insight, 77
Troupp, C., 185
Trowell, J., 230
Turner-Daly, B., 192, 193

UK Council for Child Internet Safety, 210
UN Convention on the Rights of the Child, 191
unconditional positive regard, 35, 41, 51, 53–5, 64, 66, 72, 81, 93, 94, 109, 117, 118, 138, 175, 184–5, 220
unconscious processes, 20, 34, 77, 111, 112, 147, 164, 179, 181, 183–4

Van der Veer, G., 281
Van Waning, A., 281
video-games, 210–11
visual impairment, 247, 248, 250
voluntary and community counselling services, 273–5, 276
volunteer counselling, 273
Vygotsky, Lev, 14, 117

Waddell, Margot, 206–7
Wheeler, S., 89–90
Williams, J., 284
Winnicott, D., 5–6, 7–8, 10, 23, 26, 120, 147, 148, 151
withdrawal, 106
wittering, 154
see also therapeutic 'chat'
Worden, J.W., 219
working memory, 30
worksheets, 161
World Health Organisation, 16

Yalom, I.D., 171
Yon, K., 65
Youell, Biddy, 5, 9
Young Person's Clinical Outcome Measures in Routine Evaluation (YP-CORE), 90
youth information, advice and counselling services (YIACS), 273–4

Zeigler-Hill, V., 222
zone of proximal development, 14, 117

Kolibri 360 GmbH
Ferdinand-Jühlke-Straße 7
99095 Erfurt, Deutschland
produktsicherheit@kolibri360.de